D1565266

Modern Organizations of Vocational Education

MODERN ORGANIZATIONS OF VOCATIONAL EDUCATION

Angelo C. Gilli, Sr.

THE PENNSYLVANIA STATE UNIVERSITY PRESS
University Park and London

038306

Library of Congress Cataloging in Publication Data

Gilli, Angelo C
  Modern organizations of vocational education.

  Includes bibliographical references and index.
  1. Vocational education—Administration. 2. Leadership. I. Title.
LC1047.8.G55   370.11'3   76-1883
ISBN 0-271-01223-4

To Jennifer Leigh,

*My most recent claim
to immortality*

Contents

Preface xi

I Introduction 1

  1 A General Theory of Vocational Organizations 3
    Definitions 3
    Types of Organizations 3
    Organizational Goals 4
    Organizational Structure 6
    Organizational Continuity and Growth 7
    Organizational Status 11
    Organizational Activities 13
    Organizational Communications 15
    Vocational School Effectiveness 16
    References 17

  2 Vocational Education Leadership Concepts 18
    Groups 18
    What Is a Leader 19
    Leader–Follower Behavior 20
    Attitudes of and toward Leaders 21
    Leadership Styles in Vocational Education 23
    Theories of Leadership 26
    References 28

  3 Rudiments of Vocational Education 29
    Program Components 29
    Vocational Education's Obligation for Retraining, Upgrading,
      and Updating Workers 31
    The Philosophy of Vocational Education 33
    Vocational Teachers 37
    Vocational Students 40
    Vocational Education Institutions as Organizations 42
    Prestige 44
    References 48

4 Leadership in Vocational Education 49
Leadership Concepts Applied to Vocational Education
  Leadership 49
Administration of Vocational Education 53
Vocational Leadership in the Governmental Hierarchy 55
Sources of Training for Vocational Education
  Administrators 58
The Training of Vocational Education Leaders: A Model 58
References 61

II Vocational Education Delivery System 63

5 The Vocational High School 65
Objectives and Philosophy 67
The Administration and Faculty 67
The Students 73
References 73

6 The Area Vocational School 74
Objectives and Philosophy 81
Administration 83
Faculty 88
Students 93
References 96

7 The Comprehensive High School 98
Objectives and Philosophy 103
The Student 105
The Faculty 108
Governance 109
References 111

8 The Public Community College 112
Objectives and Philosophy 115
The Administration 119
The Faculty 124
The Students 136
Major Organizational Variables 145
Technological Complexity 150
References 155

9 The Private Junior College 159
Objectives and Philosophy 161
The Students 162

The Faculty   164
Governance   165
References   166

10 Technical Institutes and Post-Secondary Vocational
      Technical Schools   167
    Objectives and Philosophy   172
    Administration   176
    The Faculty   178
    The Students   180
    References   180

11 Proprietary Schools   182
    Philosophy and Objectives   185
    The Students   188
    The Faculty   190
    Governance   192
    References   193

12 Senior Colleges and Universities   195
    Objectives and Philosophy   198
    The Students   200
    The Faculty   201
    Governance   202
    Conclusions   203
    References   204

13 Federal Manpower Programs   205
    Characteristics of Graduates   208
    Revenue Sharing in Vocational Education and Training   209
    References   215

14 Other Vocational Education Delivery Systems   216
    Problems Associated with Performance Contracting in
      Education   216
    Reference   219

III Quo Vadis   221

15 State of the Art: A Status Report   223
    A Brief Look Backward   223
    Enter Career Education   224
    And then, Competency-Based Vocational Teacher
      Education   225
    The Dual Vocational Education System   226

Varieties of Vocational Organizations 232
Sources of Leaders in Vocational Education 233
References 234

16 Models for the Future: The Ideal 235
The Students 235
Faculty 237
Administration-Governance 238
Institution 240
Funding 242
The Overall Delivery System 243

17 Models for the Future: A Prediction 246
Funding 251
The Dual System 254
Vocational Education Institutions 257
People To Be Served 259
Preparation of Teachers and Administrators 261
Competency-Based Teacher Education (CBTE) 264
Women and Minorities in Vocational Education 268
Governance Patterns 270
Research in Vocational Education 274
Competency-Based Vocational Education 276
Vocational Education for Retirees 277
Vocational Education for Leisure—Hobbies 281
Coordination of Vocational Education and Other Elements in
    Education 283
Relations Between Vocational Education and the Power
    Groups 284
Professional Vocational Education Associations 287
Unionism and Vocational Education 290
The New Institutional Configuration for Adolescents and
    Young Adults 293
The New Institutional Configuration for Adult Career
    Changes 295
The New Institutional Configuration for Part-Time and
    Continuing Education 297
The Universal College: It Can Happen If We Try! 298
References 300

Index 301

Preface

The overall purpose of this book is to provide a basis for a greater understanding of the American vocational education delivery system, especially through an examination and analysis of its various constituent educational organizations. One of the work's major premises is that the more successful and influential leaders in the field use certain basic elements of organizational theory and elementary leadership concepts, along with the fundamentals of vocational education. These basic elements are examined in terms of their application to vocational education in Part I (Chapters 1-4). These applied theories and concepts are then used in Part II (Chapters 5-14) as a foundation for examination and analysis of ten components within the vocational education delivery system, including vocational high schools, area vocational schools, comprehensive high schools, community junior colleges, private junior colleges, technical institutes and post-secondary vocational technical schools, private-proprietary schools, senior colleges and universities, manpower agencies, and other vocational education delivery systems. The unique aspects of each kind of organization, in terms of its faculty's characteristics, governing structure, financial base, students' characteristics, history, and relationships with the larger community, are described and analyzed. Selected statistics on enrollments, graduates, faculty, programs, number of institutions of each type, and so on, are provided and interpreted.

Several important developments in vocational education are given special attention here. First is the most urgent necessity to alter strategies for provision of vocational services. Uppermost in this modification is inauguration of the universal college concept, which delays the specialization portion of a student's vocational training until the individual has accepted a specific job. This strategy represents a virtual turnabout from the traditional approaches to occupational preparation and employment practices. The need for such a radical response has been brought about by the greatly increased difficulty in accurately predicting the kinds of skills and occupational expertise demanded of workers at all levels from skilled to professional. Several chapters contain substantial sections dealing with important aspects of the universal college idea.

xi

A second significant development is the establishment and continued strengthening of the dual delivery system. As is now obvious to the leadership in vocational education, funding via revenue-sharing devices, such as the Comprehensive Employment and Training Act (CETA) of 1973, have a potential for revolutionizing adult and continuing education. This development is largely in response to the substantial demand for training related to mid-career changing and periodic occupational adjustments, such as updating and upgrading of work skills. Such training will likely serve more persons and require greater funding than the traditional preparation of adolescents and other neophyte workers.

A third development relates to a perceptible change in the seat of governance from the state (which has traditionally mandated directly to local administration), to regional units, established to perform many of the earlier statewide governance functions. This curious phenomenon simultaneously contains two seemingly contradictory trends: one toward centralization and one toward localization. It appears that both local and the state levels are becoming less directly involved in administrative and governance functions as the vocational education regional units become extant. A harbinger of this trend is the prime sponsor concept embodied in the CETA of 1973 legislation.

A fourth development considered in some detail is popularization of post-secondary vocational education. This movement, which has picked up momentum recently, is largely attributed to the increased number of community junior colleges and area vocational schools. Their involvements in vocational education are examined in considerable detail, as well as possible ways of improving post-secondary vocational education, especially through the consolidation and/or coordination of the efforts of area vocational schools and community junior colleges.

Part III (Chapters 15–17), which is based largely on the preceding two parts, examines where vocational education *is* at the time of this writing and what its mode *would be* if ideal circumstances prevailed, and it offers a prediction of where it *will likely be* in 1980 and beyond. Chapter 15 reviews the state of the art in vocational education, dealing with such matters as financing, students, faculty, governance, and institutional configurations existing in the United States. What follows in Chapter 16 is a fanciful excursion into the utopia of vocational education, which should provide a useful point of comparison between what is and what could be in vocational education. The final chapter predicts what the future may have in store for many aspects of the profession. Cause for optimism is found in certain areas, no major changes are predicted for many, and extinction is predicted for some practices and even institutions. It appears, however, that vocational education as a whole is not in danger of either rapid or gradual extinction, although no large expansion is predicted either. It is hoped that some of the much-needed changes will at least begin to be inaugurated during the next decade.

I wish to acknowledge the assistance obtained from using federal statistics and several important research studies, all of which have been cited in the work. Although the ideas presented are largely based upon my own perceptions of how a course dealing with the organization of vocational education would be and has been offered, it is written in as nontechnical a manner as possible so as to be of use to educators, students, and laymen interested in vocational education and its overall delivery system in the United States. Special thanks are extended to Anna DeSantis Baran and Kathy Spicer for their consistent and most valuable help in preparation of the manuscript during the past eighteen months. Without their assistance this effort would have been more difficult and time-consuming. I accept responsibility for the positions taken and the philosophy expressed in this work, and any errors that may appear herein are to be attributed to me.

I

Introduction

1

A General Theory of Vocational Organizations

Definitions

There are many ways in which organizations can be defined, but most definitions include the idea that an organization is a special social system with a certain minimum number of elements within it. Caplow (1964) indicated that an organization has five common variables: (1) the encompassment of a group of individuals with identifiable characteristics unique to that organization, with a number of interrelationships established among them (e.g., faculty, administrators, and students in a school), (2) a name which provides it with an easily identifiable collective identity (e.g., Smith County Area Vocational School), (3) members that are easily identified both by those inside and by those outside the organization, (4) specified organizational activities (e.g., training in vocational skills); and (5) clear-cut procedures for member replacement (e.g., the predictable method of recruiting faculty and administrators used in vocational schools).

For other ways of defining organizations see Etzioni (1964), Argyris (1966), and Barnard (1938).

Types of Organizations

There are several approaches to classifying organizational types. First, they can be classified within the categories of professional, service, and nonprofessional organizations. Professional organizations are those that produce, apply, preserve, and communicate knowledge; one clue to their identification is that half or more of the staff members are professional individuals. Service organizations are those in which professionals manage the equipment and facilities, while an auxiliary staff performs the work functions. Generally, the professionals in service organizations are not employed by the organization, nor are they subordinated to the administration of that organization. Nonprofessional organizations are typically found in industry and military establishments. Professionals in such organizations function either in special positions or in special divisions within the organization.

Second, organizations can be identified by their size (Caplow, 1964). They have been categorized as giant if they have at least 50,000 employees, large if they have from 1,000 to 50,000 employees, medium if they have 30 to 1,000 employees, and small if they have fewer than 30 employees.

Third, organizations can be classified according to *who benefits* from the initiation of their ongoing practices (Blau and Scott, 1962). This approach provides four basic classifications:

1. Mutual benefit organizations. These include labor union and professional organizations.
2. Businesses. The owners (either stockholders or actual proprietors) are the prime beneficiaries because they receive the profits obtained by the marketing of their products.
3. Service organizations. This category is the one of greatest interest here because it includes schools, colleges, and universities. Service organizations are those in which the clients are the primary beneficiaries, and the students are the clients in schools and universities.
4. Commonwealth organizations. Armies, police departments, and fire departments are included in this classification. The primary beneficiary is the public at large, which receives protection and/or other kinds of required social services.

For other classification systems, see Etzioni (1961), Haas et al. (1963), and Caplow (1964).

Organizational Goals

One of the underlying reasons for establishing an organization is to achieve preselected goals. Sometimes, the achievement of initial goals provides a segmented gateway for working toward more distant goals. Thus a hierarchy of goals often exists in organizations. Most goals are part of the means–ends chain of activities found in the organized structure. At one end of this chain are the lower level goals, and at the other end are the top level goals. The highest goal is usually very general and nonoperational in nature and is sufficiently broad to encompass harmoniously all of the organization's lower level goals.

When one is trying to gain some understanding of organizational goals, it is useful to separate the goals of the participants from those of the organization as a totality. Organizational behavior is characterized by the complicated interdependence of many individuals. Individual goals and peer group goals are often different, with each individual and group working toward the attainment of some aspect of his or its objectives. Superimposed over these individual and peer group goals are those of the organization itself. The overall goals of a viable organization can be viewed as an amalgam of the participants' goals. That is, the organization is a coalition of various individual members, who are induced to contribute their personal resources to the overall group effort because they may fulfill their own needs by performing within the organization.

The possibility of conflict immediately arises when two or more people interrelate. In organizations an equilibrium must be established and maintained so that individuals can work toward attainment of goals with a minimum of conflict. The major sources of conflict in vocational schools lie in discrepancies between the goals of individual faculty members and those of the school and its board of governance. Working within an organization like a vocational school unfailingly exacts a price from the participants (faculty and to some extent the administrators as well) because of this conflict between individual and school goals. Recognizing this, vocational schools have established recruiting procedures that strive to increase the chances of bringing in new faculty and administrators who will experience a minimum of goal conflicts. A teacher's or an administrator's level of compatibility increases as he continues working in a school. Compatibility also increases through teacher and administrator turnover (those who don't fit in leave) and through a careful choice of persons for promotion (those that fit in well are rewarded by salary increases and position elevation). In some cases of major conflict a teacher or an administrator is forced out of the school system, if he or she doesn't move out voluntarily.

The goals of a vocational school may be altered for any of several reasons. For example, the vocational institution may be located in a hostile environment, and opposition toward its activities may be sufficiently strong for its administrators and teachers to feel its existence is in jeopardy (as well as their jobs). When school goals are changed in reaction to community opposition, the result is generally increasing support from the community. A good example of such a change in goals is the increased emphasis that community junior colleges gave to vocational programs when reduced enrollments and financial support made opposition to the concentration on preprofessional studies evident.

The changing of a vocational institution's goals (also called goal displacement) can occur for other less dramatic reasons. Sometimes the process of achieving the goal becomes the goal itself, and the original goal is lost or forgotten along the way. This tends to happen in older vocational schools, particularly those that have a rigid bureaucratic format. In such cases the faculty and administrator are mainly interested in the meeting of requirements and more or less ignore what the student is ultimately supposed to achieve by meeting them.

Goal displacement also occurs when a vested faculty and/or administration group seeks to preserve and strengthen its position within the school. When this effort takes precedence over all other matters in the institution, the situation becomes conducive to the replacement of original goals with new goals that are in keeping with the preservation and strengthening of the group's desires.

Another form of goal displacement takes place in some vocational schools, especially at the lower and middle worker levels, when the participants are so involved and concerned with the organization's day-to-day operations that they lose sight of what it is all about—the goals. This, in effect, is one way in which the vocational school becomes so introspective that it no longer attends to its external environment and its original goals in an adequate manner.

Sometimes goals are removed or altered over a period of time as a by-product of ongoing operations. Some of the changes result in improved relationships between the vocational institution and its external environment, while others improve the welfare of the faculty and/or administrators but are not as beneficial to the school's clients and society. A vocational school, while undergoing changes in goals over a period of years, may become more *or* less of a service organization to its community, depending on the nature and the direction of these changes.

Vocational schools strive to achieve their goals through programs. Programs are groupings of activities leading toward goal achievement, and they specify in some detail the behavior of the students, faculty, and the vocational school as a whole. In vocational schools the programs consist of curricula, courses, and other items offered to the students, or clients.

Organizational Structure

Vocational educational institutions are created so that certain objectives can be met. A broad strategy is established and that broad strategy leads to consolidation and coordination of efforts of many individuals. The establishment of the strategy leads to the development of an administrative structure with a pyramid shape.

Tables of organization are commonly used to show the structure of vocational schools, including the positions within the institution and some of the more obvious interactions between these positions. Figure 1-1 is a generalized table of organization for vocational schools and colleges. In such diagrams vertical lines usually indicate the hierarchical sequence of the positions in terms of authority. Jobs that are at approximately the same authority and prestige levels are placed in the same horizontal line. Although tables of organization fall far short of showing all of the possible interaction paths, the title of a given position is usually descriptive, and its distance from the top of the chart is a reasonably accurate measure of the authority and status associated with it. When examining the path of interaction and communication, the observer must use devices other than the table of organization.

Vocational schools, because students, teachers, administrators, board members, maintenance people, and alumni do not perform the same activities, are compound organizations. Many schools dichotomize their professionals into faculty and administration, which tend to impede communication between them. This separation of people by activities creates different status scales, as evidenced by the division of vocational school professionals into two groups: faculty and administrators. Faculty members are also identified as being in a department and as teaching a specific subject.

Larger vocational schools have a better chance of long-term survival than small ones. Many small schools are, in actuality, suborganizations of large ones. Area vocational schools and two-year colleges in states having highly centralized state control (such as Virginia, Massachusetts, and Connecticut) are examples of schools within an overall state education system. The apex of the table of organization in such cases would be the state director or equivalent. The next line would list the president or principal of each school. The third line would branch out further into the organizational scheme depicted in Fig. 1-1.

Organizational Continuity and Growth

The chances that a vocational school will continue to function and grow are enhanced if its beginning is based upon public support.

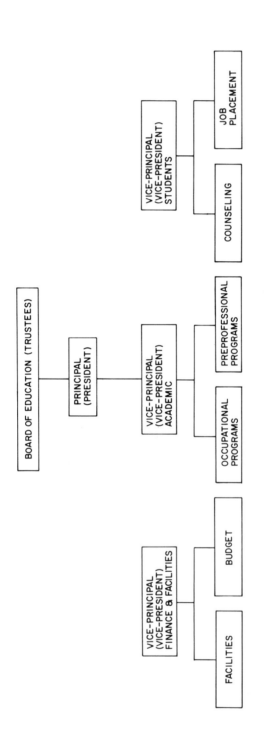

Figure 1-1. Organizational table: the pyramid.

Also, the initial action bringing the vocational institution (private or public) into existence should include norms that can be enforced by rules and regulations. Enforceable norms are vital for the effective functioning of any vocational school. Rules and regulations are established in a much stricter and more legal manner in public vocational institutions than in private and proprietary vocational schools.

There is a clear relationship between a vocational school's selectivity and institutional control. For example, should a vocational school alter its criteria for admitting students so that it is more highly selective, most, if not all, low academic ability students would be screened out. One of the management consequences of this action (if we ignore possible repercussions from the community at large) is a reduced need for special purpose faculty to accommodate that type of student. Furthermore, it may result in a higher student/teacher ratio, since more intellective students are considered easier to teach and can be placed in larger classes. In the past the more selective schools have been the ones with the greatest resources and facilities. Consider the universities that have obtained the greatest amount of financial support and resource allocations.

Students become socialized to the schools they attend. Those students who score highest in academic endeavors acclimate most readily to the organizational structure of the vocational school. Those that don't make the adjustment academically or socially are encouraged to leave (explicitly or tacitly).

Faculty members also undergo a socialization process when they accept a position in a vocational institution, although the adjustment is not too difficult for them because they are initially accepted, partially because they are somewhat similar to the majority of the faculty members already in that school. The more effective the socialization is (i.e., the more the faculty agrees with the school's objectives), the less need there is for exercise of control over the teachers.

Vocational schools are expected to socialize their students successfully into the world of work and even the world of a specific occupation. Businesses and industries select graduates of vocational programs partially on the basis of the extent to which they are socially oriented toward that industry or business (referred to as work attitude) as well as abilities and skills required for the job. Thus the business-industrial community charges vocational schools with a dual responsibility: socialization toward industrial organizations and acquisition of knowledge and skills needed for work performance.

There are two types of authority in vocational schools: administrative and professional authority. Administrative authority is based upon a power hierarchy and is clearly depicted in organizational charts. Professional authority, or the authority of the faculty, permeates vocational schools. The faculty members seek to situate themselves within the vocational school structure such that they can carry out their work with relative immunity from the routine social pressures, obtain relative freedom to innovate and experiment; and take risks without the usual social repercussions for unsuccessful endeavors. There are obvious inherent conflicts between these two types of authority, and such conflicts have resulted in the emergence of a number of governance problems in vocational schools, many of which are presently being negotiated by faculty unions and boards of education. Because of this inherent conflict many teachers fail when they become administrators in a vocational school.

In many vocational education institutions, the line of authority is not purely hierarchical but also functional in nature. For example, the principal or director of a vocational school does usually report to several authorities simultaneously, with each authority holding him accountable for a certain aspect of his overall responsibilities.

Decision making, another important factor in organizational continuity, is the key process for program selection in vocational schools. Even when the decision-making process is considered unsuccessful in terms of finding a feasible alternative to existing programs, it can still result in a change in programs and roles. The quality of the decision-making process is based upon the quality of the decisions themselves and the speed and efficiency with which they are implemented. The ways in which changes are carried out have great import for organizational continuity. A change in a vocational school can occur when:

1. New tools and mechanisms are introduced in order to improve the functions already carried out.

2. The organizational structure is altered with a view toward making it more effective through a new division of labor, chain of authority, and communication network.

3. The participants' performance is improved because of administrators' increasing interpersonal skills, the creation of more effective interpersonal and intergroup relationships, etc.

No one, of course, has discovered a foolproof method for creating desirable changes within an organization. A review of ways in which changes have been considered or studied for educational institutions has been described in several places (Blau, 1962; Caplow, 1964; Gillie, 1973).

Changes that receive the least amount of resistance in vocational schools are those that involve mutual adaptations between the faculty and the administration, and they have the best chance of becoming part of the organization. Suggested changes that originate from outside the schools meet with the greatest amount of resistance. In many cases when external influences become commonplace, the school institutes protective measures to guard against tendencies to replace its original goals. On one hand, this is desirable because it minimizes the possibility of undesirable goal displacement, but its drawback is that it presents a very substantial obstacle for making changes within the vocational school. Even though vocational schools undergo continuous changes in faculty and administrators, their overall characteristics remain basically unchanged over a period of many years.

Resistance to innovation may be reduced when (Gillie, 1970):

1. The burden of the faculty and staff is reduced.

2. The change is consonant with the values and ideals of the faculty.

3. The change offers interesting and new experiences for the faculty members involved.

4. The change does not threaten the security or autonomy of the participants.

5. The faculty members have a hand in identifying the basic problems associated with the innovative effort and subscribe to its importance.

6. The project is reasonably agreed upon by the faculty.

7. The innovators are capable of recognizing the objections and fears relative to the project.

8. Arrangements are made for feedback and additional explanation and modification of the project when necessary.

9. The involved participants develop positive relationships with one another.

10. The project is readily changed if experiences warrant such changes.

Some people feel that readiness to change can gradually become a characteristic of certain individuals, groups, and even entire organizations when sustained efforts are made in this direction. Perhaps this is a possibility for vocational educators.

Organizational Status

Contrary to logic, organizational effectiveness (i.e., the degree to which a vocational school realizes its goals) and organizational efficiency (the amount of resources used to educate a class of students) do not necessarily correlate with the status of the vocational institution. This is better understood by considering the nature of status and prestige, or the position of a vocational school compared to other vocational schools of its own kind or set.

Prestige is a component of status and can be identified by the rank order of the vocational institution, as established by a group of experts. Such a comparison must be made with vocational schools of similar kinds if it is to have any meaning. For example, area vocational schools should be compared with each other and not with other kinds of vocational institutions. Even then, the manner in which assessments of prestige are made is nebulous. Several factors seem to be involved. Some deal with the age, size, and budget of the school, others with the present condition of the vocational institution in terms of whether it is becoming larger or smaller or remaining unchanged.

Status order is an array of similar vocational schools and not of specific participants within the vocational institution, but the status and prestige of the particular school can have an effect on its members. An assistant professor at a community junior college, for example, might be considered at a status level equal to or higher than a department head at a proprietary school or area vocational school.

Self-aggrandizement is another aspect of vocational school status. Members of a vocational institution tend to evaluate its achievements more highly than outsiders do. Furthermore, the school's upper status faculty members rate its achievements more generously than its lower status members. The same tendencies were found for rating departmental status.

A group of similar organizations which are more or less seen as having similar or identical goals is an organizational set. Each kind of vocational school analyzed in Part II of this book forms an organizational set. Prestige and status are much more meaningful when used in comparing vocational schools within the same organizational set. Within this context status is a measure of a particular school's influence upon other schools in its set. Prestige is a composite opinion of experts about the relative value of that vocational institution within its own vocational school set. Establishment of a prestige order within an organizational set helps to foster communication, provides incentive, and imposes responsibility. Prestige also has some dysfunctional elements, however. It tends to distort evaluation of faculty members, can impose mobility restrictions and create other injustices, and in some cases exaggerates authority. Prestige also limits organizational adaptability in many instances. It is difficult to determine whether the advantages of prestige ordering outweigh its disadvantages. The fact remains, however, that prestige ordering develops in all vocational institution sets. How can a vocational school organizational set be identified? Three of its basic elements are a prestige order recognized by all participants, frequent exchange of personnel, and members that are engaged in at least one major activity common to all of them. For example, consider the community junior colleges. There is a recognizable prestige order among the colleges in a particular state, there is frequent exchange of faculty and administrators among them, and each is engaged in the activity of teaching post-secondary students.

A vocational school organization set has six major functions: (1) It transmits and refines the institutional model. (2) It provides a basis for allocating scarce resources (so as to minimize curriculum duplication, etc.). (3) It provides a way to identify like vocational institutions for use in experiments with organizational procedures. (4) It makes the establishment of methods for comparative appraisal and achievement easier. (5) It eases the task of diffusing new ideas, programs, and other innovations. (6) It eases the movement of faculty and administrators (i.e., job changing) between schools.

We should also consider the exchange value of statuses. When a person thinks about leaving one school or position for another, he concerns himself with the tradeoff involved. For example, a teacher may perceive himself as being in a more favorable status position in a school in one organizational set (such as the community junior college set) than he would in another set (such as the proprietary school set).

Organizational Activities

Organizations are created in order to achieve objectives with the combined effort of many individuals. The vocational schools' strategies for achieving these objectives are founded upon basic principles of public and educational administration and are dealt with in later chapters. Most of the activities going on in vocational schools are geared toward the achieving of one or more of the schools' goals.

Most teaching jobs are primarily based on performance and decision making. The hierarchical position of a faculty assignment can be ascertained with considerable accuracy by identifying the amount of decision making and actual performance involved. Higher ranking positions are primarily decision-making jobs and demand relatively little actual performance. Decision makers can be subdivided into several levels: The higher ranking ones establish and set broad policy lines, while the administrators below them in the organizational hierarchy apply the policy when making more detailed and implementable decisions. The teaching faculty does most of the actual work in vocational schools.

Each individual faculty member and administrator is concerned with both roles and activities. Activities involve a contact with the environment, whereas roles involve contact with other persons as an individual performs his job's activities. An activity deals with some kind of environmental manipulation, whereas a role involves communication with other people about things relating to the environment. Activities and roles are both governed by the school's organizational norms, which indicate the behavior expected of faculty and administrators.

A vocational school has a specified program of activity. Faculty duties are specified in that faculty members are to teach a predetermined number of credit or contact hours per week and are responsible for certain attendant activities related to the teaching assignment. The administrators' duties are also specified. Even the principal (or president) knows, at least in a general way, those activities and certainly the roles he is expected to perform. These predetermined job specifications give a newcomer clues to both the activities and the roles which are expected of him and which fit within the school's overall functioning.

In the final analysis, the quantity and quality of a teacher's or administrator's activities and roles within an organization are determined by his relationships with others. Each belongs to a primary group, where he deals directly with every other member. Primary groups are usually small. For a faculty member, a primary group could consist of two to four other faculty members who teach the same subject area he does. Vocational school faculty also belong to secondary groups, which tend to be less intimate and larger in size. In addition, faculty members and administrators establish peer groups. The peer group helps its members to obtain gratification which they fail to derive from the organization and provides for horizontal communication, particularly regarding the standardizing of the rate and quality of work. The peer group tends to insulate its membership from arbitrary kinds of evaluation, and a wise vocational education leader knows that the overall goals of the vocational institution will be met better if corrections and assignment of duties are made at the peer group level. The large global types of goals embraced by the upper administrative levels can be effectively implemented at the lower peer group level.

The concept of organizational roles has two components. First are the specified elements that indicate the "do's and don't's" associated with the faculty member's or administrator's position. Second is the discretion the participant is allowed in initiating and carrying out job-related activities. Higher level positions, such as principal or president of the school, have a very large discretionary component with little specificity, whereas faculty members have a large specificity component and a small discretionary component in their job assignments. In actuality, all positions are a hybrid of these two components, and the prevalence of one component over the other is one indicator of the relative placement of a particular position in the organizational hierarchy of a vocational school.

Organizational roles need to be specified rather precisely in order to assure that particular activities are performed. This specificity can become a source of conflict between faculty and administration in some vocational schools. While organization roles provide stability, they also bring in an element of impersonalization. Of course, this impersonalization helps the organization to survive faculty and administrator turnover, thus ensuring organizational continuity.

Perfect matches between faculty-administrators and the vocational school are probably impossible, no matter how refined the recruiting process, and an initial mismatch of minor proportions is common. With a continual adjustment on the part of both teacher or administrator and the vocational institution, however, compatibility between the individual and the school increases over a period of time.

Organizational Communications

Organizations rely heavily upon effective communications. The kind and frequency of communication are related to the number of teachers reporting to each administrator. This number is called the span of control (Caplow, 1964). In vocational schools that have a sharp distinction between faculty and administration, often accentuated by unions, mechanisms that impede communication are established.

There is always a danger that communications will become distorted. When many people handle information as it goes from the originator to the receiver, the chances of this happening are increased. Communications that have some emotional content to faculty or administration are especially susceptible to coloration or even complete blocking. An effective system of communication would minimize these blockages and would encourage rapid flow of undistorted information from the originator to the receiver. There is some question, however, as to whether a completely accurate transmittal of information from source to receiver is desirable in all instances. A toning down of information would be more beneficial in some cases than presenting it in its bald and candid form.

Vocational School Effectiveness

A vocational school seeks to be both an effective and an efficient social unit. Its effectiveness is related to the extent to which it achieves its goals, while organizational efficiency is negatively correlated with the amount of resources used to educate a class of students. When one attempts to measure effectiveness and efficiency of a vocational school, however, the outcome is deceiving. Although the outcome may be related to the school's goals, it may not be identical with them. For example, the overall goal of a vocational school is to provide selected students with occupational preparation, while the actual outcome is an annual class of graduates. The existence of graduates, however, does not ensure the achievement of the school's goal. To evaluate this achievement, one must measure the extent to which the graduates are occupationally prepared, not just count graduates. The measuring of graduate preparedness has led to such moves as curriculums based upon behavioral outcomes and competency-based teaching (discussed at length in a later chapter).

Trying to compare the efficiency of several schools is equally difficult because of the general lack of criteria for determining validity and reliability. Frequent attempts to measure a vocational school's outcomes will, in the long run, result in a distortion of its outcomes (to fit the measuring mechanism better). The result can be the faculty and administrators concentrating their efforts on those things the evaluators measure, causing overproduction of them with correspondingly less effort devoted to the less measurable (but equally important) achievements.

A vocational school can be evaluated in terms of its own goals or by comparing it with other schools within its organizational set. There are several disadvantages to evaluating any vocational school in terms of its own goals. Schools are low in effectiveness anyway, and this approach takes on a tone of social criticism, which leads the faculty and administrators to establish certain protective mechanisms, and these mechanisms block off the chances of using the evaluation to improve the school and its programs. Furthermore, attempting to measure a school's effectiveness in terms of its own goals makes it necessary for the school to identify its goals and the manner in which they are pursued, a task that is not always easy (or pleasant) to do. Evaluating a vocational school by comparing its output and production with other schools in its organizational set (the system model approach to evaluation) minimizes these drawbacks.

Still another aspect of effectiveness and efficiency is the permissible level of conflict within the organization. Conflict at certain levels is conducive to the introduction of new ideas and innovations. But it is uncertain as to when conflict becomes destructive to the organization as a whole and to its members.

There appears to be some evidence that groups in which there is a more democratic and permissive atmosphere and where the workers consequently have a role in determining goals have higher morale and tend to have a greater commitment to the organization. This then results in greater achievement by the workers. A corollary of this is that organizations which have elements of democracy and permissiveness may be more efficient and effective in the long run.

References

Argyris, Chris. *Understanding Organizational Behavior.* Homewood, Ill.: Dorsey Press, 1966.
Barnard, Chester I. *The Functions of the Executive.* Cambridge, Mass.: Harvard University Press, 1938.
Blau, Peter M., and Scott, W. Richard. *Formal Organizations: A Comparative Approach.* San Francisco: Chandler, 1962.
Caplow, Theodore. *Principles of Organization.* New York: Harcourt, 1964.
Etzioni, Amitai. *Modern Organizations.* Englewood Cliffs, N.J.: Prentice-Hall, 1964.
———. *A Comparative Analysis of Complex Organizations.* New York: Free Press, 1961.
Gillie, A.C., Sr. *Occupational Education in the Two Year College.* University Park: Department of Vocational Education, The Pennsylvania State University, 1970.
———. *Principles of Post-Secondary Vocational Education.* Columbus, O.: Charles E. Merrill, 1973.
———, Leslie, Larry, and Bloom, Karen L. *Goals and Ambivalence: Faculty Values and the Community College Philosophy.* University Park: The Center for the Study of Higher Education, The Pennsylvania State University, Report No. 13, 1971.
Haas, Eugene, Hall, Richard H., and Johnson, Norman J. *Towards an Empirically Derived Taxonomy of Organizations.* Columbus: The Department of Sociology and Anthropology, The Ohio State University, 1963.
Mayo, Elton. *Human Problems of an Industrial Civilization.* New York: Macmillan, 1933.

2

Vocational Education Leadership Concepts

There has been interest in leadership and its relationship to organizations for many years, and a number of scientifically designed studies of this relationship have been made since World War II. The leadership role is of primary interest to us because of its effect upon groups and goal achievement in the types of institutions examined in this book.

Leadership involves an interaction of individuals within a group task situation. The leadership style considered most effective depends largely upon the immediate circumstances and the environment. Contrary to common belief, a democratic style of leadership may only be the most effective leadership in situations that are moderately favorable to leadership. It has been found consistently that the authoritarian leadership style is expected by followers in many situations, and this style is considered most effective in attaining group objectives when circumstances are either highly favorable or highly unfavorable for leadership (Gibb, 1968). This revelation has considerable implication for vocational schools.

Groups

A group consists of at least two members who share a common set of norms and who coexist within defined interrelationships, where the behavior of each person affects the others. Leadership emerges only after such a group develops.

As the group develops, initially spontaneous behavior eventually becomes institutionalized. Znaniecki (1939) has described the process in the following manner:

> In the beginning of the process of group formation those activities which make it a cultural product are experienced as spontaneous performances of voluntarily cooperating individuals. But as the group is formed and its makers become its members, such activities are normatively standardized and systematized so they come to be regarded as

18

group institutions, the whole system of which constitutes the dynamic organization of the group. The function of each member consists in his obligatory active participation in group institutions; functions vary for the different categories of members.

Organizations such as vocational schools also have segmental groups within the overall or unitary group. A faculty member, for example, is a part of the unitary group identified as the professional staff of the educational institution, but he is simultaneously a member of one or more segmental groups (such as the Division of Vocational Programs, the Department of Electronics, and one or more faculty committees). In vocational schools such concurrent allegiances frequently create fragmentation of goals and, as a result, friction among certain unitary group members.

What Is a Leader?

Several definitions of a leader appear in the literature. A person may be defined as a leader by virtue of the position he holds in an organization, but that concept is disputed by some, who prefer to consider such an individual as occupying a headship position. An easily discernible mark of a vocational school leader is that he or she exerts considerable influence on associates in that vocational institution. One way of determining which teachers and administrators have the most influence on their co-workers is by sociometric choice, a method first used for this purpose more than twenty years ago (Jennings, 1950). If one wishes to study the influences of leadership types, however, the usefulness of this method is limited because sociocentrality may also indicate other factors related to friendship and popularity (Gibb, 1968). A vocational school leader is an individual whose personality is a major factor that permits him to control and direct teachers and administrators in the pursuit of goals accepted by the professionals of that school.

Attempts have been made to identify differences between leadership and headship. Four basic differences, as they apply to the vocational school setting, are as follows: (1) Headship is established and maintained through the vocational school's administrative hierarchy, and leadership develops through spontaneous recognition by fellow teachers and administrators. (2) The head person selects the vocational school's goal that is in line with his interests and capabilities, and the leader accepts goals that are internally determined by the faculty. (3) In a headship relationship faculty members have little or no feeling that they are sharing in a joint action to pursue a given goal, and in a leadership relationship they do have this feeling. (4) The head person strives to maintain a social gap between himself and the faculty and lower level administrators in order to make it easier for him to coerce the group, and the leader does not do this. Summarizing, the school head derives his authority from an extra-group power and his role is primarily one of domination, whereas the leader's authority is given to him by his fellow faculty and administrators, who then become his willing followers.

Leader–Follower Behavior

The physical and character traits associated with leadership in vocational education are not clearly known. Although some believe vocational leaders rank higher in intelligence than their followers, it is recognized that the difference in intelligence between the vocational school leader and his faculty-administrators cannot be too large. A vocational leader who is much more intelligent than his faculty-administrators could have interests and values that are not shared by his faculty and administrators. Although intelligence is desirable in terms of enlightened governing, teachers and lower level administrators prefer to be less well governed by a person they can better understand.

Investigators who have studied the personality traits of leaders, such as self-confidence, personal adjustment, dominance, extroversion, conservatism, and interpersonal sensitivity, generally agree that a good vocational school leader is self-confident. He also shows good personality adjustment in that he exercises deliberate control of his will, rarely worrys anxiously, has reduced nervous tension, and is more emotionally mature than his faculty and other administrators. Like other leaders, those in vocational education have strong needs for power, prestige, and material gain, and many of them are predominantly extroverted.

A person becomes a leader in vocational education when there is an appropriate relationship between his personal characteristics and the characteristics, activities, and goals of the school's teachers and administrators. When an individual demonstrates his capacity to contribute more than any other person to the vocational school's goals, he may become its leader, if this is not prevented by persons in the upper echelons of the school's hierarchy.

Effective vocational leaders are generally high on behavioral dimensions of consideration and initiation of structure. In vocational schools
with a high level of grievances and a high turnover rate, the leaders are
usually low in consideration and highly structured. Vocational school
leaders that are viewed by their faculty as inconsiderate are also likely
to be viewed as low in effectiveness, whereas leaders rated as considerate of their faculty and lower level administrators can indulge in high
levels of structuring or task analysis and still maintain a high level of
efficiency. High levels of consideration and initiation of structure are, of
course, desirable for vocational leaders in hierarchical structures. Also
if a vocational school leader is first highly considerate of his subordinates, he will be able later to obtain their support, which will provide
him with a sound basis for initiating structure without lowering the
level of satisfaction and morale of the faculty and staff.

Descriptions of a vocational leader's behavior vary. Faculty and lower
level administrators perceive his behavior in one way, while the
superintendent and board members view it in a different light. From
this, one would suspect that conflicting demands are often made upon
vocational school leaders from above and below.

Attitudes of and toward Leaders

One of the dilemmas confronting an intermediate level leader
has to do with his dual role. While accepting the norms and values of his
superiors, he must also capture the support of the faculty and administrators, who are his subordinates. Furthermore, he is evaluated by both
superiors and subordinates.

Evaluating leadership in vocational education is no simple task. Two
approaches are possible. One is to evaluate the behavior of the individual vocational leader, and the other is to evaluate leadership in terms
of the vocational school's outcomes. Some experts feel that good
techniques for evaluating vocational leadership are not available. The
heart of the problem is that experts don't agree as to what leadership in
vocational education is, and thus have difficulty in distinguishing good
from poor leadership.

A complicating factor is that patterns of behavior which make a person a successful leader in one type of vocational school may be inappropriate for another type of institution. The forms of leadership behavior
needed in a given vocational school depend upon the nature of that

institution's goals and the characteristics of its faculty and administrators. In addition, further differences are found between formal vocational leaders, such as specific officeholders, and informal leaders chosen by the faculty. In many of the schools examined in this book, it is difficult for informal leaders to advance to formal leadership. A leadership bureaucracy develops in some of the larger vocational schools, and as a result, the leader becomes insulated from the faculty and even some lower level administrators by his immediate staff or bureaucracy. The existence of such a bureaucracy significantly changes the relationships between the formal vocational leader and the faculty, the tendency being for the leader to move away from the interests and attitudes of teachers and other staff members. When such a problem becomes sufficiently severe, the vocational leader can lose the faculty's following, which eventually can result in complete or partial loss of his power and status. On the other hand, vocational leaders in small schools can operate in a different manner. An incoming leader of a small vocational institution must initially accept the traditions of the faculty and then carve out a leadership role for himself which will maintain the direction predetermined by the faculty. Successful small vocational school leaders are very skillful in doing this.

An important function of a vocational school leader is to see that belonging to the group is a satisfying experience for the faculty. Membership in the faculty can be made to facilitate a group action rather than individual actions. Faculty size does affect vocational leadership, however. As the faculty becomes larger, the demands on the vocational leader become greater, and so does the faculty's tolerance in accepting directions centered around the group activities.

Some roles are a part of vocational leadership in one situation and not in another, and a good vocational school leader will change his behavior, when he thinks such a modification is necessary, and in order to retain leadership. A faculty member may become a leader on a temporary basis when he takes part in group activities and demonstrates his ability to contribute to the achievement of the goal under consideration at that time.

What are some of the satisfactions associated with vocational leadership which motivate people to become leaders? Economic reward is not likely the most important, since salary differences between vocational leaders and faculty are usually small. Characteristics related to dominance are probably involved, along with the desire to achieve higher status (Maslow, 1936). Some persons may be induced to seek vocational leadership roles by the promise of large personal rewards, a personal conviction that a task is possible to achieve if one works at it, desire for personal acceptance by faculty members, the presence of a task which requires a high rate of group decisions, or their recognized possession of superior knowledge or competence relative to accomplishing the task.

Vocational school faculty members have strong needs to follow. One suspects there are occasions when a vocational faculty group pushes one of its members into the role of leader because the others are ready to embrace his leadership. Vocational faculty members become more dependent upon their leader in times of great stress and highly threatening situations. For this reason, strong vocational school leadership is often demanded during financially difficult periods.

When a leader in vocational education is successful, he helps the faculty achieve its goals, his suggestions are readily followed by the school faculty and staff, and his conduct is satisfactory to the faculty and staff.

Leadership Styles in Vocational Education

Leadership in vocational education may be described in terms of the relationships between the leader and the faculty and lower level administrators. The two broad categories of leadership style are authoritarian and democratic.

The authoritarian, or autocratic, style of leadership, in its most bald form, tends to create needs for the followers and to generate faculty behavior that seeks to meet the needs engendered by the faculty's fear, insecurity, and frustration. The most autocratic vocational school leaders probably exploit the regressive, primitive, unconscious needs of their faculty members (such as dependency and the need to obtain vicarious satisfaction through identification) to at least some degree. The authoritarian leader in vocational education, like most leaders of this variety, segregates his faculty and staff members from each other and minimizes intragroup communications so that most communications must pass through and focus upon him. This style has two notable drawbacks. First, because of the degree to which the faculty and lower level administrators are dependent upon such a leader, his sudden withdrawal from the scene can result in chaos and even breakdown of the faculty group. Second, the reduction in interpersonal communication over a period of time lowers morale to the point where the faculty and staff are less able to withstand attack and strain from external sources.

A practitioner of the democratic style of leadership seeks to (1) have maximum involvement of and participation from faculty and staff in selection of the school's objectives and activities, (2) promote a diffusion of responsibility to other administrators and faculty members rather than concentrating all authority in his office, (3) encourage the use of interpersonal contacts as a mechanism for strengthening the faculty structure, (4) reduce intrafaculty and faculty–administration tension and conflict, and (5) minimize special privilege and status differential by functioning outside the traditional hierarchical structure of the school. Faculty efforts under the direction of democratic leadership produce a smaller quantity of work, but there is greater work motivation, more originality, less aggressiveness toward the leader, toward fellow faculty members, and toward the administration, less underlying discontent, less dependent-submissive behavior, more intragroup friendliness, and increased group-mindedness. When the vocational leader's behavior has a high content of consideration and initiation of structure, the result is increased productivity and greater satisfaction with the school's work conditions. Performance tends to be of a higher quality when there is a considerable amount of stimulative interaction between the vocational leader and the faculty and other administrators.

Also related to vocational leadership style is leadership climate. There are four general types. Paternal leaders are respected, feared, and scorned. Persuasive leaders have the confidence and strong support of their faculty and lower level administrators. Arbitrary leaders are viewed as being aloof, primitive, inconsistent, untrustworthy, and generally undeserving of confidence. Weak leaders are the least desirable, since the faculty members have no respect for such a leader, derive no inspiration from him, and do not fear him.

The effectiveness of a particular leadership technique depends in great part upon its acceptance by the faculty and staff. The most efficient and desirable techniques, authoritarian or democratic, depend to a large extent on the expectations of the faculty and lower level administrators. For example, faculty members with authoritarian personalities prefer status-type leadership, accept strongly directed leadership, and hold the authoritarian leader in higher regard than the more democratic leader. There are reasons to suspect that most vocational faculty fall within this broad classification, and that authoritarian leadership, although not in its extreme form, is most suitable for most vocational schools. Furthermore, faculty members with equalitarian-type personalities are able to accept authoritarian vocational school leadership when the circumstances demand it.

Then why do some people feel that democratic leadership is superior?

Perhaps one reason is that it encourages participation on the part of all faculty and staff members, even though such participation does not necessarily result in the most efficient type of leadership. Advocates of democratic vocational leadership prefer it because it leads to a better understanding of the school's goals on the part of the faculty and staff, and the faculty and staff are more profoundly influenced by processes in which they have participated. Interactive faculty decisions are likely to receive more solid support from the faculty and staff than those mandated in an authoritarian manner. When decisions are made by the faculty as a group, they are powerful devices for changing attitudes and behavior, but such devices are available only to democratic vocational leaders, since the technique is unique to this style of leadership. Democratic vocational leadership also fosters the development of greater cohesiveness between faculty and administration.

Authoritarian vocational leadership may be required when circumstances demand emergency action. Authoritarian, managing, and directive leadership is effective under both very favorable and unfavorable leadership conditions. Conditions are very unfavorable when the vocational school leadership lacks power, does not enjoy the confidence of the faculty and staff, and the group task is ambiguous. The optimum situation for democratic leadership occurs when the conditions are moderately favorable for leadership (somewhere between the extremes).

Knowledge of the relationship between the effectiveness of leadership styles and leadership conditions has considerable implication for vocational leader training and selection. Persons predisposed to authoritarian leadership styles would be most effectively placed in situations where conditions are markedly favorable or unfavorable for vocational leadership. On the other hand, vocational administrators predisposed to democratic, considerate, human relations or a group-oriented leadership style would best serve their groups if they were placed where vocational school leadership conditions are of intermediate favorableness.

The method by which vocational leaders succeed others has implications for leadership styles as well. When a new vocational school leader moves into an institution, he should be cognizant of his predecessor's behavior and adapt himself as much as possible to established traditions. The two most frequent and important ways of becoming a vocational education leader are through group recognition, or election, and executive appointment. Vocational leaders can be sponsored by faculty election, by co-optation of the administrative group in a school, or by the board of education or trustees. Frequently, existing vocational leaders are in a position to determine their own successors, which has obvious influence on the characteristics of the school's future leadership. In such cases, the faculty and/or board is often pressured into selection of a successor who is similar to the retiring leader, even when an abrupt change is what is most needed. Leaders chosen from the upper hierarchies of the same vocational institution are frequently selected because they will best meet the needs of the board of education or trustees, and their primary obligation is to that group. A new leader in a vocational school must be cognizant of his obligations to his predecessor with regard to norms and rules established by the faculty and staff.

Theories of Leadership

Three basic theories of leadership have been proposed over the years. The first may be called the unitary trait theory. This theory proposes that leaders may be characterized as having a particular trait found in all leaders, regardless of the situation in which they serve as a leader. There are indications, however, that no such unitary trait exists. The second theory is called the constellation of traits theory. Here each leader is recognized as possessing a pattern of traits, the total of which constitutes his capacity to lead. This theory holds that the pattern would vary from a leader in one situation to another leader in a second situation. There are two arguments in favor of this theory: (1) Some individuals who have the opportunity to lead fail to do so because they lack the pattern of traits needed for leadership in that situation, and (2) most leaders, rather than being forced into leadership positions, seem to aggressively seek such assignments. But there is also evidence that argues against the plausibility of this theory: (1) Not all persons who appear to possess the necessary constellation of traits become leaders, and (2) a leader can only follow social trends already established or, at best, modify them slightly; he or she could really be viewed as a product of social forces rather than their determiner.

The third basic theory is the interaction theory. Its main tenet is that all the major variables are incorporated and integrated such that a situation develops which provides the opportunity for a certain person to lead a particular group at a specific point in time. The major variables taken into consideration in this theory include the leader's personality, the subordinates' attitudes, needs, and problems, the structure of interpersonal relationships and the group's syntality, the physical setting, and the nature of the task.

In the interaction theory, the relative role a person plays within the group is largely determined (and limited) by the group's role needs as well as by the leader's personality, ability, and skill. The role finally achieved by the vocational school leader, for example, is determined by his personal characteristics in conjunction with his standing among the faculty and staff, and that standing is highly dependent upon the degree to which his fellow group members perceive him as having the special qualities required to achieve the school's particular goal.

From this, vocational school leadership is seen to be a function of personality and social situation, in a complicated interactive network of these two factors. In reality, a vocational education leader probably has very little effect on the dynamics of the faculty and staff. One of the vocational leader's major functions is to embody and provide expression for the needs and wishes of the faculty and staff and to make positive contributions toward satisfying them. Should he fail to do this in a rather obvious manner, the faculty and staff will develop a desire to eliminate him as a leader. It is ironic that vocational education leaders are held responsible for changes in progress while simultaneously being made to conform with group norms which could make it difficult to initiate required changes. A vocational leader who is regarded as making a positive contribution to faculty-staff progress and satisfaction while simultaneously conforming to developing norms is viewed as a good leader. Such leadership behavior gives the vocational leader additional status and credits which permit him greater latitude in idiosyncratic behavior at a later time. The leader may later use such idiosyncratic behavior credits to make changes in some of the school's traditions; he may, for example, initiate a nontraditional curriculum. As long as the group perceives the vocational leader as competently moving toward the accomplishment of the group's task, as loyal to the faculty, and as one who is fulfilling the expectations demanded of him, he may indeed enjoy sufficient idiosyncratic behavior credits to challenge and possibly change some of the school's prevailing social patterns. Here lies one of the real possibilities for inaugurating internal changes in vocational education. Such leaders need to be identified and then utilized in instituting those important changes required in the vocational education delivery system. Leaders of this stripe are most likely to be found in vocational schools having benign authoritarian leadership.

References

Gibb, C.A. *Group Psychology and the Phenomenon of Interaction*, 2nd ed., Vol. 4. Edited by G.E. Lindsey and E. Aronson. Reading, Mass.: Addison-Wesley, 1968.

Jennings, H.H. *Leadership and Isolation*, 2nd ed. New York: Longmans, Green, 1950.

Maslow, A.H. "The Role of Dominance in the Social and Sexual Behavior of Infra-Human Primates." *Journal of Genetic Psychology* 48 (1936).

Znaniecki, P. "Social Groups As Products of Participating Individuals." *American Journal of Sociology* 44 (1939).

3

Rudiments of Vocational Education

The rudiments of vocational education encompass a number of elements including several program components. Traditional vocational education was divided into the seven fields of agriculture, home economics, distributive, business, technical, trade and industry, and health-related fields. Because of increased overlapping of these fields in many occupations, such a division is now viewed as dysfunctional. Program components are more realistically considered in terms of major generic work areas and the variety of institutions providing preparation for them.

Vocational education has traditionally laid claim to being the major vehicle in our society for preparing people for less than professional level occupations. Success in meeting this claim has been mixed, as has been vocational education's record of accomplishment in providing assistance for individuals who are seeking adjustments in their work skills or searching for new careers. Leaders persist, however, in seeing these responsibilities as integral elements within the framework of vocational education.

The professional vocational educator, the students, and the several varieties of vocational schools make up the foundational elements that, together, become vocational education services. While vocational education suffers from chronic low prestige, it endeavors to remedy this by improving the quality of its vocational services.

Program Components

The lack of public understanding as to what the program components of vocational education are adds to the difficulty this form of education has in being accepted on a broad basis. Vocational curricula number in the hundreds. Some of these curricula are common throughout the nation, while others are almost one of a kind. A program is often started when someone in the community or school itself thinks the

29

business-industrial concerns of that region (or state in some instances) have vacancies for the type of workers the proposed new program would produce (Gillie, 1973). Sometimes sound feasibility studies are conducted, but in many cases such judgments are made on the basis of biased views held by one or several influential individuals (educators, laymen, or both). Regardless of the quality of the need assessment, most programs are initiated in sincere attempts to prepare people for selected occupations in their community.

The programs offered cover the entire gamut of occupations below the professional level. The *Dictionary of Occupational Titles,* published by the U.S. Department of Labor, provides a good perception of the great variety of vocational programs that could be offered by the vocational education delivery system. Of interest to vocational curriculum designers is the manner in which jobs are categorized in terms of data, people, and things-related activities (U.S. Department of Labor, 1965). While jobs are categorized in that fashion for the *Dictionary of Occupational Titles,* vocational educators have traditionally identified jobs in terms of broad work areas. (The major generic work areas include manufacturing, human services, public services, and business-commerce.)

Many levels of training are found within these broad work area categories, as is a great diversity in program types. Certain vocational curricula are offered at every level of schooling. Auto mechanics programs, for example, offered in secondary schools in some places, often beginning in grade 10, are found in many community junior colleges (where associate degrees are awarded for the program), and are also available in a number of area vocational schools and proprietary schools. Examination of the curriculum content shows that some of the programs are offered at the most fundamental level, while others are relatively sophisticated and cognitive in content. Adding to the confusion is that programs of similar content often have very dissimilar titles, and those bearing identical program names frequently have different curriculum content. One of the rationales offered for such curricular inconsistency is that specific job characteristics vary from one community to another. Although such a rationale can be questioned, many of the vocational programs provide a sufficiently broad background in the occupational area to permit such variations with no serious disadvantages to the students. Closer examination of the situation shows that a more likely reason for diversity in seemingly similar curricula relates to differences in the educational and occupational background of the faculty. Instructors tend to design vocational curricula, emphasize course content, and teach in ways that directly relate to their own work and educational experiences.

More than 80 percent of the public vocational education students are found in schools at the secondary level. Subsequent chapters consider the kinds of secondary schools involved. In addition, a very significant vocational education thrust is provided by the proprietary schools and various post-secondary institutions.

When one views the entire spectrum of vocational programs available through the several public, private, and proprietary institutions, one finds a rich variety of programs at all grade levels. This is one of the most heartening facts about the present state of vocational education.

Vocational Education's Obligation for Retraining, Upgrading, and Updating Workers

A superficial view of vocational education leads one to assume that its major role lies in the preparation of youngsters for their first entry into the work world. This is certainly one of its major functions, but an equally great responsibility is the education in vocational areas of persons who are out of school.

Such education falls within the rubric of continuing and adult education. Large numbers of individuals need to be completely retrained, while others are in periodic need of occupational adjustments (i.e., updating and/or upgrading of work skills). There is some evidence that many workers will undergo four or more job changes, often requiring updating or upgrading of skills, during their working years. With a labor force of well over 85 million workers, a conservative estimate is that as many as 5 to 10 million persons annually need assistance of this sort.

Cycling individuals from one job to another, with an intervening period of additional vocational training, is the most difficult of all training processes. Persons in need of this kind of changeover and retraining are usually married with growing families to support. Some means must be devised for providing such persons with financial assistance at a realistic level from the onset to the completion of this important transition. Up to now such workers have had to resort to unemployment compensation and, in extended cases, welfare support or to draw upon personal savings. In any event, by the time the worker has completed the new training and is relocated on a new job, he and his family may be financially weakened or bankrupt. Because of the economic (and emotional) trauma involved, most workers resist such recycling.

One major attempt to ease worker recycling (i.e., mid-career job changes) and its attendant financial difficulties has been the retraining programs sponsored by the Department of Labor, first through its manpower-training programs and later through efforts emanating out of the Comprehensive Employment and Training Act of 1973. The federal funds allocated for these efforts are greater than those available from the vocational education programs offered by the public and private educational institutions (U.S. Manpower Administration, 1973). This subject receives further consideration in several later chapters, most particularly in Chapter 13.

What are the long-term effects of such a great need to recycle workers? One can only conjecture, of course, but predictions based on trends of the past ten years or so can be made. Although the public schools (secondary and post-secondary) have consistently claimed that continuing and adult education is one of their important responsibilities, efforts in the areas of retraining, updating, and upgrading have been spotty. Many institutions have made some outstanding efforts in this area, yet others have responded by replicating their regular programs or parts thereof under the guise of retraining, upgrading, and/or updating. Vocational recycling efforts have entities of their own, since the clientele consists of adults who have had previous work experience and also need substantial financial aid. A special kind of program effort is needed for them, not a mere rehash of the curriculum offered to youngsters who have little or no work experience and have relatively minor financial problems.

Vocational educators are not to be completely blamed for the bifurcation of vocational education. Vocational school programs have consistently been devoid of the means to offer financial assistance to recycling adult workers, and as a result such individuals have bumbled their way through the dilemma in sundry ways—most noticeably by entering a period of unemployment and its attendant hardships. The situation has become a concern of the Department of Labor, which originated the Manpower and Training Act of 1962 (PL 87-415), later replaced with the Comprehensive Employment and Training Act of 1973 (PL 93-203), but all this is hardly a beginning. Increasing numbers of people are in need of job recycling well before they are forced out of their present jobs. More needs to be done toward alleviating the recycling needs of millions of workers annually. The present efforts, funded by the Department of Labor, may be a harbinger of an impending new and more humanistic approach to worker recycling. Predictions regarding this movement are made in Chapter 17.

The dual effort in vocational education appears to be a natural adaptation to the characteristics of the American work force and the demand for considerable worker recycling. The question of whether the dichotomization is good or bad is no longer a relevant one, since it is an established fact and will likely become strengthened in the years ahead. A constructive adjustment to the realities of the situation is what is required. Vocational education institutions, under contract with the Department of Labor or its designated state governmental agencies, should make increasing efforts to provide courses and programs deemed necessary for certain identified recycling workers. The prime sponsors with Department of Labor funds at their disposal, on the other hand, should seek to have training functions performed at existing institutions, so as to minimize duplications and redundancy. If both constituencies focus on the intent of the whole effort, which is to ease the transition of adult workers in the recycling process, then many areas of agreement probably can be found. If this common goal is always before them, a spirit of equanimity and a desire to enter into cooperative arrangements can prevail. While cooperating with the Prime Sponsors (who are funded through the Department of Labor) in the conduct of worker-recycling programs, those in the existing vocational education system can also continue to provide preparation for initial job entry for the majority of the nation's younger people.

The Philosophy of Vocational Education

The philosophy of vocational education is embodied by the general principles or laws of vocational education. Several principles or laws are woven into the fabric .of vocational education and are accepted by vocational educators of all stripes. The two broadest and most encompassing principles are discussed in the following paragraphs.

1. *Vocational education accepts the task of providing pre-work youngsters with relevant information about the world of work and the place of the individual within it.* This principle has won broad acceptance in the vocational education community, although the manner in which educators work toward this goal varies. The show-and-tell approach to acquainting youngsters with occupations is common, and the use of guidance and counseling professionals who have specialized in occupational information and development has proved fruitful. Another approach is also a goal of secondary school industrial arts (called

practical arts in some places). That is a carefully planned student exposure to clusters of occupations through a series of shop-laboratory experiences. Industrial arts has been a common offering in comprehensive high schools throughout the country for many years. Furthermore, a kinship between vocational and industrial arts education has been clarified in recent years, and cooperative endeavors between them are becoming more commonplace.

The student's view of the work world and his place in it can also be enlarged through cooperative vocational education programs. Considerable diversity is found in the format of cooperative education efforts. One type of program provides "capstone" experiences in that after the student has acquired substantial skills in an occupational area, he is placed in a job, where he is exposed to a number of additional experiences leading to further expertise in that area. Ideally, the student's job assignment is predetermined jointly by the school's job coordinator and the business or industrial person responsible for the endeavor. In the best possible arrangements, the job experiences would supplement the skills the student has acquired in the classroom up to that point in his studies. Furthermore, close relationships between the school and various employers could reduce the number of highly specialized shops and laboratories required in the schools, and considerable savings could result when such a relationship is successfully initiated and maintained. A major drawback to the scheme is the almost Herculean efforts needed to maintain viable relationships between so many students and almost equally numerous employers. After initiation of such relationships, a tendency toward complacency sets in, which can result in specific work experiences being selected for reasons of convenience rather than optimum fulfillment of the student's objectives. Contract arrangements, in which the employers are compensated for their efforts, might reduce the hazard of complacency, especially if contracts are renegotiated on an annual basis for each cooperative education student.

A second cooperative education model is one where the student is employed for a period of time in the occupational area for which he is studying, then returns to school for a while, with a repetition of the sequence until completion of the program. Although this mode provides the student with financial resources to continue his vocational preparation, it also lengthens the time required to complete the program. Furthermore, such arrangements with employers can easily end up with students being placed in jobs that are primarily convenient for the business-industrial enterprise, and concern for optimal development of the student's skills and occupational experience becomes secondary in importance. While exposure to almost any authentic work environment can be valuable for youngsters who lack such experiences, the validity of its use in place of carefully planned training in the school shops or laboratories can be questioned.

A third variety of cooperative work experience is the situation where the student works up to fifteen hours each week while attending school at the same time. The close contractual arrangement would also be the ideal situation here, and the hazards associated with the other models also exist in this type.

A fourth variety provides a common core program for a group of youngsters, with each going into a unique cooperative work situation. In such a program twenty students involved with cooperative work experiences in as many occupations would meet several times weekly for their common core courses. This mode of cooperative education is particularly worthwhile in smaller schools which do not have large groups of youngsters interested in a single occupation. It can be a viable alternative to the traditional vocational programs, although it also contains the inherent hazards stated above.

Another alternative for providing students with exposure to and experiences in the out-of-school world is the work practicum. In such arrangements students are placed in jobs that may or may not be related to their program of study. The intent of such practicums is primarily to provide the potential worker with an experience in a work environment so as to enable him to more realistically assess his role as an employee. Work practicums can be full-time experiences for as long as a year, or they may be part-time. The better work practicums include a job coordinator, whose primary function is to be sure each student is placed in a job environment which is conducive to his occupational development.

Another mechanism for providing students with realistic job exposure is the internship. Some of the professions have utilized internships as an integral part of their training sequences. Success with internship programs seems to vary according to the internee, the school, and the employer. The medical and teaching professions have developed successful internship programs in many places. As with cooperative work programs, the internship can be an effective on-the-job-training approach when carefully planned, conducted, and supervised. A good internship effort includes practical on-the-job instruction for the internee as well as a meaningful work experience. Internships also have a number of disadvantages, including the time required of the student and the danger of his not receiving an exposure to all aspects of the occupation.

Vocational educators have consistently addressed themselves in imaginative ways to this first principle of vocational education—to provide pre-work age youngsters with relevant information about the work world and their place in it. Indications are that vocational programs will continue to make an effective thrust in the future.

2. *Vocational education accepts the task of preparing people for work in the entire nonprofessional segment of the work force.* Preparation for the professions is left to the professional schools, while preparation of workers for the other occupations is considered by vocational educators to be their responsibility. This goal of preparing all nonprofessional workers has not been completely achieved.

A very substantial amount of occupational preparation is conducted by business and industry under the general description of on-the-job training. Most efforts of this variety are responses to short-term needs of commercial enterprises, and for the most part, they are best performed on the work scene at the time they are required. Such efforts may be described as the service-station approach to vocational education. Such training is clearly oriented around the needs of industry and business, and a considerable amount of such training is always in demand. On the other hand, some on-the-job training is lengthy and more generic in scope and has been undertaken by commercial concerns chiefly because no schools in the area are willing or able to provide the kind of training required. Much of such longer-term training would likely be best done within the context of a total vocational program in an educational institution. Referral of such training to vocational schools (when available) provides two advantages. First, the employee would receive a rounded vocational education rather than a bits-and-pieces kind of skill training. Second, business and industry would be relieved of the training tasks while still obtaining the kinds of trained employees they desire. Many industries have indicated that they would prefer to be relieved of such training tasks and would rather obtain employees with initial formal vocational training.

A substantial amount of training, involving up to a million persons in some years, is conducted in the military services. There appears to be little reason for vocational schools to attempt to relieve the military of this responsibility (although there has been some talk of this), particularly in light of the extreme specialization demanded in the majority of these programs.

A major shortcoming in the vocational education delivery system has to do with worker recycling—the retraining, upgrading, and updating of adult workers. Financing of such programs, along with providing equitable subsistence funds for the recycling worker, has remained an insurmountable obstacle in this effort. Congress has elected to provide some thrust in this direction via the Department of Labor rather than the Office of Education in the Department of Health, Education, and Welfare. Perhaps some educational historian will someday unravel how this came about. Although the vocational schools' continuing education programs do provide some services for adult workers in need of recycling assistance, the manpower-training and -development activities funded by the Department of Labor will likely be the most important source of such assistance.

It appears, therefore, as noted earlier, that the major response of vocational schools will continue to be preparation of pre-work age youngsters for nonprofessional occupations, while the Department of Labor-funded primary sponsors will be the major source of continuing and adult education for recycling workers. When viewed in this perspective, it is seen that a dual system of vocational education has emerged. Although considered an anathema by some vocational educators, a bifurcated system of vocational education can be a viable mechanism for meeting the diverse vocational needs (i.e., initial training, occupational adjustments, and complete recycling) of all citizens.

Vocational Teachers

Teachers of general academic subjects generally qualify for their positions through completion of degree and certification requirements in a senior college or university. The only genuine prerequisite in most cases is that they be sufficiently prepared in secondary school to complete the prescribed college program. It is sufficient for them to bring only their basic ability with them into such a program, and no special kinds of experiential demands are made in advance. Many training programs for industrial arts (practical arts) teachers are similar in that regard, with the possible addition of summer or other short-term work or internship experiences. The recruiting of potential teacher candidates in such programs is relatively simple.

Teacher candidates for vocational subjects in most states are much more difficult to come by because of the unique prerequisites. A common one is that the candidate be deemed competent in the occupational area he plans to teach. A myriad of problems arises from trying to satisfy this requirement. A major difficulty, of course, is establishing criteria for competence in the many specialized occupations. In the past a work experience of a minimum number of years (usually arbitrarily determined by someone) beyond the training period was accepted as the basic vocational competence criterion. This guideline, although widely used, has been criticized by vocational educators and others as not being suitable to the task. Two major questions have been raised: Is the candidate necessarily competent in his specialty because he has had a required number of years of work experience? And would such a candidate develop into a good teacher merely because he has had such work experience? The rationale for demanding relevant work experience was that it would better ensure that the vocational teachers would be competent to convey, accurately and realistically, the atmosphere of the occupation and to transmit the needed skills to the neophyte worker. These characteristics are still considered highly desirable for vocational teachers. What has been, and still is, questioned is the establishment of criteria for judging whether vocational teacher candidates have these characteristics.

Some vocational educators believe occupational competency can be assessed by carefully designed examinations which incorporate both written and performance elements. Several efforts have been made in this direction. One shortcoming of competency testing is that such examinations may fail to take into account a number of obstructing factors, such as the examinee's unfamiliarity with competency testing procedures and the inability of the test instruments to cover the competencies deemed essential in an occupation. Furthermore, the introduction of such testing devices alters the real work situation, and many elements of the occupation's work environment cannot be covered by such examinations. A danger, also, is that some vocational educators may seize upon competency testing as a panacea for identification of suitable teacher candidates and become too complacent about the problem. Another shortcoming of competency testing lies in the complexity of identifying the competencies that ought to be examined. Many vocational educators believe it is impossible to validate such competencies. How does one determine the hierarchical importance of skills in an occupation? What are the absolute "musts"? How many of the competencies listed should the examination include? Jobs with similar titles and even similar job descriptions are not *exactly* the same in terms of actual on-the-job performances. Added to this dilemma is the question of when a competency is sufficiently outdated to be discarded in the examination. When should new competencies be introduced in the tests? Who regulates these green and red lights?

Having expressed concern about the drawbacks and potential traps associated with competency testing, we should also review its positive aspects. Using such examinations to determine a teacher candidate's knowledge of the vocational subject area could provide a basis for demanding less extensive work experience of the candidate. In some states and in certain occupations, a teacher candidate must have six or more years of on-the-job experience before he will be considered for certification. As a result, candidates can come only from the ranks of those who have little or no college education, since they must have been working in a nonprofessional occupation for a substantial period of time. The competency test, as a replacement for a lengthy work experience requirement, opens the possibility of establishing internships or laboratory-shop-clinic exposures for the development of nonprofessional work competencies in a condensed period of time. This is obviously a drastic change in vocational teacher selection tactics for some states and may be opposed by a few, but it does offer some real possibilities for improving vocational teacher selection and preparation.

University and senior college vocational teacher education programs have the responsibility for professional preparation of teachers, although this is being challenged in some quarters. Such programs most commonly consist of undergraduate courses and seminars dealing with methods of teaching, laboratory-shop management, principles of vocational education, curriculum construction, testing and measurement in vocational education, nature of occupations, improvement of instruction, and teaching practicums. Generally, the program includes a minimum of thirty semester hours of credit in professional vocational education course work. Course completion often meets both certification and degree requirements at the same time. Every state has one or more vocational-teacher-training programs. The content of the program's courses varies from college to college, although the overall course offerings are similar in most places.

Certification requirements for vocational teachers vary to some extent from state to state. Most often, certification is granted by the State Department of Education, but the program is administered in cooperation with or by the universities and colleges offering the vocational-teacher-training programs.

Virtually all teachers of vocational subjects have previous work experience in their teaching specialty, and because of this, they tend to be several years older than beginning teachers in the academic subjects. With increased used of competency examinations as a partial or complete fulfillment of the traditional work experience requirement, vocational teachers of the future may be younger than their present-day counterparts. Furthermore, the type of individual who aspires to become a teacher of vocational subjects may change from those who came up through the occupational ranks to persons who elected to become vocational teachers before working in their specialty.

Vocational Students

Vocational students receive lower school grades than traditional students and score lower on intelligence tests and academic examinations. The literature is replete with protestations of this basic fact, and it is unfortunate that some educators have undertaken rather elaborate attempts to masquerade this fact, rather than acknowledge that such differences exist. Traditional school grades and other academic achievements are meaningful predictors only of success for those who enter preparatory programs for professions. There is a very little basis for expecting academic achievements to be predictors of a person's successfully preparing for a satisfying nonprofessional occupation. Unfortunately, the American education system has been traditionally geared to meet academic needs of those entering preparatory training for professions.

There is a relative lack of stability in occupational choice among secondary school youngsters (O'Reilly, 1973). What this indicates is that many adolescents don't know what they want to become. A fraction of high school students do select occupations, graduate from high school programs which prepare them in the chosen area, and then accept jobs closely related to their training. Only a small minority of high school students do this, however. What are the implications? Some educators seize upon this as proof that there should be few or no vocational programs in the secondary schools. Proponents of this position strive to include a more general education for all high school students, especially those who can't succeed in the traditional academic areas, but there is a more sensible alternative.

Secondary school vocational programs ought to be of two basic varieties, neither of which is in vogue at this time. First, for the least academically inclined youngster, there should be a brief exposure to several occupational clusters, followed by early placement on a job where he will soon have successful job experiences. Such success would build his self-confidence and give him the incentive to learn other job-related activities and to find even better opportunities for a satisfying work life. The second approach, for more academically inclined youngsters, would provide a more lengthy exposure to several occupational clusters, with considerable opportunity for acquiring firsthand experience in at least one of them. On the basis of these exposures and with the assistance of enlightened vocational guidance professionals and paraprofessionals, students would eventually be placed in one of the clusters for additional and more specific training. Both of these options avoid having the student make a commitment that is difficult to revoke; instead the student is provided with a program that is flexible but also sufficiently explicit to serve as a job entry vehicle. In addition, graduates of such programs would have the choice of enrolling in post-secondary vocational programs should they elect to do so.

In terms of socioeconomic background, most vocational students come from homes with parents having nonprofessional occupations and incomes at or below the national average. The availability of low- or no-tuition vocational education at a variety of secondary and post-secondary institutions reduces this socioeconomic disadvantage. But the combination of coming from a family which is socioeconomically below average and having had relatively unimpressive academic achievements continues to present a formidable obstacle for many vocational students. The meritocratic criteria. of schools tend to deal harshly with vocational students, unless special courses and programs are provided for their nonacademic interests and more practical abilities. Well-planned and -conducted high school vocational programs are an effective response to this dilemma, and the two types proposed here should be expanded to serve an even greater percentage of secondary school youngsters.

Similar problems involving the differences between academic and practically oriented students are encountered in post-secondary school settings as well. These vocational students are in late adolescence or early adulthood, and vocational specialization is philosophically sound and realistic for them. Post-secondary vocational students are psychologically higher on the scale of readiness for job preparation than are their younger siblings in high school, and more directive measures should be taken to encourage them to prepare for a job. Vocational students who find their way into the post-secondary setting are, as a whole, a significant notch higher in academic achievement and socioeconomic background than those vocational students who don't go beyond high school. This indicates that a subtle selection process goes on between these two levels of vocational education.

Because vocational students are different from academic students, special courses and programs should be offered for some of them as early as grade 9 or 10, especially for those who appear to be likely dropouts. These programs would provide them with realistic occupational preparation, particularly if the programs were designed along the two modes described earlier.

Vocational Education Institutions as Organizations

Vocational schools can be classified as educational institutions (Blau, 1962; Caplow, 1964), and when one is categorizing all organizations in society, such gross identification is often adequate. If, however, the important elements of vocational institutions are to be identified and examined in order to establish a better understanding of vocational education, a view of vocational schools as unique organizations is helpful. Such is the approach which is incorporated here and used as a basis to examine each type of vocational education institution (in Chapters 5–14). The general concepts of organizational theory (Chapter 1) and leadership (Chapter 2) are included in the analysis. The major sources of variance between institutional types are analyzed within the context of eight broad categories (Indik and Berrien, 1968).

Category 1—Objectives and Goals. Included in category 1 are such variables as (1) the placement of goals on a mandatory versus voluntary scale, (2) the dependency of goals on formal authority (Are goals established by governing authorities?), (3) the extent to which goals are polarized (e.g., community junior colleges simultaneously stress job preparation and transfer to a senior college program), (4) the placement of goals on a remoteness versus immediacy scale, (5) the criteria for successful goal achievement (e.g., placement of graduates in program-related jobs or transfer to higher level educational institutions), (6) the placement of possibilities for goal achievement on a high to low scale, (7) the degree of competition with other vocational institutions, (8) single versus multiple institutional goals (in some schools employment of the graduate is the single goal, whereas other schools have multiple goals, since they serve a varied clientele, each having its own goal), and (9) the placement of growth emphasis on a high to low scale.

Category 2—Philosophy and Value System. The elements in this category are not usually officially stated, but they can be inferred from a variety of actions, such as the way in which certain critical decisions are made and the types of key appointments which the leaders make. The major variables in this category include the obedience of members to rules and regulations, emphasis upon the school's mission as manifested by the funds spent on achieving its goals, degree of respect for and accorded to each individual, degree to which the faculty, administrators, and students accept and conform to the mores of vocational education.

Category 3—Characteristics of Personnel. Several variables can be used to describe faculty, staff, administration, and students. Using these variables to examine each subgroup (faculty, administrators, students) as a separate entity provides a basis for making comparisons between each type of vocational school examined in this book. The variables include intellectual-educational level, extent of relevant training and experience, possession of skills required to function in one's school role, degree of motivation to participate in the school's activities, sex, age, rank or status (i.e., student, faculty member, senior instructor, professional rank, etc.).

Category 4—Description of Organizational Items. Five major variables can be included here: school size; differentiation of groups within the school (students, faculty, and administration); degree of autonomy with regard to the institution's goverance; characteristics of school governance (i.e., centralization, extent to which behavior of members is limited, span of control, availability of sanctions, flexibility, communication channels and facilities, and members' relative openness of expression); and role structure (extent of formalization and status level stratification, hierarchical relations, method of succession, congruency of status rules for entrance into and exit out of the institution).

Category 5—Technological Complexity. Variables in this category can include (1) functions, (2) products and/or services provided (day courses, adult after-work courses and training, job placement, etc.), (3) types of equipment and media used (traditional, modern, exotic, etc.), (4) utilization of specialized principles, (5) degree of sophistication in teaching, laboratory-shop activities, etc., and (6) the extent to which specialized terminology or jargon is used by professionals and clients.

Category 6—Physical Environment. The major variables within the rubric of physical environment include quality of buildings and campus, location of campus with regard to population centers, industrial concentrations, campus characteristics (sprawling, high-rise, converted factory), quality of equipment and supporting facilities, and geographical and climatic characteristics.

Category 7—The Sociocultural Environment. A very large list of variables can be included in this category, but this book considers only the following: geography, demography, curriculums and courses, age of groups within the school, socioeconomic-educational background of professional staff and students.

Category 8—Temporal Characteristics. Major variables in this category include length of courses and programs, length of school day for faculty, staff, and students, and the immediacy of goals (Is the proportion of graduates that obtain jobs in their area of specialization considered important?).

These eight categories are far from complete, and a certain amount of redundancy is unavoidable when cataloging items in such a manner. However, this categorization can serve as a general guide for examination and analysis of the several types of vocational schools discussed in Chapters 5–14.

Prestige

The low prestige of vocational education is due to a number of factors, some historical, others of a more contemporary nature. Vocational education was intricately involved with early American society in a manner that deprived it of any chance for prestige. Its incorporation in efforts to control blacks is typical, although immigrants have also been diverted from collegiate forms of education in many places. In 1794, for example, the American Convention of Abolition Societies recommended that Negroes be instructed in those mechanic arts which would keep them most constantly employed and, of course, would also subject them less to the evils of idleness and debauchery, and thus prepare them for becoming good citizens (Franklin, 1965). "Industrial education" was favored for blacks by white northerners and southerners alike in the post-Civil War period, and the philanthropic support for Negro education during that period went to the trade type of schools. Some historians feel that this policy prolonged the maintenance of political and economic supremacy by the whites (Winston, 1971). The Southern Education Association, in 1907, announced its policy that in secondary Negro education, emphasis would be placed upon industrial and agricultural occupations (Fraser, 1937). During the 1930s a number of Negro intellectuals perceived industrial education as a cynical political strategy for keeping blacks in the lower type of occupations (Miller, 1933). The industrial education endorsed by Booker T. Washington dominated the Negro education scene until after World War I and even longer in some places. Washington's position favored separatism, with an inferior position in the work world for the blacks. Along with this, of course, came the realization that industrial education was an inferior education. Vocational education has emerged with this element within its overall rubric and still suffers from it.

Because vocational education prepares people for nonprofessional jobs (i.e., lower status occupations), many persons of all races and backgrounds reject it without understanding its nature and possibilities for serving people. Most upper- and middle-class parents want their children to prepare for a profession, hoping it will provide them with a chance to move into the life-style of an elite group. But only 20 percent of the work force in the United States is in the professions (Lerner, 1970). The remaining 80 percent is employed in the comparatively less prestigious occupations. There is concern about the sizable discrepancy between the great number of nonprofessional job opportunities and the relatively small number of individuals who aspire to enter these occupations. Recent attempts to assist persons with racial, social, and/or economic disadvantages show that these individuals also want to enter the professions and shy away from occupations at the highly skilled and skilled levels. Education is viewed by many as being one of the chief vehicles for "getting ahead" (Blau and Duncan, 1967), and this is reflected in the disproportionate number who seek entry into preprofessional programs.

If one considers the human condition and our frailties, it isn't surprising to find many individuals who seek unrealistic things for themselves. This is true in career aspirations of some youngsters (and in the aspirations their parents have for them). Many persons experience the adolescent dreams of becoming a movie or television celebrity, a major league baseball or professional football player, a state governor or president of the nation. At the appropriate time in one's development, such dreams are normal, healthy, and perhaps even essential to future growth. As the individual matures, such aspirations ought to become tempered with realistic assessments of one's chances of achieving such goals. A youngster's parents ought to provide information that will introduce some realism into his occupational aspirations, but many parents find it impossible to be objective with their children. Some fathers and mothers project their own frustrated adolescent dreams upon their offspring. Comments such as "I want my son to have the opportunities I didn't have" or "I wanted to be an engineer, and since I can now afford to send my son to college, I want him to become one" are sometimes indicative of a parent's own frustrated life goals. Some parents fail to make sincere attempts to associate their youngster's abilities and interests with the requirements of the aspired-for occupation and the prospects of acquiring such a job. In many instances the youngster is not best suited by virtue of abilities and/or interests for the prestigious job his parent has in mind for him. This is a common phenomenon and is manifested by students' avoiding vocational programs. This avoidance is, ironically, counter to the parents' original intention, which was to provide their youngster with occupational preparation that would lead to an interesting and worthwhile life.

Many individuals seem to be working at jobs which fail to provide them with a sense of self-worth and importance. Familiar clichés that describe such a personal dilemma are: "I'm like a cog in a machine," "My job is unimportant, and I don't know how I really fit in the whole scheme of things," "I do the same thing a hundred times a day, five days a week, forty-eight weeks a year, and it will go on this way until I either quit or retire." Much of this difficulty can be attributed to mass production and automation, which has resulted in the breaking down of job tasks into bits and pieces, thereby depriving such jobs of meaningfulness in an overall structure. As a result, many jobs, including those at the professional level, have become impersonal, colorless, uninteresting, and even mentally debilitating over a period of time. The word is apparently out. Many nonprofessional workers know they are likely to have a job with characteristics like those listed above to a greater or lesser extent (O'Toole, 1973). Their escape, via unions and such, is to press continually for less time on the job and earlier retirement. Their major focus is on their out-of-work life, where they hope to be more successful in finding their bit of happiness, self-fulfillment, and feelings of self-worth. Such mental disenfranchisement is found to some degree in most nonprofessional occupations.

There are signs that attempts to reverse this trend are being made.

Several industrial concerns, for example, are experimenting with worker groups who learn to conduct the entire operation from input of materials to output of the final product. Very early indications are that such experiments enable the workers to feel they are a part of the entire operation and derive greater satisfaction from their jobs. Whether this is a movement of consequence in the work world remains to be seen. Workers are beginning to revolt against monotonous, depersonalized jobs, and continued pressure in this direction could force a trend toward humanizing occupations.

Considering the present state of worker interest and job satisfaction in much nonprofessional work, one can understand why youngsters prefer professional jobs if they can get them. Vocational education, which is the major delivery system for preparing people for nonprofessional jobs, is caught in the middle of this dilemma. To enroll in a vocational curriculum is at least a partial commitment to enter a nonprofessional occupation upon completion of the program. Opposition to such a commitment is commonplace, both at the high school and post-secondary school levels. So vocational education is perceived by many as being for those who can't make it into the professions. No one likes to be labeled as being in the lower half of anything, but it is a mathematical certainty that only 20 percent of the work force can be professionals. The less academically able students (i.e., those in the lower three quartiles or so) should be urged, through sundry devices, to seek preparation for a nonprofessional career. Many presently prefer to drop out of the academic mainstream, rather than face the alternatives offered to them in school; they then try to adjust to their broken aspirations on their own, often drifting from one uninteresting job to another, with long intervening periods of unemployment. If, through wise counseling and advisement, they were spared the initial failure experience, they likely could be placed in a vocational program that is reasonably congruent with their abilities and interests. But such counseling and advisement is difficult to obtain when the major thrust is to steer as many youngsters as possible into professional and academic programs. More than one high school has boasted about the percentage of their graduates who go on to college while playing down the proportion of those who completed vocational training and became employed. We see, therefore, that one of the major reasons for the lack of prestige accorded vocational education is the low value placed on the kinds of jobs for which it trains individuals.

Although some have stated that secondary vocational educators are doing a poor job of preparing people for occupations (O'Toole, 1973; *Report to the Congress,* 1974), these claims are unsubstantiated for the most part. Still the publication of such claims further damages the prestige of vocational education. Vocational educators can draw some consolation from the fact they are doing at least as good a job in their educational endeavors as are other educators in their efforts. By preparing people for nonprofessional jobs, vocational education is dealing with the less attractive aspects of the work world and is, therefore, the least attractive part of American education. That vocational education is not prestigious is a fact of life in American education, but it is not a reason to view vocational education with dismay. We should learn to deal with this drawback in ways which increase the effectiveness of vocational education. The Congress of the United States, perhaps aware of the impediments, has in recent years provided funds to assist in the development and expansion of vocational education. Federal funding for vocational education will probably continue for a long time. One way to make vocational education more acceptable is to increase its accessibility through the provision of adequate financing, and this is being done at a level that brightens vocational education's future. A second important way to improve the prestige of vocational education is to improve its overall quality.

References

Blau, P.M., and Duncan, O.D. *The American Occupational Structure*. New York: Wiley, 1967.
Blau, P.M., and Scott, L.R. *Formal Organization: A Comparative Approach*. San Francisco: Chandler, 1962.
Caplow, T. *Principles of Organization*. New York: Harcourt, 1964.
Franklin, John H. "Two Worlds of Race: A Historical View." *Daedalus* (Fall 1965).
Fraser, Lionel B. "The Dilemma of Our Colleges and Universities." *Opportunity: Journal of Negro Life* 15 (May 1937).
Gillie, A. C., Sr., *Principles of Post-Secondary Vocational Education*. Columbus, O.: Charles E. Merrill, 1973.
Indik, B.P., and Berrien, F.K., eds. *People, Groups and Organizations*. New York: Teachers College Press, Columbia University, 1968.
Lerner, W. *Statistical Abstract of the United States: 1970*, 91st annual ed. Washington, D.C.: Government Printing Office, 1970.
Miller, Kelley. "Negro Education and the Depression." *Journal of Negro Education* 2 (January 1933).
O'Reilly, P.A. *Predicting the Stability of Expressed Occupational Choices of Secondary Students*. University Park: Department of Vocational Education, The Pennsylvania State University, VDS Monograph No. 13, May 1973.
O'Toole, J. *Work in America*. Cambridge, Mass.: MIT Press, 1973.
Report to the Congress: What Is the Role of Federal Assistance for Vocational Education? Washington, D.C.: Controller General of the United States, 1974.
United States Department of Labor. *Dictionary of Occupational Titles*. Washington, D.C.: Government Printing Office, 1965.
U.S. Manpower Administration. *Manpower Report of the President, 1973*. Washington, D.C.: Government Printing Office, 1973.
Winston, Michael R. "Through the Back Door: Academic Racism and the Negro Scholars in Historical Perspective." *Daedalus* (Summer 1971).

4

Leadership in
Vocational Education

The practice of leadership by vocational educators departs from the "textbook" version described in Chapter 3, primarily because of the manner in which these institutions are established and governed. The administration of vocational education in most places (including all levels and varieties of institutions) is such that leadership is of the headship type. This form of leadership exists in all levels of governance in vocational education (local, state, and federal). Leadership-training programs provided by the universities prepare individuals to serve in such a manner, and teacher education programs lead potential vocational faculty to anticipate this type of leadership.

Leadership Concepts Applied to Vocational Education Leadership

To what extent are principles of leadership practiced by vocational educators? This section attempts to respond to this query.

The faculty, administration, additional staff, and student body make up the larger or unitary group of the vocational school. Within this larger group are a number of segmental groups. The first level of segmental groups includes:

A. Professional teaching staff
B. Professional administrators
C. Nonprofessional staff
D. Students

Each of these, in turn, is further fragmented into second (and even lower) level segmental groups, as diagrammed in Fig. 4-1.

The professional teaching staff, or faculty (first level segmental group A in Fig. 4-1), has a variety of second level segmental groups, and these in turn have several third level groups. The common second and third level groups include:

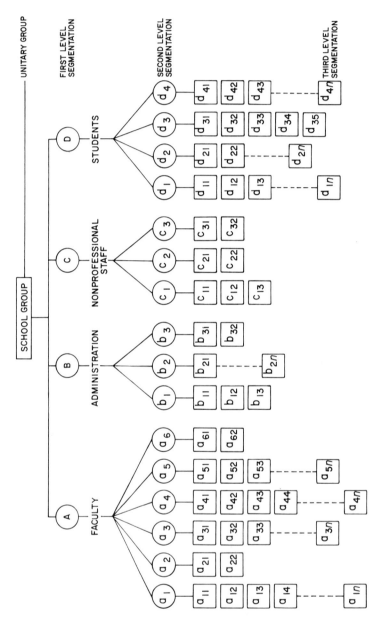

Figure 4-1. Segmentation of the vocational school group.

A1. Academic rank categories*
   A11. Full professor or instructor
   A12. Associate professor or instructor
   A13. Assistant professor or instructor
   A14. Lecturer or instructor
   A1n. Other teacher categories
A2. Appointment status categorization
   A21. Untenured
   A22. Tenured
A3. Vocational subject matter categorization
   A31. Electronics technology
   A32. Nursing
   A33. Business administration
   A3n. Other curriculum specialties
A4. Vocational divisions
   A41. Engineering technology
   A42. Health services curriculums
   A43. Business commerce curriculums
   A44. Human service curriculums
   A4n. Other divisions in the school
A5. Faculty committees
   A51. Curriculum committee
   A52. Academic policy committee
   A53. Faculty salary committee
   A5n. Other committees
A6. Faculty subgroups
   A61. Subgroups of cosmopolites. These subgroups are most strongly committed to their subject area.
   A62. Subgroups of localites. These subgroups give their first allegiance to the institution.

The administration (first level segmental group B in Fig. 4-1) tends to have greater unitary characteristics than does the faculty, but certain second level and third level segmentation subgroups are found among the professional administrators. Typical ones include:

B1. Administrative specialization categories
   B11. Instructional
   B12. Fiscal
   B13. Personnel

* Some institutions incorporate instructor categories (such as 1 through 5) in lieu of the academic ranks of professor, associate professor, assistant professor, and instructor.

B2. Administrative hierarchical categories
These categories are best seen in organizational charts, where levels of authority are shown in the vertical plane, similar levels are shown horizontally, and administrative posts advisory to one another are joined by broken or dotted lines.

B3. Administrative subgroups
B31. Cosmopolite. These groups are committed to the profession as their primary loyalty.
B32. Localite. These groups are loyal first to the school where they are employed.

The nonprofessional staff is also fragmented into a number of second and third level segmental groups, including the following:

C1. Job specialty categories
C11. Secretaries
C12. Maintenance staff
C13. Clerical staff associated with administrative subcategories
C2. C21. Union
C22. Non-union
C3. C31. Male
C32. Female

The student body is also fragmented into several secondary segmental groups. Some of the more common ones are:

D1. Program categories
D11. Electronics
D12. Business administration
D13. Nursing
D1n. Other programs
D2. Grade level
D21. Freshmen
D22. Sophomores
D2n. etc.
D3. Family socioeconomic background
D31. Upper class
D32. Upper middle class
D33. Lower middle class
D34. Upper lower class
D35. Lower lower class
D4. Student status
D41. Full-time student
D42. Part-time student
D43. Adult or continuing education student
D4n. Other status categories

The leader in most vocational schools has been appointed to a headship position by the board of education or trustees. In only uncommon instances is he elected by his peers. In a vocational school the major group goals are generally determined externally by the board of trustees or school board, and the individual who is to be the leader comes into the school with some understanding of what these external goals (e.g., to prepare electronics technicians) are.

While the head's role is that of domination to some degree, it can be made democratic to some extent. The head can turn over some of the leadership responsibilities for establishing ways to implement goals to the faculty and in some cases even to the students. For example, while it may have been determined externally that there will be a two-year associate degree program in electronics technology, much of the curriculum development and actual content can be left to the faculty. When such a policy is utilized to as great an extent as possible, the faculty may more readily become willing followers rather than being passive about or even hostile to the school's higher level goals. A mark of a good leader in a vocational school is the presence of a faculty that is effectively performing its duties and preparing graduates who are satisfied with their programs and well prepared in their specialty areas.

There are also peer group leaders. Such an individual is more or less spontaneously recognized by his own peers as the person in their subgroup who is most capable of assisting them in achieving their goals. In a specific curriculum, for example, he would be recognized and respected in his specialized vocational subject by his peers. Such leaders can be effective instruments for achievement of school goals at the specific curriculum and course level. Successful leadership experiences at this level often whet a person's appetite for more leadership responsibilities and can result in his seeking promotions to an administrative post. Such occurrences are common enough for vocational educators to comment frequently about them—the way we reward a person for good teaching leadership is to move him out of it into administration. It is ironic that becoming an outstanding vocational teacher is an important vehicle for entering the ranks of administration.

Administration of Vocational Education

There are three periods in the evolution of the administrative theory movement, which began in earnest following World War II. These periods are from 1947 to 1954, from 1954 to 1964, and since 1964.

This new movement began at about the time the National Conference on Professors of Educational Administration (NCPEA) convened in 1947. Three years later the Kellogg Foundation provided funds for support of educational administration research and program development to be conducted in eight universities. This support continued until 1960–1962. During those years a number of educational administration studies were conducted, and several works were written on that subject, including Griffiths (1959), Halpin (1956), Moore (1957), Campbell and Gregg (1957), and Carlson (1962).

A theoretical model for analyzing educational administration as a social process tested in 1954 (Getzels and Guba, 1957) is one of the first studies in educational administration to incorporate theories and techniques from the behavioral sciences. Many of the leaders in the educational administration movement during the second period (1954–1964) emphasized three major points: (1) empirical research should be couched in well-formulated (hypothesized) theory; (2) educational administration is within the larger area of administration and should be studied and researched within that context; and (3) funding for behavioral sciences research should be utilized in educational administration practices (Kroll, 1970).

The most substantive new educational administration achievements of this period are reflected in five studies: Halpin (1956), Getzels and Guba (1957), Hemphill, Griffiths, and Fredericksen (1962), Carlson (1962), Halpin and Croft (1963). The Halpin (1956) study found that superintendents were viewed in a consistent manner by board of education members and were also viewed in a consistent, but considerably different, manner by the faculty. As mentioned in Chapter 2, this is one of the difficulties leaders must contend with in a vocational school. The Hemphill and Griffiths (1962) study, among other things, demonstrated that preservice and in-service training of elementary school principals can be successfully done with the use of the simulation technique. The importance of that finding here is that the simulation technique may also be successfully incorporated in the training of vocational administrators. The Carlson (1962) results likely have implications for vocational education leadership. He found that the cosmopolitan type of administrator is in a better position to effect a change in the school than is a localite type administrator. The major implication of this work is that should a vocational school board of governance want a major institutional change at the time they are seeking a new top-level administrator, the chances for successfully inaugurating that change would be enhanced if the board employed a cosmopolitan type of administrator. (A cosmopolitan is oriented more toward his profession than toward a particular geographic location where he happens to be practicing his profession.)

The administrator of a vocational school, regardless of level, has many job functions similar to those of a general education administrator at a corresponding level in the administrative hierarchy. The similarities relate to the routine, day-to-day aspects of school management involving such matters as finances, facilities, faculty and staff, and students. The differences between vocational and other educational administrators are related to the uniqueness of vocational education programs with regard to their occupational orientation, sources of funding (generally a tri-source in the form of federal, state, and local funding), higher per student costs because of the laboratories and shops, larger blocks of time required for laboratory-shop sessions, and a faculty whose orientation may be related more to the work world than to education. These unique elements, which set the demands made upon vocational education administrators apart from the usual demands made upon educational administrators as a whole, are the chief bases for offering graduate programs specifically aimed at preparing vocational school administrators.

Vocational Leadership in the Governmental Hierarchy

Educational leadership of varying quality is found in all governance levels: federal, state, and regional-local. This is particularly true in vocational education because of the distribution of funding among these levels (Gillie, 1973). In addition, some leadership is exercised by a number of professional associations, most notably the American Vocational Association.

Federal government leadership in vocational education has not been particularly instrumental in bringing new ideas into vocational education. Leadership at this level, by virtue of the government's pattern in the United States, where true control of vocational school operation is at the state and local levels, has been limited to the disbursing of federal funds in accordance with the formulas established by the legislative branch of the government. Vocational education leadership within the Office of Education of H.E.W. has been shuffled about because of organization structural changes that have occurred almost annually. Other leadership related to certain important aspects of vocational services are found in the Department of Labor, the place where Congress has been most generous with vocational preparation and training funds through legislation like the Comprehensive Employment and Training Act of 1973. Recent tendencies to incorporate elements of revenue sharing in such funding may be in keeping with the American tradition of permitting control of education to remain with the states and regions. Predictions relative to this trend are presented in Chapter 17.

A recent listing (AVA, 1972) showed that the U.S. Office of Education employed about seventy individuals in positions related to vocational education. Included were persons employed in the Bureau of Adult, Vocational and Technical Education, Division of Adult Education Programs, Division of Manpower Development and Training, Division of Vocational and Technical Education, Planning and Evaluation Branch, Development Branch, Service Branch, Pilot and Demonstration Branch, and H.E.W. Regional Directors of Adult, Vocational and Technical Education.

This same directory lists a total of nearly 800 key state leaders in vocational education, which averages to just over fifteen state level leaders per state. The highest level leader (i.e., the individual assigned responsibility for directing the vocational efforts in the state) is known by a variety of titles: In twenty-five states he is labeled "state director" of vocational education; eleven other states assign the title "director" of vocational education; six use the description "assistant commissioners"; five identify him as "superintendent (deputy, associate, or assistant)"; and four use "associate commissioner" of vocational education. The position titles of the other key state leaders are equally diverse, with more than 100 such titles listed for the 800 leaders included in the directory. An examination of the titles reveals that considerable variation in the format of leadership hierarchy is found in the several states. State level vocational education leadership has been viable up to the mid-seventies and has much to do with the infusion of federal funds (matched with state dollars) into the overall vocational education effort over the years.

The local or regional level of vocational administration also varies in form from one place to another. Typically, each vocational school has a cadre of administrators, varying in number from one or two in smaller institutions to twelve or more in the larger ones. In area vocational schools, private vocational schools, and some community junior colleges, the highest level administrator commonly has the title of director. Lower level administrators have such titles as associate or assistant directors and administrative assistant. The chief administrator of comprehensive high schools is most often granted the title of principal. In the community junior colleges the chief administrator most often is called president, although the titles of chancellor, provost, and director are used in some places. The pyramidal administrative structure exists in vocational schools at all levels and mode of control. Local school districts serving large populations may have a central administrative hierarchy for governance of its several vocational schools similar to that found at the state level.

Professional associations provide some leadership to the vocational education profession. Most important is the American Vocational Association (AVA) with national headquarters in Washington, D.C. It is a confederation of state vocational associations, and one of its major interests has been federal legislation relating to the funding of vocational education, although it does not maintain an official lobbying activity. The seven major objectives of the AVA are (AVA, 1929):

A. To establish and maintain national leadership in all types of vocational and practical arts education, including industrial arts and guidance services.

B. To render service to state and local communities in promoting and stabilizing vocational education.

C. To provide a national open forum for the study and discussion of all questions involved in vocational education.

D. To unify all the vocational education interests of the nation through representative membership.

E. To cooperate with other nations in the further development of vocational education, and to welcome international memberships.

F. To encourage the further development and improvement of all programs of education related to vocational and practical arts education, including industrial arts and guidance services.

G. To emphasize and encourage the promotion, improvement and expansion of programs of vocational, part-time and vocational adult education.

In addition, there are smaller professional associations that specialize in more narrow areas of vocational education, such as technical education, industrial trade and technical education, home economics education, industrial arts education, vocational guidance, research in vocational education, engineering-related technical education, and a host of others. These may be considered splinters of the overall vocational education movement, and there is considerable overlapping of membership among several of them. These associations are discussed in Chapter 17.

Many vocational educators are also members of faculty unions, a movement that has swept through secondary education since the 1960s. Although no figures are available, there is reason to suspect many vocational teachers belong to state affiliations of the National Educational Association (NEA), institutional affiliations of the American Association of University Professors (AAUP), or the American Federation of Teachers (AFT). There is, however, a clear-cut distinction between organizations of this type and the professional organizations discussed previously (Gillie, 1972).

In review, one can see that vocational education leadership is found at all levels of government as well as in state and national professional associations. Although there are elements of competition which lead to some fragmentation, vocational education leaders as a whole are essentially a cohesive group.

Sources of Training for Vocational Education Administrators

Formal training of administrators for vocational education is provided in many senior colleges and universities. It can be assumed that graduate programs in vocational education consider leadership development and administrator training as among their major program objectives.

Furthermore, many vocational leaders obtain their graduate training in graduate programs other than those in vocational education. Most common are graduate programs in industrial arts, educational administration, and higher education. An assessment of the percentage of vocational leaders who received their graduate program preparation in fields other than vocational education would indicate the discrepancy that exists between the number of vocational leaders presently available and the number actually needed.

The Training of Vocational Education Leaders: A Model

A perusal of catalogs from several of the many colleges and universities which offer graduate programs in professional vocational education shows that much diversity exists in their content. Although there probably is no single graduate program that would serve as the best mechanism for training administrative leaders in vocational education, there are basic ingredients that ought to be included in any graduate vocational leadership preparatory program.

First, about one-sixth of the doctoral program (fifteen of a total of ninety credit hours beyond the bachelors degree) ought to be allocated for graduate level exploratory courses in an area other than education. In view of the nature of the educational profession, most persons would likely seek courses in the behavioral sciences, although they ought not be restricted to it, since some individuals will have a strong desire to develop a minor in another academic area. The underlying purpose of the minor studies cluster is to broaden the doctoral candidate's viewpoints while he is delving deeply into the major area of vocational education. Well-thought-out minor programs of study would supplement and round out leadership preparation in vocational education as a whole.

Second, another part of the doctoral program (one-sixth in total credits but at least one semester in length) should consist of a carefully selected, planned, executed, and evaluated internship. The experience should be reasonably similar to the type of experience the candidate would receive in a position he intends to obtain upon graduation. A good internship requires a viable cooperative arrangement between the receiving institution or agency and the sending university. The internship should be planned to provide the internee a sequence of experiences that would give him a thorough overview of important elements of the administrative position for which he is interning. While proceeding through the chain of selected experiences, the internee would be provided with an opportunity to perform the duties as well as observe others doing so. Also, to assure maximum benefits from on-the-job encounters, the internee, his on-the-job mentors, and (when feasible) his major university adviser should participate in an ongoing seminar in which experiences are discussed and evaluated within the context of vocational education leadership. Only in this manner can the internship become an intentional learning and practicum situation. A considerable amount of time and energy is required of the several people involved in the internship, but such an approach is achievable and in the long run will help to prepare a superior group of vocational education leaders.

From a practical point of view, the internship has several disadvantages: (1) The internee is often required to move to a new geographic location for the internship. This is often difficult, particularly for the many doctoral candidates who are married and have school age children. Relocating one's family for a six-month or one-year internship creates a family hardship, and so does leaving one's family behind during the internship period. (2) The internee requires a salary considerably higher than that traditionally offered to graduate assistants. There is some question as to who ought to assume this expense. If the institution in which the internee has been placed is participating in the kind of internship described here, it might be assumed that the institution is providing as much of a service to the internee as the internee is providing to the institution, and the question of internee financial support goes unresolved. And yet the internee needs funding to meet ordinary living expenses. One point of view is that internee salaries ought to be derived from special vocational education leadership funds and considered an integral part of the graduate program budget. (3) The internship lengthens the time required to complete the total doctoral program, and doctoral students traditionally strive to finish their degree as quickly as they can. But a true profession should require that the candidate practice his profession for a period during his professional studies in order to ensure that he is competent in the practical applications of the profession. There are elements in vocational education administration and leadership that should not be entrusted to courses alone. The internship described above would tie the theoretical constructs developed in the course work in with the daily tasks of administering and serving in a leadership position in a vocational institution or educational agency.

The major field of concentration and internship together constitute about one-third of the program. Half of the program (about forty-five credits of the ninety hours total) would be devoted to developing those areas needed for the potential vocational education leader to function successfully on the job. There are fifteen basic elements within this specialty block: (1) principles of leadership, (2) principles of organization, (3) application of principles 1 and 2 to vocational education administration, (4) the various kinds of institutions in which vocational education is found and their place in the overall vocational education effort, (5) principles of vocational education and their application to various types of vocational institutions, (6) basic principles of vocational education budgeting and financing, (7) the politics of vocational education, (8) characteristics of vocational education faculty and administrators, (9) characteristics of vocational education students, (10) theory of vocational education curriculum construction, (11) skills and practice in becoming a good consumer of vocational education research, (12) principles of determining the feasibility of starting, stopping, and altering specific vocational programs, (13) principles and practices of decision making, (14) principles and practices of disseminating innovations in vocational education institutions, (15) principles and practices in vocational education facilities planning.

There ought not be vocational doctoral programs that specialize in a subject matter area (such as technical, trade and industrial, home economics, or business), although such specialization may be appropriate for masters degree programs (where the likelihood of the graduate assuming an administration position in one of these specialization areas is greatest). A doctoral graduate may expect to acquire a position which encompasses administering several vocational specialties. The leader at this higher administrative level needs a repertoire of knowledge and conceptionalizations that provide him with a broad and cosmopolitan picture of vocational education.

The remaining one-sixth (fifteen credit hours) of the doctoral program would be the dissertation. This should be a closely and expertly advised experience in which the candidate identifies the topic he is to investigate, analyzes his findings, draws conclusions, and makes suggestions. Such an experience is an important practice in problem solving, particularly when the selected topic is a practical and worthwhile one.

In conclusion, the university vocational doctoral programs are the major source of leadership in vocational education at the federal, state, and local levels. This being the case, it is important that the programs in which the leaders are trained have an overall framework which includes the components described here.

References

AVA, *Articles of Incorporation*, 1929.
AVA, *State and National Leadership in Vocational Education: 1970-71 Directory*. Washington, D.C.: American Vocational Association, 1972.
Campbell, Ronald F., and Gregg, Russell, T., eds. *Administrative Behavior in Education*. New York: Harper, 1957.
Carlson, Richard O. *Executive Success and Organizational Change*. Chicago: Midwest Administration Center, University of Chicago, 1962.
Dennis, E.A. *Industrial Teacher Education Directory*. Sponsored by American Council on Industrial Arts Teacher Education and National Association on Industrial and Technical Teacher Education, 1973.
Getzels, Jacob W., and Guba, Egon G. "Social Behavior and the Administrative Process." *School Review* 65 (Winter 1957).
Gillie, A.C., Sr. *Principles of Post-Secondary Vocational Education*. Columbus, O.: Charles E. Merrill, 1973.
————. "Vocational Mission Versus Employment Concerns." *American Vocational Journal* 47 (October 1972).
Griffiths, Daniel E. *Administrative Theory*. New York: Appleton-Century-Crofts, 1959.
Halpin, Andrew W., ed. *Administrative Theory in Education*. New York: Macmillan, 1967.
————. *The Leadership Behavior of School Superintendents*. Columbus: College of Education, The Ohio State University, 1956.
————, and Croft, Don B. *The Organizational Climate of Schools*. Chicago: Midwest Administration Center, University of Chicago, 1963.
Hemphill, John E., Griffiths, Daniel E., and Fredericksen, Norman. *Administrative Performance and Personality*. New York: Bureau of Publications, Teachers College, Columbia University, 1962.
Kroll, Arthur M. *Issues in American Education*. New York: Oxford University Press, 1970.
Moore, Hollis A., Jr. *Studies in School Administration: A Report of the NOEPA*. Washington, D.C.: American Association of School Administrators, 1957.

II

Vocational Education Delivery System

5

The Vocational High School

In this work the category vocational high school includes specialized vocational secondary schools that consider themselves outside the rubric of area vocational schools or the comprehensive high schools in one respect or another. The institutions considered in this chapter are listed under two classifications in a recent directory (Osso, 1973): (1) specialized vocational: a secondary school used exclusively or principally to provide vocational education to individuals available for full-time study, and (2) combination specialized secondary and technical vocational: a school used exclusively to provide vocational education on a full-time study basis to persons who are in or have left high school.

A listing of these schools for 1971 is given in Table 5-1. There are 354 specialized vocational and 195 combination specialized secondary and technical vocational schools, resulting in a total of 549 institutions. Unfortunately, it is difficult to place some schools in the vocational high school category because many of those included in these two types (e.g., specialized vocational and combination secondary and technical vocational) are also listed as area vocational schools (*AVS Directory*, 1973). Therefore, the number of institutions that fall within the vocational high school category is considerably smaller than the total given in Table 5-1. Also, only seventeen nonpublic schools are classified in the vocational high school category.

Of interest is the total number of secondary schools (by state and mode of control) that offer vocational programs. Table 5-2 shows that a total of 17,460 secondary schools offered vocational courses in 1971, most of which were under local public control. Less than 600 of this total were nonpublic secondary institutions.

Secondary vocational education has traditionally been divided into seven broad vocational fields: agriculture, distributive, health-related fields, home economics, business and office, technical, and trade and industrial. In 1971 the most programs were offered in home economics, followed by business and office, trade and industrial, agriculture, distributive, technical, and health-related. The distribution of secondary school offerings in each of the seven fields nationally and by state are given in Table 5-3. Of interest is that the total number of secondary

TABLE 5-1 Number of Secondary Schools Offering
Occupational Curriculums, Type of School
and Number of Area Schools,[a] by State or
Other Area of Control: Aggregate United
States, Fall 1971

State or Other Area of Control	Specialized Vocational[b]	Combination Specialized Secondary and Technical Vocational[c]
Alabama	21	2
California	5	1
Connecticut	1	16
Illinois	24	3
Indiana	7	2
Kentucky	1	58
Massachusetts	33	10
Michigan	9	3
Minnesota	16	—
Missouri	16	10
New Jersey	16	14
New York	57	2
Ohio	25	—
Oklahoma	15	—
Pennsylvania	33	13
South Carolina	27	—
Tennessee	9	6
Virginia	—	21
Puerto Rico	7	19
States and areas not listed[d]	31	13
Grand Total	357	199

[a] A public school approved by the state board for vocational education to provide instruction in occupations for residents of an area usually larger than a local administrative unit.

[b] A school at the secondary level used exclusively or principally to provide vocational technical education to persons available for full-time study.

[c] A school used exclusively to provide vocational education to persons available for full-time study, who are in or have left high school.

[d] Those states and other areas of control having less than five schools in both categories are included here.

Source: Extracted from Osso (1973).

vocational programs offered throughout the United States in 1971 was just under 50,000, an average of about three for each secondary school reporting offerings in vocational education.

In addition, about half of the more than 17,000 secondary schools offering vocational curricula also provided special vocational programs in 1971. These were distributed among five special categories: disadvantaged, handicapped, cooperative work study, work study, and group guidance. Table 5-4 gives this distribution by state.

Objectives and Philosophy

The objectives and philosophy of secondary vocational schools embrace certain elements found in the comprehensive high schools and other elements common to the area vocational schools. They subscribe to the philosophy of preparing secondary school age youngsters for a vocation through one or more of the vocational curricula identified in Table 5-3. Generally, if the school offers programs in five or more occupational areas, it can be classified as an area vocational school, according to the definition of such institutions found in the federal legislation (the Vocational Education Amendments of 1968, PL 90-576). Those schools that meet the federal criteria are classified as area vocational schools and are considered in Chapter 6. But as already indicated, there are special purpose secondary vocational schools that do not offer a sufficient variety and/or number of vocational curricula to be termed area vocational schools. It can be assumed, however, that the limited number of vocational programs is the only major difference between them and the area vocational schools. Thus the basic philosophy and overall objectives of this kind of vocational institution is, for all practical purposes, similar to that of the area vocational schools, and the reader is urged to refer to Chapter 6 for a discussion of institutional objectives and philosophy.

The Administration and Faculty

The organizational format of these institutions is similar to other locally controlled secondary schools. A local board of education, elected in many places, serves as the governance board for the matters of finances, hiring of professional staff, and planning of facilities. The chief agent of the board, often called the superintendent, appoints, with confirmation by the board of education, the director or principal of the school. The vocational school functions as one of the secondary schools in that school district. Certification requirements for teachers and administrators are imposed by the state board of education. In most states vocational professional personnel have certification requirements that are unique to vocational education.

The present mode of certification in some of the vocational areas pro-

TABLE 5-2 Number of Secondary Schools Offering Occupational Curriculums, by Control and by State or Other Area: Aggregate United States, Fall 1971

State or Area	Total	Public			Nonpublic	
		Federal	State	Local	Religious	Other
Alabama	422	1	9	407	4	1
Alaska	46	4	9	33	—	—
Arizona	128	—	—	116	7	5
Arkansas	364	—	4	360	—	—
California	807	1	2	792	9	3
Colorado	145	—	—	145	—	—
Connecticut	163	—	19	128	1	15
Delaware	47	1	46	—	—	—
Dist. of Columbia	30	—	—	29	—	1
Florida	500	—	—	498	2	—
Georgia	358	—	—	358	—	—
Hawaii	61	—	58	—	2	1
Idaho	166	—	1	161	4	—
Illinois	818	—	7	726	55	30
Indiana	286	—	4	273	7	2
Iowa	358	—	—	358	—	—
Kansas	265	—	—	265	—	—
Kentucky	407	—	60	324	19	4
Louisiana	459	—	—	459	—	—
Maine	128	—	1	127	—	—
Maryland	307	—	4	299	—	4
Massachusetts	237	2	5	217	9	4
Michigan	643	9	190	422	19	3
Minnesota	407	—	4	390	8	5
Mississippi	337	—	—	337	—	—
Missouri	347	3	5	326	10	3
Montana	140	1	2	129	8	—
Nebraska	430	—	3	384	43	—
Nevada	43	1	4	36	2	—
New Hampshire	64	—	1	58	—	5
New Jersey	337	—	1	313	15	8
New Mexico	108	6	95	7	—	—
New York	1,292	1	5	1,174	52	60
North Carolina	340	—	—	340	—	—
North Dakota	150	2	2	139	7	—
Ohio	854	—	2	833	11	8
Oklahoma	426	—	—	426	—	—
Oregon	175	—	—	173	2	—
Pennsylvania	750	—	—	703	35	12
Rhode Island	21	—	3	15	2	1
South Carolina	290	—	—	290	—	—
South Dakota	151	2	1	148	—	—
Tennessee	365	4	301	54	5	1
Texas	1,181	—	1	1,180	—	—
Utah	146	—	—	146	—	—
Vermont	66	—	2	58	1	5

Table 5-2 (*continued*)

State or Area	Total	Public Federal	Public State	Public Local	Nonpublic Religious	Nonpublic Other
Virginia	423	1	12	405	3	2
Washington	363	—	—	363	—	—
West Virginia	219	—	4	211	4	—
Wisconsin	322	3	41	262	10	6
Wyoming	73	—	2	71	—	—
Canal Zone	2	2	—	—	—	—
Guam	1	—	—	1	—	—
Puerto Rico	474	11	436	—	8	19
Trust Territory	16	—	15	—	—	1
Virgin Islands	2	—	2	—	—	—
Grand Total	17,460	55	1,363	15,469	364	209

Source: Extracted from Osso (1973).

vides the teacher with the security of permanent certification quite apart from acquiring the bachelor's degree. Heavy emphasis is placed on related work experience, and the requirements for taking certification-related courses are such that, should the vocational teacher so elect, he or she may be free to discontinue all studies upon receipt of permanent certification. As long as this mode of certification exists, it may be very difficult to motivate such individuals to continue their professional studies up to at least the baccalaureate level. Evidence of this is seen in the great number of faculty members in vocational programs who do not hold bachelor's degrees (Kay, 1970). A clear endorsement of a minimum educational requirement for vocational teachers (i.e., at least a bachelor's degree) at the time of employment (with an appropriate deadline for those presently employed) would quickly remedy this unfortunate situation, which contributes to the low prestige accorded vocational programs in education. Such a move can be urged, however, only when a good case can be made for it. Such a case would have to indicate clearly that requiring vocational teachers to obtain a baccalaureate degree would in turn make them more successful in helping vocational students cope with their roles in the world of work. Making such a case would require careful analysis and then the creation of a model for an undergraduate vocational-teacher-training program based on this analysis.

Historically, the basic rationale for certification of public school teachers, supervisors, and administrators has been to ensure profes-

TABLE 5-3 Number of Secondary Schools Offering Occupational Education Programs, by Vocational Program and by State or Other Area: Aggregate United States, Fall 1971

State or Area	Agri-culture	Distri-butive	Health	Home Eco-nomics	Business and Office	Tech-nical	Trade and Indus-trial
Alabama	234	111	48	350	181	41	157
Alaska	1	13	5	40	41	2	32
Arizona	42	52	7	115	109	3	47
Arkansas	243	38	6	336	63	1	49
California	309	293	183	673	758	143	528
Colorado	71	39	42	105	114	18	105
Connecticut	17	57	34	38	130	—	70
Delaware	11	26	9	42	42	9	33
Dist. of Columbia	1	15	4	15	15	1	13
Florida	204	140	48	442	225	27	170
Georgia	186	92	—	274	210	—	90
Hawaii	25	16	—	61	38	—	17
Idaho	85	25	4	154	124	29	100
Illinois	454	375	234	690	733	216	644
Indiana	144	88	45	233	146	39	137
Iowa	230	57	—	261	49	—	52
Kansas	158	43	12	172	40	—	46
Kentucky	164	86	21	297	172	12	59
Louisiana	242	76	—	439	337	—	30
Maine	—	11	11	119	83	6	32
Maryland	52	74	30	260	210	15	158
Massachusetts	13	63	36	133	149	62	143
Michigan	156	298	122	535	496	123	452
Minnesota	213	93	23	324	110	7	98
Mississippi	202	56	26	311	57	3	129
Missouri	173	111	63	273	241	67	195
Montana	60	15	2	111	83	5	52
Nebraska	131	40	—	397	410	—	109
Nevada	15	7	5	34	34	4	28
New Hampshire	12	14	5	51	59	2	38
New Jersey	29	198	52	300	310	59	242
New Mexico	69	44	20	87	82	18	62
New York	171	459	109	1,000	1,060	517	1,070
North Carolina	238	209	37	332	139	—	273
North Dakota	89	17	3	125	55	3	13
Ohio	316	385	109	653	422	2	350
Oklahoma	346	49	25	294	64	13	129
Oregon	104	51	21	35	139	—	104
Pennsylvania	223	157	58	571	670	86	161
Rhode Island	8	9	5	15	10	7	14
South Carolina	184	118	19	59	209	—	217
South Dakota	60	34	6	145	39	12	19
Tennessee	207	125	28	317	211	43	195
Texas	873	420	47	1,089	300	28	434

Table 5-3 (*continued*)

State or Area	Agri-culture	Distri-butive	Health	Home Eco-nomics	Business and Office	Tech-nical	Trade and Indus-trial
Utah	50	46	8	145	89	1	80
Vermont	23	14	9	63	30	—	22
Virginia	188	191	49	397	299	2	210
Washington	160	94	16	327	223	1	78
West Virginia	99	47	38	166	120	55	130
Wisconsin	182	96	28	213	274	34	226
Wyoming	61	16	6	70	71	—	10
Canal Zone	—	—	—	—	2	—	2
Guam	—	—	—	—	—	1	1
Puerto Rico	53	65	27	391	104	35	207
Trust Territory	8	—	2	15	3	—	16
Virgin Islands	1	1	2	2	2	2	2
Grand Total	7,650	5,269	1,749	14,196	10,386	1,754	8,080

Source: Extracted from Osso (1973).

sional competency. Considerable thought has been devoted to the advantages and weaknesses of certification. The most recent trend, which appears to be a fad, is competency-based certification. While the basic idea is a good one, the danger lies in the selection of the skills and knowledge to be assessed. Vocational education, with one of its major underpinnings being the teaching of skills and provision of knowledge associated with the vocational specialty, at first glance appears to lend itself to easy measurement of objectives. In fact, however, the most important components of vocational education deal with matters of the mind, such as attitudes toward learning new work skills and techniques. Competency-based certification in vocational education could tend to encrust certain skills into the fabric of vocational teacher education and thus deprive the profession of much of its present flexibility. The preparation of professionals for vocational education ought to be sufficiently pragmatic to provide for optimum development of each individual teacher and administrator. The competency-based idea works the other way around; all who aspire to enter the profession must achieve a minimum level in a series of competencies, regardless of the unique contributions each of these individuals can bring to the profession. The matter of competency-based teaching is dealt with in Chapter 17.

TABLE 5-4 Number of Secondary Schools Offering Special Vocational
Programs, by Type of Program, and Number of Schools
Offering No Special Programs, by State or Other Area:
Aggregate United States, Fall 1971

State or Area	Dis-advantaged	Handi-capped	Cooperative Work Study	Work Study	Group Guidance	No Special Programs
Alabama	79	55	91	52	60	223
Alaska	41	5	27	2	—	5
Arizona	1	—	51	24	12	65
Arkansas	1	—	—	—	—	363
California	354	343	130	137	160	319
Colorado	—	11	37	39	—	105
Connecticut	8	29	—	—	15	115
Delaware	15	13	25	17	17	8
Dist. of Columbia	5	4	16	14	11	7
Florida	370	173	272	62	49	71
Georgia	329	328	57	22	3	10
Hawaii	3	4	10	17	—	41
Idaho	18	16	34	18	30	98
Illinois	236	256	454	174	267	222
Indiana	51	48	119	52	64	115
Iowa	1	—	156	—	—	202
Kansas	30	11	54	22	14	170
Kentucky	199	28	64	57	—	167
Louisiana	44	—	100	—	1	334
Maine	19	15	41	—	—	74
Maryland	63	33	32	2	5	199
Massachusetts	30	42	83	74	42	73
Michigan	109	120	313	129	99	237
Minnesota	56	41	7	2	5	328
Mississippi	111	6	44	—	145	124
Missouri	54	45	99	61	62	168
Montana	18	6	17	17	9	97
Nebraska	136	99	44	—	2	276
Nevada	7	1	17	5	2	20
New Hampshire	29	16	30	16	9	18
New Jersey	68	88	222	77	57	87
New Mexico	18	13	37	23	27	48
New York	136	140	267	158	93	851
North Carolina	22	33	248	—	1	77
North Dakota	57	10	36	31	63	48
Ohio	428	1	155	37	20	409
Oklahoma	31	8	107	1	13	295
Oregon	96	99	77	100	—	47
Pennsylvania	150	143	190	72	118	410
Rhode Island	11	6	8	4	8	4
South Carolina	93	93	77	77	115	90
South Dakota	18	8	26	12	21	102
Tennessee	53	42	89	60	81	176
Texas	94	33	134	50	142	898
Utah	26	17	14	9	13	112

Table 5-4 (continued)

State of Area	Dis- advantaged	Handi- capped	Cooperative Work Study	Work Study	Group Guidance	No Special Programs
Vermont	4	10	20	11	—	42
Virginia	16	11	103	—	3	298
Washington	4	15	39	47	360	2
West Virginia	36	16	20	44	82	100
Wisconsin	65	73	119	69	96	113
Wyoming	14	7	16	4	3	52
Canal Zone	—	—	—	—	—	2
Guam	—	—	1	—	—	—
Puerto Rico	99	41	45	47	40	288
Trust Territory	15	—	8	1	3	1
Virgin Islands	2	2	2	2	1	—
Grand Total	3,973	2,657	4,484	1,951	2,443	8,806

Source: Extracted from Osso (1973).

The Students

As with administrators and faculty, students at these institutions are similar, for the most part, to those found in the nation's area vocational schools. See Chapter 6 for characteristics of these students.

References

AVS Directory, 1973. Washington, D.C.: Department of Health, Education, and Welfare, Office of Education, 1973.

Kay, E.R. Vocational Education: Characteristics of Teachers and Students, 1969. Washington, D.C.: National Center for Educational Statistics, 1970.

Osso, N.A. Directory of Secondary Schools with Occupational Curriculums: Public and Non-Public, 1971. Washington, D.C.: Department of Health, Education, and Welfare, Adult and Vocational Education Surveys Branch, 1973.

6

The Area Vocational School

Area vocational schools (commonly called AVS's or AVTS's) are those schools that fall within a broad definition found in the Vocational Amendments of 1968 (PL 90-576). Within the rubric of area vocational schools are four types:

1. A specialized high school used exclusively or principally to provide vocational education to persons who are available for full-time study in preparation for entering the labor market.

2. The department of a high school used exclusively or principally to provide vocational education in no less than five different occupational fields to persons who are available for full-time study in preparation for entering the labor market.

3. A technical or vocational school used exclusively or principally to provide vocational education to persons who have completed or left high school and are available for full-time study in preparation for entering the labor market.

4. The department or division of a junior college, community college, or university which provides vocational education in no less than five different occupational fields, under the supervision of the state board, leading to the student's immediate employment but not leading to the baccalaureate degree.

Requirements include the school's availability to all residents of the state or an area of the state as designated and approved by the state board; and in the case of a school, department, or division described in 3 or 4, it must also admit as regular students those who have left high school as well as those who have completed high school. This chapter describes and analyzes the elements found to be common among area vocational schools.

The number of area vocational schools has rapidly increased since the passage of the Vocational Act of 1963 (PL 88-910). The growth for years 1973 through 1975 in each state and nationally is given in Table 6-1. The number of AVS's throughout the United States increased by 776 schools (a 46 percent growth) between 1971 and 1975 (as compared with the number of community junior colleges which grew from 1,111

74

TABLE 6-1 Number of Area Vocational Education Schools by State for Selected Years

State	1973	1975	State	1973	1975
Alabama	83	101	Nevada	5	17
Alaska	9	9	New Hampshire	31	34
Arizona	14	14	New Jersey	37	34
Arkansas	22	35	New Mexico	8	9
California	118	124	New York	71	72
Colorado	12	15	North Carolina	56	57
Connecticut	19	20	North Dakota	6	6
Delaware	6	10	Ohio	130	132
Dist. of Columbia	6	7	Oklahoma	24	26
Florida	34	78	Oregon	18	18
Georgia	71	120	Pennsylvania	89	92
Hawaii	17	21	Rhode Island	8	8
Idaho	6	6	South Carolina	50	51
Illinois	49	55	South Dakota	6	6
Indiana	37	43	Tennessee	49	48
Iowa	25	25	Texas	132	152
Kansas	14	14	Utah	12	14
Kentucky	62	82	Vermont	15	15
Louisiana	31	31	Virginia	105	105
Maine	20	21	Washington	125	161
Maryland	88	88	West Virginia	39	56
Massachusetts	80	87	Wisconsin	38	38
Michigan	71	77	Wyoming	7	7
Minnesota	49	50	American Samoa	1	1
Mississippi	55	68	Guam	1	1
Missouri	53	53	Puerto Rico	16	16
Montana	5	5	Trust Territory	1	1
Nebraska	10	14	Virgin Islands	2	2
			Total	2,148	2,452

Source: AVS Directory, 1975.

in 1971 to 1,203 in 1974, an increase of just over 8 percent during that three-year period).

Table 6-2 gives an indication of the level of AVS offerings. One distinct feature of the AVS's is their diversity in program offerings (i.e., secondary, post-secondary, and adult). Almost 400 of them offer programs of all three types, and those schools lend themselves more readily to the universal college configuration examined in other sections.

With 2,452 area vocational schools and 1,203 community junior colleges* in the fifty states, vocational education leaders have a multidimensional challenge.

* Almost 500 community junior colleges are also listed as area vocational schools, resulting in some duplication in the count.

TABLE 6-2 AVS Offerings by Program

Program Type	Number of AVS's
Secondary	713
Post-secondary	237
Adult	8
Secondary–post-secondary	8
Secondary–adult	561
Post-secondary–adult	530
Secondary–post-secondary–adult	375

First, continuous efforts must be made to minimize unnecessary duplication of programs. Various efforts to do this through coordination and cooperation are being made in several places, and the problem is of considerable concern to state legislators and vocational education leaders.

Second, vocational education leaders must design and implement realistic formulas and other approaches for determining financial allocations to these institutions. The problem is very complex in some states because of the existing variety of financing mechanisms. A number of states, for example, provide local and state funding for the area vocational school through a combination of the ways in which other public primary and secondary education are funded. Added to local and state monies are the federal funds received through Vocational Education Amendments of 1968 appropriations. Finances therefore are usually obtained by a combination of local-regional real-estate-based taxation, state-legislated appropriations, and federal funds. In many states community junior colleges receive both local-regional and state funds through allocations separate from those for AVS's. Both AVS's and community junior colleges are vocational schools, and in many states community junior colleges are dependent upon local-regional real-estate-based taxation although with separate budgets for partial funding; and the state appropriations part of the two schools' budgets are quite commonly separate from one another as well. Therefore, the total requested amounts for these two types of institutions are arrived at separately. Should the appropriations for AVS's and community junior colleges be combined at both local-regional and state levels, each would more or less be forced to consider what the other is doing. Such an approach is not too far afield, if one considers that many of the institutions identified as community junior colleges are also classified as area vocational schools. Furthermore, almost 1,150 of the approximately 2,450 area vocational schools (slightly over 45 percent) offer post-secondary curricula (either in conjunction with secondary level programs or as post-secondary only).

Area vocational schools, then, by including both secondary and post-secondary levels of vocational education, constitute an interstitial position in the national framework of vocational education. This is the third dimension of the challenge facing vocational education leaders. Rather than being viewed as a problem, however, the interstitial characteristics of the area vocational school ought to be considered as an opportunity to develop new types of vocational institutions. A particularly exciting possibility is a configuration called the universal college (Gillie, 1973), which would include grades 11 through 14 on a regional basis and could offer a rich array of vocational curricula at various levels. The universal college concept is considered in later chapters as well as in the following paragraphs.

The universal college would provide a core, or cluster, of vocational subjects. There would be a judicious blend of group and individualized instruction designed to maximize each student's achievement. The length of time spent in the core would vary according to the individual student's ability, with maximum time allowed in higher level cores and correspondingly shorter lengths of time in the lowest level cores. For example, level 1 (the highest) could have a maximum length of three years, although some of the students would be counseled to seek employment and would be placed in a job and others would be counseled to obtain some other kind of additional education anytime after entry into that level. The same would be true for level 2, which might have a 1.5-year maximum length, and level 3, with a maximum length of 6 months. A generalized version of this model is shown in Fig. 6-1. Such a mechanism would provide opportunities for students to remain in the vocational core of their choice, with the possibility of moving vertically (in terms of cognitive ability needed) within the core. To illustrate the point, a youngster interested in electronics would have three possibilities: the first level, which would provide high level paraprofessional training and ultimately lead to the associate degree, the second level, which would place him in a job by the end of grade 12, and the third level, which would result in job placement before completion of grade 11. The combined efforts of an area vocational school and a community junior college could provide such a program, as could an area vocational school that offers both secondary and post-secondary level vocational instruction.

Area vocational schools have grown in number largely as a result of federal legislation affecting vocational education. The first urging to construct regionalized vocational institutions came in 1958 under the

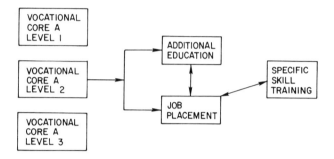

Figure 6-1. The universal college paradigm (limited to one vocational core for simplicity).

impetus of the National Education Defense Act (PL 85-864). Major funding to implement this construction did not come, however, until passage of the Vocational Education Act of 1963 (PL 88-910), which in turn was succeeded by the Vocational Education Amendments of 1968 (PL 90-576). Many educators agree that area vocational schools are the creatures of federal intentions toward vocational education. This is not meant to minimize the efforts that several states made to provide direct support of vocational education. California, for example, like a number of other states, introduced special state legislation to provide an easier mechanism for establishing vocational schools. This is partially the result of the legislature's recognizing the difficulty our vocational schools have in being recognized and accepted by the public. Broad legislation, providing for regional vocational centers, exists throughout the states, where responsibility for planning, operating, and financing AVS's has been delegated to regional (sometimes county) school superintendents, who include these activities in their local district planning.

There are a number of advantages to area vocational schools. Chief among them is that they provide an opportunity for people from a large geographic area to jointly plan and finance training opportunities for greater numbers of youngsters and adults than would be possible with single efforts scattered throughout smaller school districts. The regional approach, with its broader administrative base, is able to provide more extensive auxiliary services, and because of increased school size, the regional school can provide vocational preparation for a greater range of occupations. Also, curricula equipment and various educational services can be consolidated. An additional advantage, perceived by some, is that a properly managed area vocational school is better able to adjust to changing curricula than a smaller one-district-based school.

The impact of area vocational schools on rural poverty areas, such as the Appalachian region, has been cited in the literature (Sanders and Dennis, 1971). Several states have conducted studies during the past decade to identify effective ways of providing comprehensive vocational education. Most of these investigations indicate that typical high schools can offer only one or, at the most, several vocational programs, chiefly because of their size and the costs associated with such programs. Area vocational schools are considered the most viable approach to addressing this vital need. Some educators believe the introduction of area vocational schools in economically depressed regions would, in addition to reducing the secondary schools' dropout rate, help attract industry into the area. Partially in response to this idea, the federal Appalachian funds appropriated about one-fourth of their finances through June 1970 ($105 million out of $401 million) for construction of 261 vocational education facilities in Appalachia.

Because of the federal funding, AVS control comes from three sources: federal, state, and regional-local. Oklahoma is a typical example of how funding for area vocational schools is actually a three-way arrangement. A total of $34 million was allocated for area vocational schools in Oklahoma during the 1971–1972 year. Of this, 7.1 million were federal funds, 5.4 million were state funds, and 21.6 million were local funds. The tri-level method of funding does introduce governance complications (Gillie, 1973).

The fundamental question of what makes up the best preparation for a vocation and at what ages such preparation ought to be provided has been decided by Congress to some extent, as indicated by the manner in which it has appropriated money for vocational education. Congress apparently feels that such education ought to be going on primarily at the secondary level, but with a substantial effort from the post-secondary institutions as well. The question of separating vocational education from the rest of education is still unsettled. At least one study found that vocational education is offered under the most favorable conditions in separate vocational schools like the AVS's (Kaufman et al., 1967). The advantage is not that the separate school provided better training, but students were more effectively shielded from the many condescending and negative attitudes toward vocational education that are prevalent among students and faculty in the comprehensive high schools. Such findings lead many vocational educators to believe that the area vocational school, rather than the comprehensive high school, is the optimum institutional mode for secondary vocational education.

Vocational education for rural regions has been of considerable concern to legislators and educators, and for good reasons. The combined population of all of America's cities with a population of more than half a million would account for only 16 percent of the total population, and contrary to what is commonly believed, this has not changed materially during the past forty years. The most rapidly growing segment of our population is found in the smaller cities (10,000–50,000), which have increased by 50 percent since 1920. Seventeen states do not have a single county with a population density greater than 500 per square mile (500 per square mile is the official density measure used to classify a region as a suburban area, and 1,000 per square mile is the measure for classification as an urban area). Twenty-three states have an average population density of less than fifty people per square mile, and thirty-seven states have average densities of less than 100 per square mile. The size of the rural population in the United States is equal to the combined population of every city whose population exceeds 80,000, and its size is equivalent to the total population of America's 100 largest cities (Swanson, 1970). No country in Europe and only one in Latin America (Brazil) has a total population which exceeds the rural population of the United States. These figures point to a very significant rural segment in the United States. An astounding finding is that if the United States did not have an urban population, its rural population would meet the criteria for its being classified as an underdeveloped country! More than half of the rural families have incomes below $3,000; about two-thirds have substandard housing; and rural adults are below the national education attainment norm by about three years. In view of these conditions, area vocational schools in rural regions could have a substantial impact on the inhabitants.

But many more area vocational schools need to be placed in rural areas. As late as 1968 a study found that only 9 percent of the area vocational schools' enrollment was from small schools and villages (Amberson, 1968). There are indications, however, that area vocational schools will become a more significant component in the education services for rural sectors.

According to the 1970 census, 26.5 percent of the population lives in rural areas. Of this number (54 million), 9.7 million live on farms; the remaining are employed in manufacturing, mining, lumbering, recreation, colleges, state and county institutions, and military installations. While 10.4 percent of persons in metropolitan areas were below the low-income level in 1971, 17.2 percent of those living outside metropolitan areas were in that category that year. Surprisingly, the national rate of unemployment, 5.6 percent, was only slightly below that found in the rural regions (5.9 percent). Furthermore, a large percentage of the rural work force is believed to be underemployed. The effect of modern technology upon farming has created much of this dilemma. Between 1950 and 1972 farm output increased by 38 percent, while the demand for farm manpower decreased from 199 to 89 (where 1967 = 100; Lerner, 1973). A major outcome has been unemployment and under-employment, particularly for those who refuse to move out of their communities and/or have no specific skill or training beyond low level agricultural skills to take with them to other places.

The rural poor have several characteristics in common (HEW, Office of Education, 1970). They come from broken homes or homes without an able-bodied breadwinner and from large families. A disproportionate number of them are elderly. They lack access to adequate medical and dental care, and experience a high premature death rate. Many are nonfarmers living in small towns and villages or in remote or isolated areas. And they chronically lack access to suitable employment. In 1967, 3.1 million rural Americans were functional illiterates, and in 1960 more than 2 million rural youths between the ages of fourteen and twenty-four dropped out of school before graduating from high school. This is a disproportionate number of secondary school dropouts from the rural group, as compared to national averages. Rural schools are apparently unable to attract and hold the better qualified teachers (which may be partially attributable to low salaries). An important question is whether the area vocational school will be one of the vehicles to help resolve this very severe poverty problem.

The area vocational school has also become more common in urban areas, particularly in the North and the East. Although the American public has a strong attachment to the comprehensive high school idea, the high dropout rates seem to provide incentive for developing more AVS's. The AVS is considered a viable approach to vocational education at both secondary and post-secondary levels.

Objectives and Philosophy

There are four basic types of area vocational school. The first is the shared-time variety, in which students receive their general education under the auspices of their hometown high school and their vocational courses in the area vocational school. The second kind is a vocational department of a comprehensive high school or community junior college or university which offers vocational preparation in five or more occupational fields. The third is the self-contained vocational or technical school, often called a single-purpose school (as opposed to a comprehensive institution). The fourth variety is the residential area vocational school, of which there were sixty-nine in 1975 (*AVS Directory*, 1975). There are advocates for each type of area vocational school.

The major objectives of area vocational schools are to provide training leading to employment, upgrading, and updating in specific occupations and to serve youngsters and adults from more than one community or district. Most area vocational schools offer adult and continuing education of one type or another.

In many states the AVS's are seeking to meet the vocational needs of the rural population. For well over a decade, many young people and adults have been leaving the farms for the cities and towns to seek jobs. Many rural youngsters leave high school without acquiring the skills and training required for successful entry into the labor market, even at the lowest skilled levels. The rural area vocational schools, by offering vocational education facilities for several widely distributed school districts and counties, are helping to counteract this difficulty. In many areas, such as Appalachia, additional federal and state funds are provided for development and operation of area vocational schools, because of the very limited ability of the cooperating districts to support such endeavors.

There has been some consideration of the place of vocational education in the future. Recommendations include: (1) an extension of some type of vocational education into the elementary and middle schools, (2) increased attempts to implement the vocational cluster concept, particularly for low ability students, (3) expansion of cooperative vocational education and part-time programs into all vocational areas, (4) development of a more intensive vocational-counselor-training program so that specially trained counselors will be available to meet the special needs of vocational students, and (5) the provision of more area vocational schools so that they will be easily accessible to more youngsters and adults.

A debate is going on about how to measure program effectiveness in vocational education. Some take the position that the criteria for program effectiveness should include the percentage of graduates who work in the occupation for which they are trained, the salaries they earn, the employers' ratings of them (their job satisfactoriness), and the level of job satisfaction that they express. Some educational authorities take issue with using such factors to measure effectiveness because a host of other elements extraneous to the vocational program enters into these considerations. The question of evaluation remains, and reasonable approaches to it seem to be elusive at best.

The manner in which AVS's were defined in the Vocational Education Act of 1963 (PL 88-910) and the Vocational Education Amendments of 1968 (PL 90-576) did much to establish their philosophy and objectives, as indicated in the first section of this chapter. The definition of AVS's is sufficiently broad so as not to restrict their accountability merely to whether or not the graduate enters the vocation for which he was specifically trained. Many vocational educators believe that training in one job area may, indeed, be the basis for employing an individual in a second job area. The most important criterion, most vocational educators will agree, is whether the graduate is successful in entering an occupation that is satisfactory to him. In addition, the area vocational schools have three other major objectives: to provide occupational upgrading and updating so that individuals can accommodate themselves to the changes required by new technology and employment practices; to provide opportunities for mid-career changes for adults; and to prepare certain persons for enrollment in more advanced vocational programs.

Administration

Some area vocational schools are governed at the state level. The administrative control of such schools and their programs rests largely with the state board for vocational education (which is appointed by the state board of education). Placing the control of AVS's with the state board of vocational education has been strongly recommended in the Vocational Amendments of 1968. Included within the jurisdiction of such a state board is authority to select the school locations, designate areas in the state to be served, purchase and accept title to land, build and/or renovate facilities, determine curricula, employ educational personnel, and operate a sufficient number of such state schools to serve the needs of that state. In certain cases this board may delegate responsibility, to some extent, to local or regional boards of governance. Figure 6-2 is a generalized block diagram of an AVS governance structure.

Operational costs are met through the state-allocated educational funds. In some states students are required to pay tuition, but this is not typical. AVS's may be organized according to several different patterns.

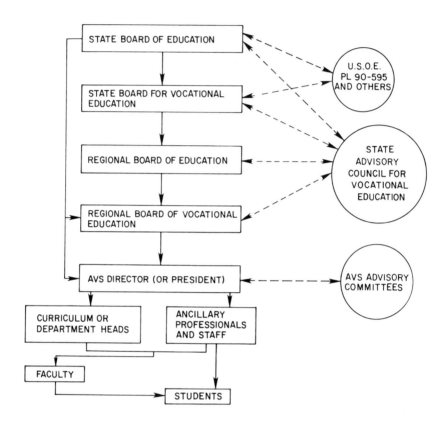

Figure 6-2. Generalized block diagram of AVS governance structure.

A common mode is one in which the AVS serves a designated geographic or political area. In such cases the state is usually divided into regions by area or population concentration or according to political boundaries (such as counties), and an area vocational school is strategically located within the designated area. In another pattern specialized schools are established. One specialized school, for example, would feature one or several clusters of occupations for students from the entire state, and another school would specialize in other occupational clusters, also for everyone in the state. Frequently, with this system some students have to travel a considerable distance from home or, in some cases, take up residence near or at the school. In spite of this disadvantage, the pattern does enable the state to establish programs of the most expensive and exotic kinds.

Another alternative to having state-controlled AVS's is to vest control with regional governing boards. The regions usually establish a special area board, with representatives from each county or school district within the region served by the AVS. The board's general governance format is basically similar to that of the state-controlled area vocational school, except that much of the funding and other governance factors emanate from the regional board.

Some patterns involve local-regional cooperation. A common approach has been for several school districts to come together and pool their resources in a variety of ways. Typically, they have joined together to operate a single, but separate, vocational school to serve students from all parts of the cooperating districts. Like the other models, this type of AVS is also administered by a special board for vocational education. Such a group is usually made up of representatives from each of the participating districts, and is generally stratified in a proportional manner so that the composition of the board and the amount of local district financial support reflects the population of the school districts in the consolidated region.

For example, districts A, B, and C may have respective high school populations of 1,500, 2,500, and 4,000. Since the percentage of the total number of high school students in the consolidated region enrolled in each district is to be reflected in the composition of the regional board, the representation would be as follows:

$$\text{District A} = \frac{1,500}{1,500 + 2,500 + 4,000} = \frac{1,500}{8,000} = 18.75 \text{ percent}$$

$$\text{District B} = \frac{2,500}{1,500 + 2,500 + 4,000} = \frac{2,500}{8,000} = 31.25 \text{ percent}$$

$$\text{District C} = \frac{4,000}{1,500 + 2,500 + 4,000} = \frac{4,000}{8,000} = 50 \text{ percent}$$

The three districts would likely round these percentages off to 20 percent, 30 percent, and 50 percent. Having determined these, they would probably establish a ten-member board (with two representatives from District A, three from District B, and five from District C). One of the first tasks of the newly formed board would be to arrive at an interdistrict funding formula, which would reflect the number of vocational students from each district.

Another approach would be to determine the membership on the basis of the amounts of total public education budgets of the three districts. Still other approaches, utilizing such factors as per capita income per district, population density (or sparcity) of each district, and overall taxing capability of each district, might be used in determining the amount to be contributed by each district.

Another variety of AVS is the self-contained vocational school. This type of area vocational school, besides providing various vocational curricula, also offers the general education courses found in comprehensive secondary schools and extracurricular activities such as athletics and social and subject-related clubs. The major difference between the comprehensive high school and the self-contained vocational school is the absence of pre-collegiate curricula in the latter, although the graduates of both are awarded the traditional secondary school diploma. The self-contained area vocational school qualifies, like the other varieties of AVS considered here, for federal aid for both construction and operational expenses. There are several disadvantages to this type of AVS, the major ones being that some students have to travel farther to attend such a special school and some youngsters have difficulty initially breaking away from their previous school and neighborhood ties.

Still another variety of area vocational school is the shared-time vocational training center. These schools usually include separate facilities that house the shops and laboratories required for vocational programs. Quite often, but not always, classrooms for general education studies are excluded in such facilities. Students are transported to the AVS school for their vocational work and take their general studies courses at the hometown high school. The turnabout time (i.e., the length of time spent in each school before changing) varies, with a half day at each school being common when long travel distances are not involved. Other common options are a one-day turnaround, a two-week turnaround, and a three-week turnaround (Gillie and Hutchinson, 1974). The high school diploma is most commonly issued by the sending (or hometown) high school.

Studies of the characteristics of AVS administrators are not common, but one investigation included almost 600 AVS directors in twenty-four states (Polk, 1969), which provided an initial basis for developing a tentative profile of personal, educational, and experiential characteristics of AVS directors. It was found that positive relationships existed between a director's success and his: (1) graduate preparation in vocational education, (2) undergraduate preparation at a private college or university, (3) number of years of experience in vocational education, and (4) membership in five or more professional organizations.

An examination of secondary vocational programs conducted in 1963 found that 667 secondary schools offered three or more vocational

TABLE 6-3 Geographic Distribution of
Vocational Schools in 1963

Section of the Country	Number of Schools	Percentage of the Total
New England	72	10.8
Mideast	162	24.3
Great Lakes	100	15.0
Plains	48	7.2
Southeast	196	24.4
Southwest	54	8.1
Rocky Mountains	8	1.2
Far West and Pacific	27	4.0
Total	667	100.0

choices at that time. Their geographic distribution is shown in Table 6-3 (Eninger, 1968). Of this number 177 had enrollments of less than 500; 284 had between 500 and 1,500 students; and 206 had enrollments exceeding 1,500.

Principals of vocational schools were queried about the major problems they encountered, and they gave the following: lack of qualified teacher replacements (31 percent), low level of teachers' salaries (24 percent), "dumping ground" reputation of vocational programs (21 percent), quality of students in vocational education (20 percent), shops in need of major rehabilitation (19 percent), and inadequate student-counseling services (18 percent). Over 90 percent of the vocational teachers surveyed rated students in their classes as average to high average in motivation, an overall rating found to be considerably more optimistic than that given by the administrators included in the investigation.

Other findings showed that principals believed their school board members had sufficient interest in vocational education, teacher turnover was not excessive, student–teacher ratios were favorable, their vocational teachers were qualified, school plant appearance was generally good, and shop material and supplies were generally sufficient.

School board members' attitudes toward vocational education were examined, and the following was found: 59 percent of the members had highly favorable attitudes toward vocational education, as evidenced by their active attempts to expand offerings; the rhetoric of 35 percent indicated they were in favor of vocational education, but they sometimes failed to give it active support; and 6 percent were either uncommitted or displayed unfavorable attitudes toward vocational education.

There is concern about sound planning for vocational education. Russo (1969) indicated that a new planning system is needed to identify and define community goals and aspirations, educational objectives, human resources, financial resources, a program of action, alternatives, decisions, and evaluation procedures. Some of the data needed to plan vocational facilities adequately include socioeconomic and ethnic composition of the immediate and adjacent communities, civic and social aspirations of the various groups in the community, educational posture of the community, business and industrial outlook for the community (positive or negative growth), potential employment opportunities and basic job entry requirements, students' aspirations, existing school facilities and capabilities, vocational programs needed, anticipated support from leaders in the business community, involvement and input that can be expected from community leaders, and the impact expected from utilization of advisory and craft committees.

Valentine (1971) has suggested a systems approach to vocational education administration. In a prepared guide to assist such attempts, he proposed: an introduction to the systems approach for analyzing administrator responsibility, a problem-solving and a decision-making model, an administrative profile of the tasks and functions performed by administrators in the decision-making process, and specific models for each of the major administrative functions pertaining to planning, development, implementation, and evaluation of the effectiveness of vocational programs.

Faculty

The national rate of growth in the number of vocational students and teachers between 1963 and 1969 is given in Table 6-4. The student–teacher ratio remained relatively constant during these years, indicating that the increase in vocational teachers apparently kept up with the growth in the number of students. The average secondary vocational class consisted of twenty-one students. This average was approximately the same for each of the seven vocational fields (i.e., agriculture, distributive education, health occupations, home economics, office occupations, technical, and trade and industrial).

The typical vocational teacher is male and in his early forties. If we assume that sixty-five is the usual retirement age, the typical vocational teacher has twenty to twenty-five years remaining in his teaching career. Since he (or she) had less than ten years of teaching up to that point in time, average vocational teaching careers appear to range from

TABLE 6-4 Enrollments and Teachers in
Vocational Education:
National

Year	Enrollments (millions)	Teachers (thousands)
1963	4.2	85
1964	4.6	85
1965	5.4	109
1966	6.1	124
1967	7.0	133
1968	7.5	147
1969	8.0	167

Source: U.S. Office of Education. *Vocational and Technical
Education Annual Reports.*

twenty-five to thirty-five years total. In 1969, about 25 percent of the
vocational teachers were under thirty years old; 44 percent were in the
thirty-to-forty-four-year-old category; and 46 percent were forty-five
years of age and older. Also, 14 percent had twenty or more years of
teaching experience; 22 percent had fifteen or more; 37 percent had ten
years or more; and 62 percent had five years or more. These data include
all teaching; vocational teacher experience was found to be less for
teachers in each of the seven categories. The distribution of the age
span of vocational education teachers and the length of time they will
spend teaching indicates that a considerable amount of in-service
teacher education will be required to keep these teachers up-to-date.
This, of course, has considerable implication for the future role of vocational teacher education.

Let us now consider the vocational teachers' academic qualifications.
About 74 percent hold the bachelor's degree; about 33.3 percent have
the master's degree or better; and about 13 percent hold only the associate degree or its equivalent; in addition, 18 percent of the male and
6 percent of the female vocational teachers hold no academic degree.
The justification for employing persons without a baccalaureate degree
is probably based upon their previous work experience. This lack of a
degree appears to be more commonplace with the older teachers (5
percent of those under thirty, 13 percent in the thirty-to-forty-four-
year-old group, and 16 percent of those forty-five and over). As a whole,
the younger vocational teachers have sought to become qualified to
teach in the vocational areas by acquiring an academic degree,
whereas older teachers, in many cases, have moved into the teaching
profession after a considerable number of years working in a vocational
area. (This, of course, can be viewed as a mid-career change.)

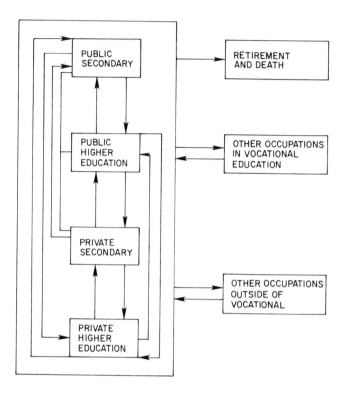

Figure 6-3. Transfer flow chart.

About half of the vocational teachers hold vocational teaching certificates, while the other half hold regular teaching certificates. Vocational teaching certificates are favored by the older male vocational
teachers, probably because the certificate's requirements emphasize
work experiences and play down academic credits. Most female vocational teachers have regular teaching certificates. In terms of vocational specialties, two-thirds of the teachers in the trade and industrial
group and more than half of those in the technical and health-related
fields hold vocational certificates, while regular teaching certificates
prevail in the four remaining vocational specialties.

An aspect of teaching in vocational education that has not been
studied intensively is teacher turnover. Sources of vocational teachers

include institutions of higher education, other occupations inside education, and other occupations outside education. Vocational teachers, like other types of teachers, leave the profession because of retirement, death, other occupations outside education, and other occupations in education. The movement of teachers into and out of vocational education is diagrammed in Fig. 6-3.

No study of the number of vocational teachers that transfer into and out of the profession nationally is known to this writer, but a study of turnover of public elementary and secondary school teachers in 1959–1960 found that 8.1 percent of the total teaching staff left the teaching profession during that year (Lindenfeld, 1963). The separation rate was similar for all but the very small schools (with enrollments of less than 600), where it was higher. No relationship was found between average salary level and separation rate or between pupil–teacher ratio and separation rate. This figure of 8.1 percent turnover may be too high for the national experience in vocational education, particularly for the mid-1970s or for future projections, but it serves as a ueful point of reference.

Combining of the factors described here with several assumptions provides a crude index of the number of vocational teachers needed in the years ahead throughout the nation. The following projections are based on certain arbitrarily chosen original figures. In assumption x a no-growth position is examined, and in assumption y an annual vocational teacher growth of 2 percent is considered.

PROJECTIONS

Total vocational teachers: 167,000*

Assumption x: No increase in overall number of teachers needed.

Estimate x

a. For each year from 1975 to 1985, a 5 percent turnover will require 8,350 new teachers annually.

b. For each year from 1975 to 1985, an 8 percent turnover will require 13,300 new teachers annually.

Assumption y: Vocational education enrollment will increase 2 percent annually.

* Source: U.S. Office of Education. *Vocational and Technical Education Annual Reports.* This is the 1969 figure, which is considerably below the number of vocational teachers in the 1970s.

Estimate y

a. For each year from 1975 to 1985, a 5 percent turnover plus 2 percent overall increase will require about 11,700 new teachers annually. This discounts the compounding effect of a 2 percent annual increase.

b. For each year from 1975 to 1985, an 8 percent turnover rate plus 2 percent overall annual increase will require about 16,600 new teachers annually. Again, the compounding effect of the annual 2 percent increase is discounted.

The ratio of teachers to administrators and other nonteaching professionals (excluding librarians, guidance staff, and psychological staff) in the public elementary secondary schools for the period from 1963 to 1967 was about nineteen teachers to one administrator (Silverman and Metz, 1970). If this ratio is applicable also to vocational programs, the number of administrators and other nonteaching professionals amounts to about 5.3 percent of the total vocational teacher supply. Therefore (using the 1969 vocational teacher total of 167,000), there are about 8,850 vocational program administrators.

If we assume a no-growth situation and the turnover rates described above for teachers, a total of 440 annual replacements will be required for the 5 percent replacement rate and about 710 administrators annually for the 8 percent turnover rate. With the 2 percent annual growth assumption added to these turnover rates (and if we ignore the compounding effect of the annual 2 percent growth rate), these figures become about 620 for the combined 5 percent replacement plus 2 percent growth rates, and 890 for the combined 8 percent replacement plus 2 percent growth rates. These estimates may be conservative, however, since 1969 vocational program enrollments were used. (The assumption being made here is that vocational enrollments in the late 1970s and the 1980s will be considerably above this number.)

Since data come from various sources, there is no direct way to project the number of new teachers and administrators that will be needed in the future. The previous paragraphs described several of the major elements that go into determining the needs at a given time and gave a conservative estimate.

Perhaps the most direct approach is to use projected enrollments. The first step is to estimate what the enrollment would have to be in a given year in order to provide training for everyone who will begin new jobs that year. Furthermore, the "in-and-out" enrollment of persons seeking to update and upgrade their skills so as to maintain their qualifications in their fast-changing specialties must be taken into consideration. Predictions have been made that adult vocational education services will be utilized by a larger percentage of the civilian labor force from 1975 and thereafter. But, as analyzed in Chapter 17, it is yet to be determined whether such mid-career change efforts will be conducted under the auspices of Department of Labor funds (thereby possibly bypassing the public vocational schools) or within the framework of the public educational institution described in Chapters 5–14.

Students

From 1950 through 1970 the number of children aged five to nineteen in the continental United States increased from 34.9 million to 59.5 million, a 70 percent increase. From this group will emerge those individuals who will seek initial job preparation during the next decade. Although there has been a decline in the birth rate in the United States since 1957, some experts believe a cyclical rise in the birth rate, temporarily postponed by liberalized abortion laws, will take effect within a few years (Davis, 1973). But even with a continuation of the decrease in births, a reduction in the population of the five-to-nineteen-year-old group would not be experienced for many years. The rate of increase will likely decrease, and that will create a leveling off of the total numbers, but actual numbers will not decrease dramatically for some time (Lerner, 1970). Thus the changes in birth rate will not have a severe immediate effect on the numbers of new vocational students.

Adult and continuing education is also contributing to increased enrollment of vocational students. Worker retraining, or mid-career changing, is becoming more widely recognized as a major vehicle for overcoming job dissatisfaction and other dysfunctional elements in our work force (O'Toole, 1973). The major impetus for the desire of many workers to make mid-career changes is derived from three societal developments: (1) There is an increasing rate of technological, economic, and cultural change—a commitment to one lifelong occupation is no longer as feasible as it was with past generations. (2) Workers now live long enough to have a forty-year working life—a long time to spend in a single career. (3) Many low level workers have increased expectations which can be achieved by changing careers. Vocational education is an available societal mechanism for making mid-career changes. Although basic financial support (most importantly, a living allowance that provides the recycling worker with sufficient funds to support his family at the level to which he is accustomed) has not been fully worked out on a widely accepted basis, the need for such provisions has been recognized for some time (O'Toole, 1973; Striner, 1972; Holt, 1971; Okum, 1963).

In light of these societal pressures, one can expect an increase in mid-career changes. The potential magnitude of this phenomenon is substantial. If the average individual has a working life of forty years and is to make one career change during that time (an extremely conservative estimate), it can be predicted that about one-fortieth (2.5 percent) of the work force, which presently exceeds 84 million, will be involved in career changing in any single year. Translated into numbers, more than 2 million adults would be engaged in such career preparation annually. This approaches the entire community junior college enrollment of 1972 (*AACJC Directory*, 1975). In addition, many workers will seek training to upgrade and update themselves in their present jobs, which could easily amount to another 2.5 percent of the entire work force—an additional 2 million or more. It is reasonable to assume that there will be an increase in adult vocational education enrollments to as high as 5 million individuals annually.

Another source of vocational students in the immediate future will be youngsters in the fifteen-to-twenty-year-old group. With continued federal support of vocational education (e.g., PL88-210 and PL90-576) some states may expand vocational programs, so that the majority of secondary students will receive some type of vocational education. Approximately 7 million students were enrolled in federally reimbursable vocational education classes in 1966–1967 (Silverman and Metz, 1970). These were categorized as 3.5 million secondary students, 0.5 million post-secondary students, and 2.9 million adults. During the same period 16.5 million students were enrolled in secondary (grades 9–12) schools (Silverman and Metz, 1970). If about three-fourths of secondary students were provided with some form of vocational education, the secondary school enrollments in vocational education would increase to 12 million. There are indications, with the increase in the number of area vocational schools to over 2,100 in 1972 (*AVS Directory*, 1973) and the corresponding increased demand for vocational preparation, that secondary vocational education enrollments will continue to increase. This coincides with the reality of the situation, in that only 20 percent of the population can expect to enter the professsional ranks (Lerner, 1970). This predicted continued growth is substantiated by the increase in secondary vocational programs in 1969 to 8 million (Kay, 1970). Added to this is the continued growth of post-secondary vocational education, particularly in the 1,140 community junior colleges and many of the area vocational schools. One study reported that about 40 percent of the community junior college enrollment is in vocational programs (Gillie, 1973). Should this trend continue upward, as is expected, the number of vocational students in community junior colleges will grow until more than half of their enrollments will be in vocational curriculums (see Chapter 8).

The number of students in vocational curricula is likely to increase in absolute numbers because of: (1) the greater acceptance of recycling workers, or mid-career changes, as a necessary component in the national economy, (2) the increase in the number of persons seeking updating and upgrading of vocational skills for their present occupations, (3) a greater proportion of secondary school students having access to vocational education, perhaps up to 75 percent of the total, and (4) an increase in the number of students in post-secondary vocational curriculum, maybe 50 to 75 percent of college enrollments.

A study conducted by Schreiber (1964) determined the percentage of students graduating, based on grade 10 enrollments and certain characteristics. The major emphasis of the report was on holding power. Returns were received from 128 cities, representing 96 percent of all cities with populations over 90,000 and 27 percent of the national population (based on 1960 census). The findings showed that forty school systems had separate vocational high schools, and one-half of these indicated a gain in holding power. (Fifty-one percent of the pupils who were enrolled in vocational schools in grade 10 in 1960 graduated in 1963.) The larger cities had the least holding power. Forty of the 128 large city school systems had vocational high schools. Nine of the sixteen school systems with populations greater than 600,000 had separate vocational schools, and that percentage decreases for school districts with smaller populations: In the 300,000 to 600,000 group, 32 percent had separate vocational schools; in the 200,000 to 300,000 group, 31 percent had separate vocational schools; and in the 90,000 to 200,000 group, 25 percent had separate vocational schools. About 7.6 percent of the total grade 10 enrollment sampled (38,000 pupils) were enrolled in vocational schools. Fifty-one percent of these pupils (about 20,000 out of 38,000) graduated from vocational schools three years later. During that same interval of time, however, about 71 percent of all pupils in grade 10 (362,000 of 511,000) graduated in 1963. In other words, the completion rate of the overall school population was higher than that found in vocational schools. Although this study indicates there is little evidence to support the notion that vocational programs have fewer dropouts than schools in general, there is probably a very selective process going on in that many of the students urged into vocational programs were potential high school dropouts initially. The 50 percent that did not drop out may, in fact, be many more students than would have remained if they had been left in other curricula. This should be investigated more carefully in future studies.

Another investigation found that occupational backgrounds of vocational students' fathers were distributed as follows: professions—10 percent, clerical sales and technical—10 percent, skilled occupations—41 percent, semiskilled occupations—19 percent, unskilled occupations—17 percent, and miscellaneous—3 percent (Eninger, 1968). More than half of the vocational students sampled in this study came from families whose fathers were in skilled and unskilled occupations. Although vocational students were not identified as coming from the below average intelligence group, the study did find that vocational students performed substantially below the normative performance levels in achievement and aptitude tests (reading, arithmetic, and language).

Female students are heavily concentrated in health and office occupations and home economics, while males predominate in agriculture, technical education, and trade and industrial (Kay, 1970). Nearly half of the secondary vocational students were in the twelfth grade, and a third were in the eleventh grade. Males were about equally divided between these two grades, whereas twice as many females were in the twelfth as in the eleventh grade. Also, 20 percent of all vocational students were classified as individuals from minority groups.

References

AACJC Directory, 1975. Washington, D.C.: American Association of Community and Junior Colleges, 1975.

Amberson, M.L. *Variables and Situational Factors Associated with High School Vocational Education Programs.* Unpublished doctoral dissertation, The Ohio State University, 1968.

AVS Directory, 1973. Washington, D.C.: Department of Health, Education, and Welfare, Office of Education USOE, DAVTE, 1973.

Davis, K. "Zero Population Growth: The Goal and Means." *Daedalus* 102 (Fall 1973).

Directory: Area Vocational Education Schools: Fiscal Year 1975. Washington, D.C.: Department of Health, Education and Welfare, Office of Education, Division of Adult, Vocational, and Technical Education, 1975.

Eninger, M.D. *The Process and Product of T and I High School Level Vocational Education in the United States.* Washington, D.C.: Educational Retrieval Information Center, ED024797, 1968.

Gillie, A.C., Sr. *Principles of Post-Secondary Vocational Education.* Columbus, O.: Charles E. Merrill, 1973.

———, and Hutchinson, J.P. *Cooperation and Facilities Sharing in Pennsylvania Vocational Education.* University Park: Department of Vocational Education, The Pennsylvania State University, 1974.

HEW, Office of Education. *Vocational and Technical Education in Rural America*. Washington, D.C.: Department of Health, Education and Welfare, Office of Education, 1970.

Holt, C.C. *Manpower Programs to Reduce Inflation and Unemployment: Manpower Lyrics for Macro Music*. Washington, D.C.: Irvin Institutes, 1971.

Kaufman, J., et al. *The Role of the Secondary Schools in the Preparation of Youth for Employment Period*. University Park: Institute for Research on Human Resources, The Pennsylvania State University, 1967.

Kay, E.R. *Vocational Education, Characteristics of Teachers and Students 1969*. Washington, D.C.: National Center for Educational Statistics, 1970.

Lerner, W. *Statistical Abstract of the United States: 1970*. Washington, D.C.: Bureau of the Census, 1970.

———. *Statistical Abstract of the United States: 1973*, Washington, D.C.: Bureau of the Census, 1973.

Lindenfeld, F. *Teacher Turnover in Public Elementary and Secondary Schools: 1956–60*. Washington, D.C.: Government Printing Office, 1963.

Okum, A. "The Gap Between Actual and Potential Output." In *1962 Proceedings of the Business and Economic Section*. Washington, D.C.: American Statistical Association, 1963.

O'Toole, J., Chairman of the Special Task Force. *Work in America*. Cambridge, Mass.: MIT Press, 1973.

Polk, A.J. *Characteristics of Directors of Area Vocational-Technical Schools*. Washington, D.C.: Educational Retrieval Information Center, ED031601, 1969.

Russo, M. "Concepts and Procedures for Systematic Planning of Vocational Facilities." *American Vocational Journal* 44 (1969).

Sanders, G., and Dennis, W.A. *The Impact of New Area Vocational Schools on the Appalachian Region*. Washington, D.C.: Department of Health, Education, and Welfare, Office of Education, 1971.

Schreiber, D. *Holding Power/Large City School Systems*. Educational Retrieval Information Center, ED022892, 1964.

Silverman, J.J., and Metz, S. *Selected Statistics on Educational Personnel*. Washington, D.C.: Department of Health, Education and Welfare, Office of Education, OE58041, 1970.

Striner, H.E. *Continuing Education as a National Capitol Investment*. Washington, D.C.: W.E. Upjohn Institute for Employment Research, 1972.

Swanson, G. *Organization and Administration of Vocational Education for Rural Areas*. Raleigh, N.C.: National Center for Occupational Education, 1970.

Valentine, I.E. *Administration of Occupationl Education: A Suggested Guide*. Fort Collins: Department of Vocational Education, Colorado State University, 1971.

7

The Comprehensive High School

The comprehensive high school is the most common mode of secondary education in the United States. Such institutions can be defined as high schools having several departments, including vocational. Of the 17,660 secondary schools offering vocational curricula in 1970, 16,494 are classified as comprehensive high schools. The distribution of these schools by state is given in Table 7-1. In that same year there was a total of 29,122 secondary schools in all states (Lerner, 1973), of which just under 61 percent offered vocational curricula.

A brief review of several statistics relative to vocational education in secondary institutions is of value in helping to identify the role of this form of education within the context of American education. Federal outlays for vocational education increased from $355 million in 1965 (5 percent of the total education budget for that year) to an estimated $2,368 million in 1973, which was 13 percent of the total education budget for that year (Lerner, 1973). Thus while the federal outlays for all of education increased 2.56 times, total allocations for vocational education at all levels increased nearly 6.35 times, an indication that federal subvention for vocational education has been increasing at a rate considerably faster than allocation increases for education as a whole.

Secondary school enrollments increased from 10.25 million in 1960 to 15.17 million in 1972 (Lerner, 1973), a rise of 47 percent during that twelve-year period. Census bureau projections for 1980 secondary school enrollments vary from a low of 14.80 million to a high of 15.13 million. In either case, secondary school enrollments are not expected to rise, but indeed may actually decrease slightly by that year, and further enrollment reductions can be expected by 1985.

Also of importance, since training efforts should reflect these facts, are statistics dealing with the distribution of the major occupational groups in the civilian work force. From 1950 to 1973 the total labor force increased from 62.21 million (59.9 percent of all persons sixteen years and older) to 87.47 million (60.8 percent of all persons sixteen years and older). During that time span, persons who remained out of the labor force because they were "keeping house" increased only modestly, from

98

TABLE 7-1 Secondary Schools Offering Occupational Curriculums: Total and Comprehensive High Schools by State

State or Other Area of Control	All Schools	Regular or Comprehensive[a]	State or Other Area of Control	All Schools	Regular or Comprehensive[a]
Alabama	422	395	New Hampshire	64	60
Alaska	46	45	New Jersey	337	305
Arizona	128	126	New Mexico	108	106
Arkansas	364	359	New York	1,292	1,209
California	807	751	North Carolina	340	338
Colorado	145	145	North Dakota	150	149
Connecticut	163	131	Ohio	854	829
Delaware	47	40	Oklahoma	426	411
Dist. of Columbia	30	17	Oregon	175	172
Florida	500	474	Pennsylvania	750	661
Georgia	358	357	Rhode Island	21	19
Hawaii	61	61	South Carolina	290	263
Idaho	166	163	South Dakota	151	143
Illinois	818	776	Tennessee	345	342
Indiana	286	276	Texas	1,181	1,177
Iowa	358	357	Utah	146	146
Kansas	265	265	Vermont	66	63
Kentucky	407	348	Virginia	423	393
Louisiana	459	459	Washington	363	363
Maine	128	128	West Virginia	219	217
Maryland	307	287	Wisconsin	322	315
Massachusetts	337	186	Wyoming	73	71
Michigan	643	630	American Samoa	—	—
Minnesota	407	390	Canal Zone	2	2
Mississippi	337	337	Guam	1	—
Missouri	347	315	Puerto Rico	474	304
Montana	140	140	Trust Territory	16	11
Nebraska	430	428	Virgin Islands	2	2
Nevada	43	37	Total	17,460	16,494

[a] A school with several departments (e.g., English, science, vocational) offering a diversified program to meet pupil needs.

Source: Osso (1973).

32.91 million to 35.30 million. Considering the population rise during this time (152.3 million in 1950 to 209.7 million in January 1973), one assumes that a greater proportion of women are electing not to be "housewives" as their major occupation. Confirmation of this trend is the fact that the female labor force, as a percentage of the female population, increased from 31 percent in 1950 to 43.6 percent in 1972 (Lerner, 1973). The total female labor force between 1950 and 1972 increased from 17.80 million (27.8 percent of the entire work force) to 32.94 million (37 percent of the entire work force in that year). It is clear that women are entering the labor force in proportionately greater numbers, and the stereotype of the male as the sole family provider is beginning to crumble.

Vocational education enrollments have increased from 5.30 million students to 10.50 million (in 1971), probably in large part because of the significant increase in federal funding during that time.

During the two decades from 1950 to 1970, total high school enrollments increased from 6.66 million to 14.72 million and college enrollments went up from 2.21 million to 7.41 million. An approximate comparison shows that vocational enrollments represented 61 percent of the total secondary school–college enrollment in 1950, and this decreased to about 47 percent of the total secondary school–college enrollment in 1970. While this reduction was occurring, post-secondary vocational enrollments increased to 1.01 million of the total 8.79 million post-secondary enrollments in 1970 (11.5 percent of the total number of vocational students, and 13.6 percent of all college students that year).

The total expenditures for federally aided vocational programs increased from $605 million (of which 26 percent were federal, 31 percent were state, and 43 percent were local funds) in 1965 to $2,347 million in 1971 (about 17 percent federal, and the remaining 83 percent, state and local funds). These figures show that the federal contribution decreased proportionately from 26 percent of the total vocational education funding in 1965 to 16.9 percent in 1971 (Lerner, 1973). This could be interpreted in several ways. The positive view is that the primary purpose of federal intervention was to get the state and local governments going in terms of supporting vocational education. Having done this, the federal government is pulling out of the funding picture to let the state and local governments pick it up. The negative view is that the federal government does not want to remain on the vocational education scene and wants to move gradually out of it. In any case, the federal portion of support for vocational education is decreasing.

Although these statistics may convey to the reader the feeling that vocational education in the secondary schools is doing well, one should remember that four years or more of college training is required for not more than 20 million individuals out of the total work force of 87 million. That is, only 23 percent of the entire work force is in the professions. Seventy-seven percent of the work force should be receiving some form of vocational education for nonprofessional work preparation, either in secondary school or in one of the several kinds of post-secondary institutions. These figures show that vocational education is reaching only a fraction of the population that should obtain this form of job preparation (47 percent presently instead of 77 percent).

Although secondary schools are not categorized in federal data in the way they are identified here, it can be assumed that a substantial portion of secondary school vocational students are found in the 16,494 comprehensive high schools offering occupational programs.

Traditional nonvocational education is not economically beneficial for some youngsters (see Jencks et al., 1972), and many more of them should be encouraged to enroll in vocational curricula. Some educators question the common American belief in "as much education as possible for everyone" because more isn't necessarily better—the *kind* of education a person receives is more important than the amount. Vocational education, especially in the comprehensive high schools, may see a further increase in enrollments as more educators, parents, and youngsters see the logic of these findings and more students are counseled to enter vocational programs at ages fourteen to sixteen. This approach is used in several western European countries, and some American educators believe our society could benefit from their experience.

Educators have argued for and against complete separation of vocational education from the rest of education for several generations, but solid proof that one approach or the other is most beneficial to vocational students still eludes us. Proof has been found, however, that vocational students suffer less from unfavorable comparisons with academic students when separated from them (see Kaufman et al., 1967; Ashby, 1971; Gillie, 1973). A belief in separatism is manifested in the comparatively rapid growth of area vocational schools during the last decade or so (see Chapter 6), although this trend has been greatly influenced by the infusion of federal funds (such as Public Laws 88-210 and 90-576) for the establishment and support of separate vocational facilities. The fact remains, however, that these funds could have been used to develop vocational programs in the comprehensive high schools, and yet many opted for the separate area vocational school. Those that take the other side of the issue believe that vocational education at the secondary level ought to be integrated within the comprehensive high school. The integration position has also made its impact upon American secondary education, for there are more than 16,000 such institutions out of a national total of over 29,000 secondary schools.

A second issue, tangentially related to the one stated above, is that of generalized versus specialized vocational education. Those advocating generalized vocational education believe that the characteristics of many jobs change so rapidly that it is difficult, if not impossible, for vocational curricula to keep up to date. In addition, some advocates of general vocational education believe the specific training ought to be left to the employers. On the other hand, those who endorse specialized vocational education believe that society requires a large number of individuals prepared to enter middle and high level skilled occupations immediately after graduation from high school. The argument has persisted for a long time largely because there is evidence of need for both types of vocational preparation. Unless a new configuration for secondary vocational education takes hold, it is likely that both of the old forms (i.e., general and specialized) will continue to be provided in various secondary institutions. There is a new vocational mode that satisfies the concern of both groups, called the universal college model, which has been described in other chapters and elsewhere (see Gillie, 1973).

The earlier claims made for the comprehensive high school were strikingly similar to those made by the community college theorists in the 1950s and the 1960s. Keller (1953), for example, offered the following definition:

> The comprehensive high school is a school where *all* pupils of secondary school age may have their aptitudes and interests tested and/or they may learn those things for which they are well equipped and which will be of use to them in later life. [P. 11]

It was later realized that such comprehensiveness can be achieved only in schools that have substantial enrollments (Conant, 1959; Keller, 1953). Conant (1959) offered twenty-one recommendations for improvement of American high schools. Only one of those recommendations (that they offer diversified trade and vocational programs) specifically dealt with vocational education, even though the study was supposed to be concerned with all curriculum components in comprehensive high schools. The primary focus of Conant's study of the American high school appears to have been the academically gifted student (see Diederich, 1964). Many vocational educators believe, although it cannot be positively documented, that vocational education in many comprehensive high schools has been relegated to a second class status.

The philosophy of providing comprehensive offerings in the secondary schools and in the community colleges appears to be cut from the same cloth. The similarities appear to extend to the desire to have vocational and academic studies exist side by side in the same institution. Although the achievement records for each of these school types (i.e., comprehensive secondary schools and comprehensive community junior colleges) are still being examined, present findings point to some undesirable side effects. Vocational students are put down by the academic students in many places (see Ashby, 1971; Gillie, 1973; Kaufman et al. 1967). Some educators believe it is undesirable to combine vocational and academic studies in one institution, and they advocate separate schools for the two purposes. The emergence of a strong area vocational school system in many states at least partially stems from this desire. It is unlikely, however, that this dilemma will be completely resolved, since separatism in vocational education also has its disadvantages. Chances are there will always be several forms of secondary vocational education in the United States. Such a mélange of delivery systems for secondary vocational education will probably enhance the viability of the overall effort.

Objectives and Philosophy

Conant (1959) conveniently divided all American high schools into two broad types: the specialized and the comprehensive varieties. In doing so, he elected to overlook some of the finer characteristics found among certain secondary institutions which have been identified in this work. One can assume, based on Conant's own words, that this decision was made so as to enable him to concentrate his efforts on the comprehensive high school.

The comprehensive high school is unique to American education, and as a result our educational system differs considerably from the European tradition, where education is terminated for 80 percent of all students by age fourteen to sixteen. The basic philosophy of the American comprehensive high school is to provide equality of opportunity for all and also equality of status for all honest labor. The extent to which this philosophy has been implemented is shown by the increase in 1972 of the median school years completed by twenty-five-to-twenty-nine-year-old Americans to 12.7 years for whites and 12.3 years for blacks (Lerner, 1973), a significant increase since 1960. Also, the percentage of Americans attending college sharply increased from 0.9 percent in 1930 (1.10 million) to 3.5 percent in 1970 (7.14 million). The proportionate rise in college enrollments indicates that the American public's endorsement of post-secondary education which is accessible to more of its citizens (including many who don't fall within the rubric of scholars) is being implemented. Many educators point to the recent enrollment increases as evidence that American education is more equalitarian than the European education system. To that extent, at least, the public secondary school system in the United States reflects the philosophic tenet of equal opportunity by attempting to provide education that serves the needs of all youth living in that school district. The single secondary institution that attempts to provide the required diversity of curricula is known as the comprehensive high school.

A great number of schools which labeled themselves comprehensive high schools in 1971 also reflect another aspect of secondary school philosophy in the United States. Most Americans believe that public subcollegiate education is a local responsibility and the manner in which the community conducts its system of education should be independent of state and federal influences. The community autonomy idea has been seriously eroded in the past decades, as state and federal funds have been offered to and accepted by local communities. Complete community independence of state and federal influence in the control and management of their schools is more a quaint memory of conditions that existed in years before the equalization of education was considered a serious issue at state and federal levels. Local responsibility for education and community independence have been eroded to some extent, as serious attempts to equalize educational opportunities for all youngsters through special state and federal formulas increased. In spite of these incursions, however, local school district boards still have considerable freedom in some aspects of local school management.

Although there are several variations in public school patterns (such as the 6-3-3, 8-4, and recently talked about 6-4-4 configurations), the comprehensive high school is customarily regarded as encompassing grades 9–12 (Conant, 1959). Limitations are placed on the comprehensiveness of a high school, however. The existence of specialized high schools (such as AVS's) alongside comprehensive high schools necessarily limits the breadth of the program in the comprehensive high school, and some communities do not wish to support vocationally oriented programs in their secondary schools (particularly in suburban areas and high income residential areas of the larger cities).

The Conant study (1959) sought to determine whether a comprehensive high school satisfactorily fulfilled three major functions: (1) to provide a good general education for all students as future American citizens, (2) to provide a sufficient variety of adequate quality programs in which most of the students could learn useful skills, and (3) to provide adequate course work for those who should be studying advanced academic subjects (such as foreign languages and advanced mathematics). Only eight of the more than 100 schools that Conant visited were, in his estimation, satisfactorily fulfilling these three objectives. One major recommendation he made was to eliminate small high schools by forming consolidated school districts. Many states were making considerable progress in this direction before he conducted his study, and such progress still continues.

One of the critical elements in the intelligent management of comprehensive high schools is the quality of the school board members and educators. School board members should be intelligent and devoted citizens who understand that their function is policy making (and not administration). Also, the chief administrator (superintendent) and high school principal must be highly qualified education administrators. If the school is to enjoy high morale and be viewed favorably in the community, faculty members must be employed on the basis of their teaching qualifications with absolutely no political influence.

Part of the philosophy of the comprehensive high school is to separate youngsters only when deemed absolutely necessary. A response to this is the attempt in many high schools to keep all youngsters, regardless of their curriculum placement, in common courses (such as English, social studies, and other general education courses) required for graduation. This approach has been and still is practiced in many comprehensive community junior colleges as well. Superficially, this approach appears to be most egalitarian, but it can result in placing youngsters with very large differences in academic ability in directly competitive situations. Such an environment is considered harmful to the scholastic development of students possessing lesser academic abilities.

Although Conant (1959) concluded that American secondary education could be made satisfactory with no radical changes in its basic pattern, empirical evidence leads some educators to challenge that conclusion. The comprehensive high school is under serious scrutiny, especially by vocational educators who see a chronic disinterest in occupationally oriented curricula in these schools.

The Student

The high school student is an adolescent in our society, and the literature is replete with descriptions of and discussions about the dilemma of adolescents in American society (e.g., see Coleman, 1961). Prior to the industrial revolution, the typical youngster of secondary school age was introduced to the world of work by his parent or a neighbor. His initial entry consisted of a learning period, which in some occupations was a formal apprenticeship. The adolescent female was likewise introduced to the household chores and responsibilities expected of women in that era.

But industrialization has created several fundamental changes in the work scene since those times. First, fathers and neighbors no longer work at agricultural and cottage industries in full view of their children. Instead, fathers leave home for the entire day and perform their occupational tasks in places where adolescents have no opportunity to observe or to share in the activities. Second, with industrialization occupational specialization has increased, and an extended period of training is required for many jobs. Third, the tradition of passing an occupation on to one's offspring is virtually impossible to maintain, since the worker is not the proprietor of the business or industry where he expends his occupational efforts. These three elements, along with a number of other factors, have combined to disenfranchise adolescents from the world of work.

The situation creates social hardships for adolescents in all industrial societies. The transition from dependency (upon parents and social institutions like the schools) to personal economic independence has become much more difficult for adolescents in recent generations. Educators have long recognized that isolation of adolescents in their own peer societies has accentuated the pull youngsters feel between their families' mores and the adolescent peer group values. Generally, educators and other adults have not succeeded in influencing the mores and drives of adolescent societies. Serious attempts are being made, however, to find ways to influence adolescent groups so they will adopt the values and mores that adult society desires of them. While there has not been a major breakthrough that is applicable to all adolescent groups, success has been achieved in certain localized instances.

What goes on in the American high school? Friedenberg (1959) described four major types of social processes: (1) Our youth is Americanized there. (2) Most youngsters become certified for white-collar jobs, while a minority of the students receives some elementary preparation in the sciences which will help them achieve college-based goals. (3) The students obtain some of the knowledge, intellectual skills, and attitudes (i.e., general education) deemed necessary for intelligent living in traditional Western civilization. (4) Through administration and record keeping of various youth activities a dossier is established on each young American (which includes information about his or her intellectual achievements, medical history, etc.).

A fundamental obligation of the entire American educational movement is to provide adolescents with a basic philosophy that will enable them to make sense out of their lives and to communicate successfully with others like themselves. In other words, the social purpose of the American high school is to help create a nation of young people who can clearly see where they are heading and who agree on what they see when they look in certain directions. It is universally agreed that the high school is an indispensable tool for spread of the common culture of America.

Americans' expectations of their secondary schools are mixed. Some want them to continue functioning as if they were melting pots (i.e., of various ethnic, religious, and racial groups). Major interest seems to be focused on uniformity and mediation. The dual ideas of success and contentment are still uppermost in the milieu of the American high school, although the high school prepares the more intelligent youngsters for success better than it prepares the majority for contentment. One of the major difficulties is a lack of common ground between secondary school educators and adolescents in their out-of-school society. As a result, many high school youngsters experience great difficulty in dealing with the demands made upon them by the school and in relating these to their out-of-school adolescent world. These difficulties are even more severe for that large fraction of adolescents classified as culturally deprived (see Riessman, 1962; Jencks et al., 1972).

Adolescents at the other end of the spectrum also present difficulties for the secondary school because of their great deviance from the intellectual norms. It is widely believed that a person's intelligence level is a complex product of heredity and environment (see Gardner, 1962; Jencks et al., 1972). The extent to which each affects the final outcome is widely debated, but the belief that cognitive ability is largely an inherited gift still persists in some places and will likely continue to do so. American schools and society place maximum value on the possession of high intelligence, and those occupations demanding the highest level of ability are accorded the greatest prestige. American high school teachers must hold back the temptation to coax the more talented youngsters into a specialization before providing them with ample opportunity to sample all areas of knowledge. Teachers tend to foster a desire for specialization by encouraging the more cognitive adolescents to enter specialized academic fields (perhaps akin to those of the coaxing educator) before affording them a broad treatment of other subjects. If talented youngsters delay specializing, the likelihood of their final career choices being in harmony with their long-range interests and their abilities may be increased.

Students in the comprehensive high school include those with the full spectrum of abilities and interests found in our population. The vocational student is somewhere in the lower to lower middle region of the general intelligence range. Serving such a diverse population will always be a difficult task at best and an impossible one in secondary schools that are limited in size and financial resources.

The Faculty

The manner in which secondary school teachers are to be prepared has long been a subject of debate. The controversy has created chronic defensiveness on the part of teacher educators (Corey, 1958). If some agreement is to be found, those on each side of this issue must have complete understanding of the opponent's position. (That is, each side must feel that the other side has stated its own position accurately.) Should this precondition ever be achieved, the possibility of resolving the teacher education issue would be improved.

What is the basic difference between the beliefs of the two major groups? One group can be correctly identified as an anti-teacher-training group which believes the major aim of public education is to teach certain important skills or specific subject matter, and students who cannot learn these things easily don't belong in the classroom. The subscribers of this elitist position believe that anyone with a reasonable amount of intelligence and competence in their subject matter can automatically teach. It then follows, according to this kind of reasoning, that little or no training of teachers is necessary. This view is held by a surprisingly large number of persons, including many specialist professors who provide part of the education that future teachers receive in their teacher-training programs.

The other group believes that the curriculum in American education requires considerable variation and flexibility because of the students' diverse backgrounds, motivations, and needs. In order to function effectively in this kind of setting, teachers must be trained to perform the different, complex, and dynamic tasks involved. From this position it follows logically that there is as great a need for professionally trained teachers as there is for professionally trained persons in the medical and law fields. An improvement in the education of professional teachers would likely help to still the voices of this group's opponents. The issue is manifested in two traditions of teacher education (e.g., see Woodring, 1957). The first and older tradition, which still controls the education of some college teachers, is the academic or liberal arts version of teacher education. This is the one which subscribes to the elitist point of view for American education. The second tradition upholds the legitimacy of the professional educator—one who is trained as a teacher. The former normal schools and present state colleges adhere to this tradition. Universities, on the other hand, have attempted to combine the two philosophies by designing teacher education programs that stress both academic competency and professional teacher preparation. Present results are mixed, but attempts to synthesize the conflicting views need to be continued.

The training of vocational teachers, as pointed out in several other chapters, requires the additional element of occupational experience on the part of the potential teacher. Thus the preparation of vocational teachers is even more complicated than the training of nonvocational teachers. Furthermore, the demand for previous work experience virtually ensures the drawing of teachers from the ranks of the upper lower and lower middle classes only, and precludes the entrance of more intellectually oriented individuals into the profession of vocational teaching. This severe narrowing of the source of vocational teachers may have some deleterious effects upon vocational education in general. (Chapter 17 comes back to this point.)

Governance

The public elementary and secondary schools in democratic societies are at least partially controlled by local interests, as opposed to the complete central control found in typical totalitarian societies. This situation permits a certain amount of interplay between diverse groups as they attempt to influence certain characteristics of the local system of education. The interplay quite often takes the form of conservative and liberal groups attempting to have their points of view dominate the local educational scene. The plurality of interests has both good and less-than-good aspects. A major attribute is the possibility that the real educational needs of the local community will be made known, fully discussed, examined, and provided for. On the other hand, should the predominant group in a community be one of older persons with grown-up children and fixed or only slowly increasing incomes, the group may want a stable tax rate and no further increases in allocations for public education. Although this may be all right in localities where good educational systems are in operation, a chronically poor district may elect to perpetuate an already inferior school system. Local control can be hazardous for public education because noneducational factors can be deciding factors in determining the amount of public appropriations allocated for education.

Nationally, public elementary and secondary education is a mélange of independent state systems, and within each there is a host of local units that are also highly independent. State control is exercised in certain matters, but much discretion is still left for local or regional boards of education. There is, however a discernible trend in local districts to consolidate with their neighboring districts and form regional school districts in order to increase efficiency and economy. In 1945 there were more than 100,000 local school districts in the United States, and there were around 10,000 in 1970. Indications are that this trend toward regionalization is continuing.

The move toward increased regionalization has been given impetus by the federal government to some degree and the state governments to a much greater extent. As states have provided additional funds for public education, they have exercised increasing control by giving the regional boards of governance various guidelines and requirements regarding certain educational matters. The introduction of state and federal money for local education does not necessarily lead to a takeover by the external agency, however. Funds from the state and federal governments can be disbursed regionally so that much of the local autonomy is preserved. Categorical monies can be provided, for example, for scholarships, research support, new facilities, and even partial subsidization of teachers' salaries. State and federal funds provide a local school with some basis to resist the more unreasonable and reactionary demands sometimes made by local pressure groups. A careful blending of funding sources, if properly designed and implemented, can result in a public education system that has some of the advantages of both centralized and decentralized school systems.

In many states this has been occurring to some extent with support for vocational education, where federal and state funds are allocated to local or regional school districts, under certain guidelines provided in each state's master plan for vocational education. It appears that this judicious blending of three funding sources is effectively working to provide accessibility of vocational education for an increasing proportion of comprehensive high school students.

References

Ashby, E. *Any Person, Any Study: An Essay on Higher Education in the United States*. New York: McGraw-Hill, 1971.
Coleman, James S. *The Adolescent Society*. New York: Free Press, 1961.
Conant, James B. *The American High School Today*. New York: McGraw-Hill, 1959.
Corey, Stephen M. *The Future Challenges Teacher Education*, 11th Year Book. Oneonta, N.Y.: American Association of Colleges for Teacher Education, 1958.
Diederich, Paul B. "The Conant Report". In *Student, School and Society: Crosscurrents in Secondary Education*. Edited by John A. Dahl et al. San Francisco: Chandler, 1964.
Friedenberg, Edgar Z. *The Vanishing Adolescent*. Boston: Beacon Press, 1959.
Gardner, John W. *Excellence*. New York: Harper, 1962.
Gillie, A.C., Sr. *Principles of Post-Secondary Vocational Education*. Columbus, O.: Charles E. Merrill, 1973.
Haskew, Lawrence D., and Tumlin, Inez W. "Vocational Education and the Curriculum of the Common School." In *Vocational Education. The 64th Year Book of the National Society for the Study of Education*. Part I. Edited by Melvin L. Barlow. Chicago: The University of Chicago Press, 1965.
Jencks, C., et al. *Inequality: A Reassessment of the Effect of Family and School in America*. New York: Basic Books, 1972.
Kaufman, J., et al. *The Role of the Secondary Schools in the Preparation of Youth for Employment*. University Park: Institute for Research on Human Resources, The Pennsylvania State University, 1967.
Keller, Franklin J. *The Double-Purpose High School*. New York: Harper, 1953.
Lerner, W. *Statistical Abstract of the United States, 1973*, 94th annual ed. Washington, D.C.: Bureau of the Census, 1973.
Osso, N.A. *Directory of Secondary Schools with Occupational Curriculums: Public and Non-Public, 1971*. Washington, D.C.: Department of Health Education, and Welfare, Adult and Vocational Education Surveys Branch, 1973.
Riessman, Frank. *The Culturally Deprived Child*. New York: Harper, 1962.
Woodring, Paul. *New Directions in Teacher Education*. New York: Fund for the Advancement of Education, 1957.

8

The Public Community College

The origins of the community junior college movement are over a hundred years old (Gillie, 1970). The school's earliest purpose was to serve as a "junior college" where local youngsters with adequate qualifications could receive their first two years of a college education. The major advantages of the earlier junior colleges, at least in the minds of their founders, were that they eased the financial burden of sending gifted youngsters to college in some distant place and enabled the weeding out of less capable students before they went on to the universities (Tappan, 1851; Folwell, 1909; Lange, 1917). These continued to be the major objectives of many junior colleges until well into the twentieth century.

Vocational programs were introduced in a few junior colleges before 1920, and the increase in the number of such curricula was slow. There were about 4,000 occupational programs in the community junior colleges in 1941 (Hill, 1942). Progress in this direction (i.e., increasing the number of vocational programs) has continued to be slow right into the 1970s.

After World War II, probably in large part due to the impetus the GI Bill provided to higher education, two-year colleges began to appear in many places. During the 1950s the name "community college" and its announced equalitarian goals captured the imagination of educators and the public. The movement enjoyed its greatest growth during the 1950s and 1960s. By 1970 the number of new community junior colleges appearing annually was tapering off. In 1974 there were about 1,200 two-year institutions (*AACJC Directory*, 1975).

During the period of greatest growth, the literature was replete with claims that the community junior colleges were going to meet the needs of virtually all kinds of persons in sundry ways. The announced purposes, as made by exuberant and well-intentioned community junior college educators, were simply too far-fetched to be achieved in any real sense. One of the most publicized claims was that they were open-door colleges, but in all too many cases the very high attrition rates demonstrated that, in actuality, they were revolving-door colleges. Also, in some places where they were purported to be comprehensive schools, a closer examination revealed their offerings were limited to mostly liberal arts courses with only one to four poorly designed occupational programs. To call such schools comprehensive was ludicrous, as were a number of the other claims. Some of the community junior college advocates suggested that the teaching going on in these schools was superior to that found in other kinds of post-secondary institutions. Another contention that was equally unsubstantiated was that a small school offers the student a better educational environment. In actuality, many smaller schools have poorer physical and learning facilities and can attract only lower quality faculty (as indicated by the faculty's previous professional experiences and educational background). The community junior colleges' role in providing a thorough guidance and counseling program, especially for students who are unsure of their vocational goals, was oversold in too many places (as evidenced by the high student–counselor ratios). Such services in many community junior colleges were no better than those available in the typical comprehensive high school. But all the above happened with the best of intentions. Young institutions historically have tended to overstate their intentions, only to find a few years later that some of their goals were unrealistic and impossible to achieve. The result would be an adjustment in their operations (i.e., goal displacement). In some cases the original claims were made to sell the idea to the public and its governance board so as to obtain the large sums required to pursue the colleges' goals. Colleges that began this way often experienced a wave of public disenchantment later on, when it became obvious that some of their claims were not materializing.

This is especially true with regard to competition between transfer-oriented and vocational curriculums. Many educators and laymen became concerned when the majority of the transfer students didn't graduate in two years. It appears that many youngsters were admitted into transfer programs primarily on the strength of their desire to enter rather than on the basis of an honest assessment of their chances of getting through the curriculum. These dropouts (the euphemism was "non-persistors") were unable to enter senior colleges and, tragically, had no vocational skills to enable them to obtain good jobs. Added to this was the damage done to their self-concepts. A strong guidance and counseling program—manned, planned, and conducted by carefully selected professionals with a high regard for and considerable knowledge of subprofessional occupations—could help prevent such personal failures by urging such persons into vocational programs consistent with their abilities and interests as well as labor market realities. For this approach to succeed, however, the college would have to have a substantial offering in vocational programs.

Many community junior colleges, admittedly with the dual persuasion of state-federal vocational dollars and declining enrollments in higher education, are expanding their occupational program offerings. The Vocational Education Amendment of 1968 (PL 90-576), for example, permits a community junior college to qualify for funding if it establishes a division which offers at least five types of vocational programs. With such a division, the community junior college would then qualify as an area vocational school. There were 1,150 post-secondary schools, which include many community colleges, out of the total of 2,452 area vocational schools which met the federal qualifications in 1975 (*AVS Directory*, 1975). An added incentive for increasing vocational program enrollments is the decreased interest in community college transfer-oriented programs. Since the number of college age youngsters available for post-secondary schooling is tapering off each year, senior colleges and universities find themselves facing the prospect of decreased enrollments. Some of the senior institutions have adjusted their entrance requirements downward in attempts to stabilize their long-term enrollment. Many youngsters with middle level abilities, who in previous years would have had to enroll in a community junior college because there were no vacancies in senior colleges or universities, are now able to get into such schools. The easing of entry into senior colleges has led to substantial decreases in community junior college enrollments. As this trend became clear, some of the community junior colleges increased their vocational offerings and enrollments. Although this is a bitter alternative to some community junior college educators, it appears to have gained considerable acceptance during the early 1970s.

Although many community junior college personnel (administrators, faculty) and students have identity problems (Is the school a high school or a college?), these schools are viable institutions. In spite of the criticism leveled at them, they have served some segments of post-secondary students well. Many educators believe they could do even better if they eased up on the idea of being primarily "collegiate" in the traditional academic sense and wholeheartedly embraced the notion of serving the vocational preparation needs of post-secondary youngsters and adults of all ages. This would enable them to become a unique post-secondary educational institution on the American educational scene. There is evidence to support the belief that community junior colleges are becoming more vocational, probably due to the kind of forces described above, and that by 1980 they may very well be the post-secondary institutions providing the most equal opportunities in the United States.

Objectives and Philosophy

The open-door philosophy is widely subscribed to, if one is to believe writers and theoreticians who are pro-community junior colleges, and appears to be the very basis for many of these institutions' objectives. Typical of this position is the following statement (Knoebel, 1970):

> The basic philosophy of the colleges is to provide the opportunity for every adult individual to pursue education to his fullest potential and interest. Each community college provides opportunity to learn in an occupational curriculum, transfer curriculum, or community service program.

Stating objectives is one thing, however, while translating them into actual performance requires careful planning, considerable energy, and abundant finances. In many places the financing patterns for community junior colleges are not designed for the optimum achievement of institutional goals (Gleazer, 1973a). Ideally, the state (or region) should first determine what the community junior colleges are to do within the overall educational system and then set out to plan a financial scheme that would enhance implementation of the goals. One writer urges these institutions to assume leadership in emphasizing the basic aim of post-secondary education, which is vocational and ranges from actually preparing students for work to teaching them the life-style associated with a particular type of work and determining how such an occupation fits into the student's long-term life plans (Millard, 1973).

The 1972 assembly of the American Association of Community and Junior Colleges (Gleazer, 1973b) urged a continued commitment to the concept of comprehensiveness so as to provide educational opportunities for all. This concept calls for the offering of a broad spectrum of programs in order to meet a wide variety of individual needs. Some community junior college educators even encourage aggressive action in seeking out potential students, identifying their needs, and designing educational programs to meet those needs. Those who subscribe to this believe students should be of all ages and abilities. Some community junior college proponents strongly encourage increased enrollment of (1) youngsters who seek college credits before completing high school, (2) baccalaureate degree candidates who want to develop a marketable skill, (3) older citizens and others who want to develop leisurely pursuits or a new occupation, (4) women who are entering the labor market for the first time or who seek to return after having children, (5) veterans and servicemen, (6) recent high school graduates who seek job entry for the first time, and (7) the disadvantaged of all types.

It was also stated at the 1972 Assembly of the American Association of Community and Junior Colleges (Gleazer, 1973b) that other institutions were competing with community junior colleges for students, and that they needed to be more flexible and imaginative in developing programs if they were to obtain their share of new students. A subtle anti-university tone was evident in the suggestion that independent research and development groups ought to be established to assist in identification of student clientele, identification of the social and educational training needs to these students and determination of the extent to which such needs are being met. The anti-university "we can do it better ourselves" exhortations are residual echoes of the adolescent stage of community junior college development in the United States. It would be ironic and wasteful to ignore the educational research capabilities of the universities as the most viable vehicle for conducting this type of research.

Much has been written in the literature about the heterogeneity of the community junior college student population (Gleazer, 1973c; Cross, 1971). Some claim these institutions have made progress in use of the behavioral objectives approach to individualized instruction (Gleazer, 1973b), while others urge community colleges to do more with new instructional modes and programs (see Cross, 1971; Roueche, 1968).

It has been claimed consistently that community junior colleges are primarily devoted to teaching. If this is so, the community junior colleges ought to study their faculty, students, and the learning process on a continuing, long-term basis (Brawer and Cohen, 1969). Furthermore, more intensive attempts ought to be made to identify students' abilities and aptitudes, assess their deficiencies and potentialities, and assist them in rationalizing their aspirations (Collins, 1967). Some of these internal, ongoing studies and assessments could be carried out by an office of institutional research in the community junior college. Until recently, the community junior colleges have been slow in establishing research staff for continuing in-house research (Roueche and Boggs, 1968). But a 1973 study showed that about 12 percent of the community junior colleges sampled had at least one full-time research staff member for such efforts (Gillie, 1973), and 1975 study indicated that 20 to 25 percent of the community junior colleges have at least one full-time institutional research person (Gilli, 1975).

Medsker (1960) was one of the earlier leaders in the movement to announce the community junior colleges' roles and objectives. Johnson

(1964), another community college theoretician of that period, described the major roles of these institutions as follows: (1) to prepare students for transfer to universities and other senior institutions, (2) to serve as a multipurpose institution, (3) to serve as an open-door college, (4) to accept guidance as a major responsibility, and (5) to be colleges of their respective communities, located within commuting distance of their students. These roles are essentially the same as those described earlier by Medsker and others, and many community junior college leaders have subscribed to them repeatedly over the years.

The question of the extent to which the community junior colleges are in fact meeting the needs of all students has been raised (see Roueche, 1968; Ashby, 1971; Cross, 1971). Some educators believe the community junior college curricula must be changed in order to meet the scholastic demands of students who seek entry. The literature points to the difficulty in maintaining transfer programs alongside of vocational ones. By adopting the principle of comprehensiveness in this manner, the community junior colleges make themselves "vassals of the four-year colleges" (Ashby, 1971). Inasmuch as 75 percent of the students in many community junior colleges enroll in transfer-oriented courses and aspire to enter senior colleges, the community junior colleges cannot enjoy real independence from other elements in higher education. Preoccupation with academic courses forces them to conform with the academic patterns of senior colleges and discourages real experimentation and innovation in academic programs. This constraint is further complicated by the fact that many community junior college teachers would prefer to teach in a senior college and express a strong preference for academic (as opposed to vocational) courses (Medsker and Tillery, 1971). Vocational programs are bound to suffer under such circumstances. The most effective way to ease this dilemma is to de-emphasize the academic by fiat and,simultaneously accentuate the vocational programs and continuing education efforts (Ashby, 1971; Gillie, 1973). The solution may not be all that simple, however, because of the advent of transfer vocational programs where the senior institution could end up dictating to the community junior colleges as to the content of the first two years of a baccalaureate vocational program.

Another reaction to the sometimes exuberant claims of community college educators has come from the National Association of Manufacturers. In the concluding remarks of a recent publication, the association stated (*NAM Public Policy Report,* 1973):

> The National Association of Manufacturers believes that community
> colleges exist to provide increased opportunities for post-secondary

education and training to meet the needs of students and employers. To help assure that occupational programs of these institutions meet these needs, industry encourages: 1) the collection and publication of more adequate data to guide program planning, evaluation and policy decisions; 2) closer cooperation between community colleges and employers in establishing performance objectives and curricula in occupational programs; 3) development of accreditation procedures more applicable to occupational education programs.

Such an interest from an organization like the National Association of Manufacturers, rather than being viewed as an intrusion into the privacy of the community junior colleges, should be interpreted as an interest of the manufacturing community in the product of the community junior colleges, particularly in terms of the colleges' vocational efforts. This is probably a harbinger of the pressure that will be brought to bear upon community junior colleges to become more seriously involved with vocational aspects of post-secondary education.

The members of boards of trustees of community junior colleges have been identified as conservative (Rauh, 1969). They agree in large part that the community junior college is: a facility for all who want to attend, a school to train for employment, and an institution to meet community needs, and that money should not be an obstacle to attendance. A mild contradiction was found in that 92 percent of the trustees sampled believed there should be opportunities for higher education for anyone who seeks it, but at the same time 67 percent felt attendance at their community junior college is a privilege and not a right. The trustees, like the faculty and administration, are subject to two opposing forces—a group which regards the community junior college as an extension of the common school system and another which views it as part of the higher education establishment. The very essence of the community junior college is to make education democratic, to make education beyond high school available to all who want it without regard to their economic means. When such a mission is adopted, it virtually necessitates accepting students with a wider range of abilities (with emphasis on the lower ability students) and providing more curriculum offerings than found in public universities. On the basis of the students' academic aptitude and curricula based on classical university models, community junior colleges might be classified as second rate by some educators and laymen. But since the community junior colleges' intention is to be responsive to social needs, intellectual growth, personal development, and vocational training, they can achieve excellence and become superior institutions in their own specialized ways. The serious adoption of vocational education as their major goal would enhance their chances of achieving excellence.

The Administration

The role of college presidents has been studied and discussed for many years, and the community junior college president has recently come under similar scrutiny. Some authorities take the position that ideally each two-year college president ought to be the educational leader of his institution and not merely a manager or custodian type of president. Proponents of this position believe a president who is an active educational leader of the college is most likely to be successful in leading that institution toward achievement of its goals (Cohen and Roueche, 1969). Since the primary reason for starting and maintaining a community junior college is to educate students (with achievement of the trustees', administrators', and faculty's needs and aspirations being secondary), the president's major effort should be in the area of educational leadership.

Although pleas have been made that presidents should be the real educational leaders in the community junior colleges, in reality they very often do not have supporting mechanisms to enable them to function in such a manner (even if they so desired). For example, institutional research, which when viably conducted can be the most important tool for the development, improvement, and evaluation of college programs, products, and students, is going on at significant levels in only a minority of community junior colleges (Gillie, 1973). When true institutional research is lacking, administrative decisions regarding curriculum development, organizational change and innovations, and other aspects of the school's activities are likely to be based on a blend of wishful thinking and imitation of others. The absence of institutional research precludes the utilization of pretested processes and techniques that render measurable results. Presidents are charged by their boards of trustees with responsibility for shaping and implementing educational policies and are held accountable for the success or failure of the community junior college in serving their creators and providers—society at large. Some feel this demands a president who is an educational leader.

The literature indicates general agreement on the point that the presidency is the most important position in the college. While agreement is lacking as to whether he should be the top educational leader of the school, there is some consensus that the president has considerable influence in determining educational policy. Some educators view the president as the principal faculty member among other things and want him to function actively as such (Alden, 1965):

> Although he is not active as a teacher or scholar, the president can and must function as an educational leader. The emphasis here is on the leader, where the most important responsibility is to create a climate in which other people can be scholars and teachers.

The president is viewed as the professional on the board of trustees, which is most commonly made up of amateurs in the field of education. Trustees usually charge him with the responsibility for leading the overall educational enterprise (Rauh, 1969).

Hillway (1959) surveyed professors from ninety-three colleges and twenty-four states to identify desirable characteristics of college presidents. Responses were obtained from over 400 of about 500 professors. The most desirable characteristics identified were integrity in personal and professional relationships (24 percent), intellectual ability and scholarship (22 percent), ability to organize and lead (20 percent), democratic attitude and methods (11 percent). The same respondents cited four major undesirable characteristics: a dictatorial, undemocratic attitude (24 percent), dishonesty and insincerity (15 percent), weakness as an educator and scholar (15 percent), vacillation in organizing and leading (15 percent). Also of interest is how the college president is viewed by the trustees. One study found that trustees considered it most vital for a president to be an educational leader (52 percent), management executive (45 percent), public relations expert (22 percent), money raiser and businessman (16 percent) (Hillway, 1961). It is interesting to note the basic differences in the college president's most desirable characteristics as perceived by his followers (faculty), on one hand, and those to whom he reports (trustees), on the other hand. In many colleges the expectations these two groups have of the president are sufficiently divergent to place the position of presidency in jeopardy.

How do presidents see themselves in their leadership role? Some presidents consider themselves as educational leaders in the community and on campus (Shannon, 1962). They also view themselves as the major official for fund raising, public relations, and diplomacy, and they believe the college's central administration is the major source for determining how something can be done (rather than having it stopped). One may suspect college presidents are cognizant of the discrepancy between faculty and trustee expectations of them. Being aware of the discrepancy is a step in the direction of resolving the dilemma, although some expectations of faculty and trustees are sufficiently contradictory to exclude the chances of true resolution. The faculty, the trustees, or in some cases both will find the president falling short of their expectations.

The realities of situations surrounding the presidency are such that he can become so burdened with routine administrative tasks that his role narrows down to being a social, diplomatic, financial, and administrative person with the exclusion of activities related to scholarship and educational leadership (Brickman, 1961). Some presidents, perhaps most notably those in less well supported colleges, spend more time searching for funds than leading their faculty and trustees. While some would rather resign than serve in such a style (many apparently have), others feel the job of college president has undergone considerable change, and his role as educational leader is an outdated one. Some who hold such a view feel the president has to be concerned with governmental relationships (local, state, and federal) and the public, and should also devote a considerable portion of his efforts to establishing and maintaining constructive educational attitudes among faculty, lower level administrators, and students. In addition, the chief administrator must be a good manager of an institution that is becoming increasingly more complex. The trustees in some instances have viewed the president's position as similar to that of a small town mayor, with its myriad duties and responsibilities, rather than that of an educational leader (Taylor, 1959).

The role of president in some places is more that of a manager than that of an educational leader. Developing college policies is among the most important responsibilities conveyed to him by the trustees of some colleges but not in others. Although most presidents have earned doctorate degrees, relatively few of them are active scholars, judging by the number that engage in scholarly writing and publication (Gilli, 1975). Most presidents have been full-time or part-time administrators for an average of eight years (Bolman and Wolfe, 1965; Gilli, 1975), which indicates that they have been away from the real "firing line" of scholarship for quite some time.

Another view, which is counter to the belief that the president ought to be an educational leader, projects him as a coordinator or balancer of decisions made throughout the institution. Demanding that the president focus his major efforts on being a good manager and fund raiser means educational leadership in the college must be lodged in another position. One can conjecture as to whose role this should be, with possibilities ranging from an academic dean, vested with sufficient authority to serve in such a capacity, to a faculty senate type of arrangement. Several modes of educational leadership have been tried in one or more colleges—with the puzzling results that the same plan fails in one place and succeeds in another. The best leadership configuration has much to do with sundry elements present in the college at that time.

The community college president, in all probability, is even less apt to take on educational leadership than his counterpart in the senior college. This cannot be stated as an absolute certainty, however, since many of them do not have their responsibilities spelled out in formal statements, nor do boards of trustees of community junior colleges have official board policies on such matters. One consequence of this nondirective approach is that many presidents are not called upon to produce periodic reports for any group within their purview—trustees, faculty, or students. Furthermore, the typical community junior college president is not assigned responsibility for, nor does he address himself to, matters concerning educational leadership. It appears that a study of the feasibility of vesting responsibility for educational leadership in some other office or group is in order (or perhaps there should be a study of the feasibility of changing the nature of the presidency).

Some community junior college theorists still think there is merit in trying to develop presidents into educational leaders. These theorists suggest that (1) the job description of the presidency should contain a category relating directly to educational leadership; (2) the president ought to describe all budget and campus expansion requests in terms of their effect on student learning; (3) the tenure of the president should be specific so there can be a rotation of the person in the office—some feel the chances of innovations coming from the top are improved when there is a periodic and predictable change of presidents; (4) the president should delegate his authority for fiscal management to a competent business manager; (5) boards of trustees should encourage the president to push for experimentation in educational programs, particularly in the vocational areas, by tolerating failures in such attempts; (6) the board of trustees should encourage the president to take the initiative in articulation of college programs, especially between vocational students and the business-industrial community; (7) boards of trustees should strongly encourage their presidents to attend conferences, workshops, and seminars that could provide them with new ideas; (8) trustees should support a strong program of institutional research on teaching and learning so the president has reliable data upon which to base decisions.

The administration needs to deal with a number of other factors. First, there are tensions between students, faculty, and the administration which come about in a natural manner. The prevailing view of student-faculty power is that the administration administers by making tactical decisions and recommendations based upon major policy decisions made previously by students and faculty acting jointly. Viewing this statement carefully, one identifies what might be considered a natural alliance between faculty and students in their desire to seek freedom from administrative rules and regulations. Students, in turn, also exert pressure on faculty to support them in more militant types of situations. By and large, however, such situations have been restricted to the larger state colleges and universities, although they did appear in a few community junior colleges in the late 1960s and early 1970s. And it was later claimed by some who analyzed those episodes that the students were really revolting against impositions placed upon them by the faculty rather than by the administration. Some feel that administrators spend more time trying to placate their faculty than they do trying to appease any other group in the school, including the students. The student activism movement of the 1960s and early 1970s has brought about a change in the students' position on community junior college campuses (Lombardi, 1969). Indications are, however, that some of the effects of that movement, particularly those relating to curriculum, are transitory in nature and will eventually disappear when such pressure is removed from the faculty and administration.

Multi-campus districts in the larger cities are increasing, and they encounter a host of unique administrative problems (Kintzer et al., 1969; Palola and Oswald, 1972). The chief administrator in multi-institutional community college districts is often called the chancellor. Other frequently used titles include vice-chancellor, vice-president, and director (most common). The title of director has been used in conjunction with the areas of business, instruction, vocational and technical training, buildings, and research in community junior colleges. Many large districts monitor all of their campuses with a central staff, and central offices are most often located apart from any of the campuses themselves.

Johnson (1964) has published procedures for the establishment of a community junior college, and he identified six areas of educational administration: curriculum and instruction, staff personnel, student personnel services, finance, plant and facilities, community services and relationships. The school president is expected to be knowledgeable about statewide planning and coordination for community junior colleges. Some disagreement as to location of authority relative to statewide planning has appeared recently. Some feel there should be strong centralization with very little college autonomy, and others take the opposite point of view (Gillie, 1973).

It is a truism that a dichotomy exists between practitioners and theorists of administration. The practitioners (i.e., the community junior college presidents and their various deans and department chairmen) may not be aware of the considerable number of theories developed in educational administration that relate to their job functions. Such practitioners may depend upon their own personal experiences to determine their actions as administrators rather than search out theories relating to those actions. There is always a danger of the separation of theory from practice to the detriment of sound practice. The ideal combination, of course, is to utilize modern theory in the improvement of practice. An administrative practice works for reasons that ought to be known to the administrator; otherwise he may not be maximizing the benefits that can be derived. At the same time, a practice that should work in theory but doesn't in actuality should be examined so as to find out why it doesn't. (That is, the extraneous elements that altered the original setting need to be identified and understood.) The ideal training program for administrators combines theory and practice such that the most viable leadership is provided for community junior colleges. This position appears to be finding increasing acceptance (Richardson, Blocker, and Bender, 1972).

The Faculty

One of the fastest growing segments of the community junior college movement in the 1970s was the multi-campus urban college. Several studies of the development of the urban community junior college have found that acquisition of appropriate faculty is a continuing problem. An effective faculty for such institutions is generally categorized as one that is sensitive to the feelings and problems of others, knowledgeable about daily affairs and problems of ghetto life, willing to have its work regularly monitored, and able to make behavioral adjustments based on constructive feedback (Palola and Oswald, 1972). Urban community junior colleges should establish meaningful cooperative endeavors with social and service community organizations, and initiate development of such organizations where they don't exist. The ideal situation would be one where the college functions as one of the community organizations concerned with and dedicated to solving the diverse problems of ghetto residents. The role of the faculty in this framework is radically different from what one would find in the conventional community junior college in a middle-class setting. The question of whether such faculty members can be found and/or trained in sufficient numbers remains unanswered.

There is some concern about the lack of minority faculty members, although progress has been made in the hiring of more minority members since the late 1960s and early 1970s. Simmons (1972) has suggested an internship arrangement designed along the lines of the academic internship program of the American Council on Education. The setup would be like that for any good internship program. The minority group faculty members in the program would be placed in community junior colleges or state agencies where prearrangements had been made so that the intern would become actively involved in high level policy and decision-making activities.

Staff development is a critical issue in community junior colleges, but there is considerable difference of opinion as to how staffs ought to be developed. Much energy has been expended in dealing with this issue, as indicated by the frequent referral to it in the literature. Some take the position that the community junior college should assume the primary responsibility for development and conduct of in-service programs for faculty (O'Banion, 1972). The advocates of this approach believe that staff development ought to be coordinated internally, and that a person with a title such as assistant to the president, academic dean, or staff development officer or a special committee of the academic council should be assigned authority for its administration. The most viable in-service programs are those conducted on a continuous, year-round basis and not merely one-week workshops conducted during the summer or between semesters. Continuous staff development can help faculty members to improve the ways in which they promote student development. This could be the basis for a reward–nonreward system (reward results only if there has been good teaching) for faculty performance in place of the traditional merit-rating system (which has not been notably successful).

A significant portion of a community junior college's research and development funds should be earmarked for staff development (Blake, 1972). Should this become the main thrust of research and development in community junior 'colleges, it could help reduce the anti-research feelings that exist and result in governance boards looking more favorably upon allocation of funds for research and development. A direct advantage to faculty members is that the program would enhance their ability to meet current and future responsibilities, and possibly to avert the obsolescence that can overtake a community junior college. In-service educational experiences that will result in improvements in the teaching–learning process for all faculty members can be selected (Sims and Bounds, 1972). This is rather important because the community junior college faculty members with varied backgrounds, especially those with no prior knowledge of these schools, should become familiar with the mission and commitment of the community junior college. The place of unionism in staff development raises some interesting questions. Nelson (1972) has suggested that collective bargaining be used as a basis for establishing mutually acceptable opportunities for professional development and responsibilities for in-service training.

Perhaps some of the poor teaching that goes on in some community junior colleges has to do with the use of the term "college" in connection with these institutions (Wilson, 1973). The use of that term in describing the community junior colleges could create unfavorable comparisons between these colleges and the senior colleges and universities. It might be better to enlarge the community junior college image to that of post-secondary education instead of merely a component of higher education. In this way, the activities of the community junior college could be more broadly conceived as including technical institutes, proprietary schools, industrial education enterprises, some area vocational schools, and governmental training programs. Even without this broadened mission, various faculty members in the same college are working toward contradictory goals. Although some difference between faculty members is indeed healthy, differences should not be so great as to result in a high level of contradiction, which can reduce student learning and development. The possibility of this dysfunctional condition arising can be reduced by an intensive, comprehensive, and continuing staff development program.

An effective staff development program, regardless of whether it is conducted on site or at a university, should assist the faculty in achieving higher levels of the several attributes believed to be important for community junior college teachers: understanding, flexibility, patience, practicality, sense of humor, creativity, and preparation. Although every faculty member cannot have equal amounts of these seven qualities, a wise selection of teachers would result in a good balance of them within the entire faculty (Pearce, 1966). Fear of and aversion to innovations are present among community junior college faculty (Evans and Lippman, 1967), as they are throughout the teaching profession. In view of the clientele to which the community junior colleges address themselves, one of their most important challenges is that of providing a consistently superior program of instruction (Johnson and Howe, 1970). The commitment to teaching should be the community junior college's counterpoint to the university's commitment to research. Several surveys have failed to detect any significant innovations in the field of community junior college teaching. Eight kinds of development in community junior college teaching are in constant need of attention: (1)

definition of the college's instructional objectives, (2) incorporation of a systems approach to instruction, (3) improvements in program instruction so as to increase its flexibility and overall utility, (4) better use of technological aids to learning, (5) design of better special facilities for large-group instruction, (6) use of students to teach other students, (7) refinement of techniques for sensitivity training and encounter groups, and (8) better use of cooperative work–study modes of education. Movement toward the above could be the vehicle for community junior colleges to depart from the traditional bill of fare in American education. Community junior college faculty members, in order to better accomplish the mission of their institutions, ought to define specific instructional objectives as a basis for curriculum development, improvement of instruction, and for launching, conducting, and evaluating teaching innovations. They should involve students much more than is presently done in their own learning and in conduct of college affairs. Faculty members ought to become more involved in the utilization of educational technology in teaching and learning. Also, greater progress needs to be made in the direction of enabling students to learn and advance at their own rate of intellectual progress.

Very little appears in the literature about the adjunct faculty in community junior colleges, even though 40 percent of the more than 120,000 faculty members in 1971–1972 were in that category (*AACJC Directory*, 1975). Perhaps this is indicative of the relative unimportance of these faculty members in the eyes of their full-time colleagues. But some community junior college leaders see the adjunct faculty in a different light, as indicated in one brief report (Bender and Hammons, 1972). Adjunct faculty members may be employed because: (1) such faculty possess skills and/or experiences which are either unavailable or not feasible to acquire on a full-time basis, (2) they can be used during peak enrollment periods (such as the fall semester) and then released when enrollments are down, or (3) they are potential full-time faculty members who need a proving ground because they have had no previous teaching experience in community junior colleges. Although adjunct faculties do include their share of individuals who accept such positions merely to supplement their incomes, many persons seek these part-time positions because of their desire to teach. Those who come for the latter reason are apt to be receptive to opportunities for self-improvement and can be adventuresome in trying out new ideas in the classroom and laboratory.

Community junior college faculty members, like those in other educational institutions, have been concerned about the students' evaluation of their teaching. Although the facts are not all in, and likely never will be, evaluation of a faculty member is one indication of the student's satisfaction as a consumer of that teacher's product (Rodin, 1973). But to move beyond that, to use students' reactions as a major basis for ascertaining the amount they have learned from the teacher is lacking in both validity and reliability. The topic of teacher evaluation is laden with emotion to begin with, and injecting the possibility of students being allowed into the picture further aggravates the situation. Deegan (1972) has cited several problems associated with student evaluation of their mentors: (1) the failure to relate students' abilities for evaluation to criteria for and goals of evaluation, (2) inadequate evaluation instruments, (3) poor rate of survey returns by the students, and (4) tendencies toward disseminating the findings in ways that are inappropriate and even disparaging to the faculty.

Evaluation with little or no direct input from the students is the lesser of two evils as far as many faculty members are concerned. California was one of the earliest states to mandate that every permanent faculty member in the community junior colleges be evaluated at least once every two years. In response to this, a study of faculty in the ninety-four public community junior colleges of that state was conducted in 1972. The results showed that researchers could not agree as to what constituted valid evaluation criteria. Certain characteristics appeared consistently for the highly rated teachers, however, and they were: (1) ability to relate to students, (2) ability to arouse student interests, (3) friendliness, (4) empathy, and (5) knowledge of subject matter (Schulman and Trudell, 1972). Many of the researchers queried on this matter stressed that the most valid criteria for teacher evaluation is the effect of teaching upon the learner (Schulman and Trudell, 1972). The respondents also agreed that the purposes of evaluation, in addition to improving instruction, were to provide a basis for school leaders to make judgments as to the teacher's effectiveness in preparing subject matter for presentation, to determine the effectiveness of the teacher's instruction methods, and to decide whether or not the teacher should be retained in employment. Implicit in the last purpose is the possibility of replacing faculty tenure with an objective evaluation process, although one can question the chances of such a move succeeding (in view of the present status of unionism and collective bargaining in community junior colleges).

Historically, it has been difficult to evaluate faculty because both the purposes of teaching and the criteria upon which measurements should be based have been too ambiguous (Brawer and Cohen, 1969). Perhaps a first step would be to define teaching as a process that causes learning. From this definition the basic criterion would be a demonstration of students' learning that is attributable to the teacher's efforts. This is perhaps a bit simplistic because it is difficult to establish clear lines between something learned and the precise cause of the learning. Thus many more factors need to be included in any faculty evaluation scheme. Community junior college instructors, like teachers at most academic levels, are not accustomed to the idea of examining the results of their efforts in terms of changes in their students. Many present forms of evaluation do not lead to an enhancement of student learning. If, however, faculty evaluation is properly designed and conducted, it could serve a number of important purposes. Chiefly, it could urge faculty to move in certain directions. When the faculty members see that evidence of student learning is gathered systematically and consistently, they are likely to redirect their efforts to increase the causation of learning. Also, good faculty evaluation would study the sequence of learning activities and the methodology involved in their presentation, thereby providing concrete information for feedback to the teacher so that he can change and/or improve his techniques. In addition, a good evaluation strategy would rate the teacher within the context of the total learning environment—we are all too familiar with the extremes: A teacher functions poorly in what is potentially an excellent setting with the latest in educational technology or a teacher functions brilliantly under the most adverse learning conditions. The approach considered here would minimize rewards or penalties that might be accrued because of effects of the learning environment that are beyond the teacher's control.

An increasing number of college faculties are turning to unionization. In mid-1973, 304 institutions were bargaining collectively, in 205 units, with representatives of their faculty. The National Education Association (NEA), American Federation of Teachers (AFT), and American Association of University Professors (AAUP) are the three national bargaining agents. Over one-third (136) of the higher education institutions involved are two-year colleges, with ninety-two represented by the NEA, forty-one by the AFT, and three by the AAUP (Ladd and Lipset, 1973). There is considerable debate about the benefits and possible dangers of college unionism. Traditionally, one of the marks of the profession is the high degree of self-regulation, which provides the membership with a sense of individual standing. Unions have had difficulty gaining a hold in places where feelings of professionalism run strongest, as seen by the fact that only fifty-two four-year colleges and universities are included in the total of 304 institutions. Opposition to collective bargaining and faculty unionism is strong in many places, and many of the elections failed to support unionism. Proponents feel the movement will grow because of the financial pressures on higher education throughout the country. An additional concern, relative to the public colleges, is the possibility that a unionized faculty may bargain directly with the state legislature. Such a move would result in a loss of academic autonomy for those schools, and the adversary labor–manager relationship would come to a sharp focus. Faculty attitudes toward unionism vary according to the individual instructor's attainments. The less productive teachers are more likely to endorse the principles of collective bargaining than are their more productive colleagues. An interesting development in the early 1970s was the reduction of differences between the NEA, AFT, and AAUP. The future of faculty unionism will likely remain unclear for some time to come, but during this period it will be one of the most turbulent areas in higher education. Also, one can assume that faculty unionism is most likely to spread in the community junior colleges because the faculty has less control over more aspects of the working conditions than in many senior colleges and universities. Should unionism become extant in community junior colleges, these colleges will undergo significant changes—primarily in the direction of assuming more of the characteristics found in secondary and primary schools.

Criteria for hiring community junior college faculty are partially determined in about ten states by virtue of required certification (Gillie, 1973). In most places hiring is based primarily on the judgment of persons charged with the responsibility for faculty selection, although they in turn may rely heavily upon recommendations of other faculty members and administrators. The most common general criteria (if one is to believe the advertisements in the professional journals and the Sunday edition of *The New York Times*) is the acquisition of a master's degree and a belief in the mission of the community junior colleges.

The characteristics of community junior college faculty have implications for these institutions and their students. An individual will undergo a personal conflict when made to behave in ways that are inconsistent with his personality. One way to minimize such conflict is first to define carefully the community junior college's goals and then select teachers whose personal aims coincide with the institutional goals. Goal conflict between the individual teacher and the community college is an important component of the antagonism that can exist in such institutions (Brawer, 1968). A potential faculty member should be informed in advance of his institutional responsibilities. Should this be done, the likelihood of matching faculty members and colleges with compatible goals is increased.

In addition to being cognizant of institutional goals, the faculty

member should know himself well enough to understand his preferences and dislikes. Some educators feel that team teaching can be
made into an effective method for encouraging teachers to develop their
own personalities, fulfill their own needs, and also improve the manner
in which they relate to students.

When preparing community junior college teachers, the university
teacher-training programs should teach them as much as possible
about higher education in general and two-year colleges in particular.
Teacher trainers must be aware of individual differences in potential
teachers and should coax them into teaching roles that are congruent
with their basic personalities. Teaching methods need to be examined
closely with an eye on the learning process. Teacher trainers need to
acquire knowledge of the student, his potential for learning, his resistance to learning, and the ways in which desired student changes can
be brought about. Another important aspect of teacher training is to
provide the potential teacher with freedom to advocate his point of view
(at least to some extent), to promote his special interest, and to attempt
to win over disciples of his own.

Sorely needed is more longitudinal demographic data, so that we can
better understand teachers and how they grow in the profession over a
long period of time. A series of investigations into teacher–student interactions within prescribed environments ought to be conducted soon.
Of particular interest in this regard would be identification of the most
successful teachers in groups of students with whom they are congruent, dissimilar, or some mixture of each.

There were nearly 100,000 two-year college faculty members in
1969–70, with just under 70 percent holding the master's degree and
less than 7 percent holding the doctorate. During that year the mean
faculty salary was $8,000 in private two-year colleges and just under
$11,000 in public community junior colleges. The community junior
college salaries then were somewhat higher than those of public school
teachers but lower than those found in universities. The community
junior college instructor also holds a middle of the road position as far as
teaching load is concerned. His twelve- to fifteen-hour weekly class load
is less than that of the secondary school teacher but more than that of
the university professor.

Several studies have found that teachers with greater academic preparation and those assigned to academic types of teaching positions (as
opposed to vocational) tend to be among the faculty members most
dissatisfied with the community junior colleges and most likely to view
the senior colleges and universities as their reference group (Hammel,
1967; Gillie, Leslie, and Bloom, 1971).

Several studies have developed faculty categories. One such endeavor led the investigators to classify the faculty members into three groups: pioneer settlers, pioneer adventurers, and jobholders (Gusfield and Riesman, 1968). The pioneer settlers were career-oriented planners with firm professionalism. They were viewed as conservative, career-oriented young fogies by their peers. They emphasized efficiency in their work and insisted on teaching materials closely related to research. The pioneer adventurers displayed a dissident attitude toward the first group. The pioneer adventurers were attracted to their jobs by the college's image as innovative, rather than by other career advantages (higher salaries, smaller teaching loads, etc.), and they were less committed to the values and standards of the profession than were the pioneer settlers. They had a less dedicated attitude toward their subject fields and were more oriented toward the interdisciplinary approach. The jobholder was considerably different from the first two. This type of person did not consider his teaching position as a central dimension of his life and viewed his present job as a means to other ends. His real interests were in the enjoyment of his family, leisure time, and, in some cases, another occupation.

Friedman (1967) classified community junior college teachers in terms of their prior institutional affiliation—high school teachers, graduate students, and professors. He found that most had formally taught in high school, had earned master's degrees in a specialized academic field, and were over thirty-five years old when they became community junior college teachers. The former high school teachers emphasized subject matter, did not identify themselves with particular teaching methods, and frequently held low regard for methods courses in education and professors of education (even though their own academic preparation included about twenty hours in education courses, and much of their "shop" conversation contained educational terms). The former graduate students were usually in a state of transition. They spent much of their time scaling down their expectations of student performance and strove to fill in gaps in their own knowledge (particularly in the difference between their specialties and the content required for freshman, sophomore, and remedial courses). They were less committed to teaching as an occupation than either of the other two groups and regarded the community junior college as a steppingstone position until a job in a senior college could be obtained or they could complete work on their doctorate degree. The professors had previously taught many freshmen and sophomores, and seemed to adjust readily to teaching lower division courses. The switch to a community junior college teaching position was viewed by them as a failure or a demotion, while the high schoolers viewed their move as a definite step upward. Teachers can also be categorized as subject matterists and disciplinarians (Friedman, 1967). The subject matterists derive their colleagueship from the particular college where they are employed, while the disciplinarian tends to be more cosmopolitan and looks toward nationwide associations in his profession. The majority of community junior college instructors are subject matterists.

Community junior college teachers can also be classified according to the way they conduct themselves within their own discipline. They may consider themselves as belonging to a discipline, such as electronics, but they may also work in their particular discipline at several levels of involvement such as discoverer, synthesizer, translater, practitioner, or commuter (Cohen, 1970). The discoverer is the researcher who develops theory, designs and conducts original studies, and sometimes even invents tools or techniques of investigation. The synthesizer draws on the findings of the researcher, combining them into a new knowledge deemed suitable by others in the discipline—he is often the writer of original textbooks. Both these types are likely to contribute to journals in their fields. The translater defines work areas by reviewing the synthesizer's publications and transforming them into modes of teaching. The practitioner uses tools of his discipline as if they were his own—he accepts ideas from others and rarely contributes his own. The commuter relies on popular information readily understandable to any layman within the specialization. The community junior college instructor might hold a dual disciplinary membership in that he is affiliated with a subject field and also with the discipline of teaching.

Brawer (1968) developed a typology of community junior college faculty members based on the roles they assume: the end-of-the-roaders, ladder climbers, clock punchers, and defined-purpose routers. The end-of-the-roaders may come from high school or university teaching positions, directly from graduate schools, or from nonacademic positions, but they all perceive the community junior college teaching position as both a means and an end and not as their permanent professional station. For some it represents a last resort because they were unable to hold or obtain the position they really wanted. (Many desire to teach in a university but failed to complete the doctorate.) Others opted for the community junior college because of salary considerations. For example, many liberal arts instructors would prefer a liberal arts college but can't afford such a position because of the low pay. These instructors are in the group of community junior college faculty members who would rather be in a four-year liberal arts college. The ladder climbers see their present community junior college job as a steppingstone to a bigger and better position, and perceive themselves as being there for a limited period of time only. They may also be university students working toward advanced degrees while teaching at the community junior college, and they often hold themselves aloof from instructors who view the community junior college as their terminal point. The clock punchers are more truly devoted to other fields or avocations. They view their teaching job only in terms of earning wages, and not as an opportunity to either further themselves or their disciplines. The defined-purpose routers are in many ways the most desirable type of teacher at any level of education. They have dedicated themselves to integration of self and to the attainment of their goals via their teaching. They view the community junior college as a teaching school, a place where different kinds of students come to seek satisfaction for various needs. The defined-purpose routers define their specific subject matter in terms of specific learning objectives and move their students toward a combination of goal-oriented, specified behavior and personality integration.

Other typological studies ought to be conducted to enhance our understanding of the kinds of people that go into community junior college teaching and the nature of the teaching profession in that institution. Such inquiries could help community junior college teachers identify commonalities with high school and senior college teachers and also to delineate the elements that are unique to community junior college teaching.

The manner in which community junior college teachers view occupational and academic students is of great importance, and one study included questions that assessed attitudes toward students in occupational and academic curriculums. The purpose of the study was to describe instructors possessing the most favorable attitudes, to make inter- and intra-institutional comparisons of attitudes, to determine attitudinal conditioning (which is dependent on institutional settings), and to examine values as predictors of certain teacher attitudes (Oppelt, 1967). Vocational teachers were found to view all concepts more favorably than academic teachers. Faculty members who were older and had some blue-collar work experience and multipurpose teaching experiences viewed vocational students more favorably, while those with doctoral degrees viewed vocational students less favorably. Academic instructors who worked in community junior colleges with a high proportion of vocational programs viewed vocational students favorably. Vocational teachers viewed themselves more favorably when their academic colleagues regarded them more favorably.

Many community junior college faculty members apparently suffer some role conflict. Park (1970) found they were self-centered in their value orientations and viewed their college as an obstacle to the achievement of their desired goals. He discovered that teachers separate themselves, as individuals, from their work and college and feel insecure in their understanding of the community junior college. Many even admit to not fully accepting the community junior college philosophy. Much needs to be done to determine the extent to which values and attitudes of this order lead to specified behaviors in the classroom, which in turn affect students in ways other than would be expected.

The community junior college teacher can be viewed within the dimensions of three concepts: creativity, flexibility, and authoritarianism (Cohen et al., 1972). Creativity is important because it enables the instructor to nurture creativity in students and also makes it possible for him to generate innovative instructional approaches. This ought to be particularly important in community junior colleges. Apparently, creative instructors don't find their way into community junior colleges very often, and when one does end up in a community junior college, there is some question as to whether his colleagues really want him there.

Flexibility varies from one person to the next, and even in one person shifts according to the dynamic forces impinging on him at the moment. Such fluctuation can be expected. Flexibility is a highly valued characteristic of community junior college teachers.

Nine components of the authoritarian syndrome have been postulated: conventionalism, authoritarian aggression, authoritarian submission, power and toughness, anti-introspection, acceptance of superstition and stereotype, destructiveness and cynicism, projectivity, and overconcern with sex (Cohen et al., 1972). It may be that the teaching profession tends to attract and hold people with authoritarian tendencies. The authoritarian instructor encourages either countervailing authoritarianism or subordination. When the teacher acts authoritatively and the student submits, fragmentation of the student's personality can result, and such a situation is undesirable. It appears that when an individual plays the role of teacher, it tends to bring out the authoritarian in him.

The community junior college teacher engages in several functions, including service to the school and community, student guidance, and teaching activities. Even a teaching role may be subdivided into a number of areas, such as dispensing information, establishing a classroom climate, serving as a model, facilitating student development, and managing a total instructional environment. Although every instructor functions in all of these areas, some persons are better in some areas than in others, and they tend to emphasize some functions and minimize others. Perhaps it is most important for the community junior college faculty member to be a model, mediator, and manager. Most instructors probably tend to adopt specialized styles and become most strongly identified with one of these. The community junior college professor has been viewed in several lights. In some cases he has been esteemed and respected, but in others he has been the recipient of casual derogatory remarks. Views shift with the times, and the teacher may be seen as a positive or a negative model.

The instructor who is a mediator sees his exclusive function as one of intervention with the students, and he finds himself relying heavily on the element of interaction between himself and students. The instructional manager is outcome-oriented, being concerned with the tangible, measurable, and identifiable outcomes of his endeavors relative to student learning.

The Students

Student enrollment in community junior colleges increased from 100 in 1900 to 3.527 million in 1974, of which 3.394 million were in public two-year colleges and the remaining 0.133 million were attending independent colleges (*AACJC Directory, 1975*). The increase since 1970 is 1.03 million students.

Cross (1971) conducted a study of community junior college students and extracted data from four major projects: (1) Project TALENT—a national sample of over 60,000 high school seniors tested in 1960 with follow-up studies in 1961 and 1965; (2) The Growth Study—a sample of just under 9,000 students tested as high school juniors in 1965, after data had been collected in 1961 and 1963, and tested in follow-up studies in 1967, when they were high school seniors, and in 1968, one year after high school graduation; (3) SCOPE (school to college: opportunity for post-secondary education)—a four-state sample of about 34,000 high school seniors tested in 1966 with a 1967 follow-up study; (4) Comparative Guidance and Placement Program (CGP)—a sample of just under 24,000 students tested by forty-five community junior colleges in 1969. One major finding was that community junior colleges were attracting low achievement students in increasingly larger numbers, but had not succeeded in designing and implementing programs tuned to the interests and abilities of this group.

The term "equal opportunity" means that every person should be able to make the best possible use of his talents. In education this means diverse offerings must be made available so that all persons, regardless of color, religious or economic differences, and ability, can profit from some aspect of education.

During the 1950s there were extensive talent searches for individuals who were from poor lower class families but had an abundance of academic talent and a willingness to strive. These talent hunts were for persons who met meritocratic ideals of this era, although they did not meet aristocratic criteria. The prevailing attitude in American education is still predominantly meritocratic, although some attempts are being made to reduce the barriers imposed by this approach, particularly in community junior colleges. The intermingling of meritocratic and egalitarian philosophies in the community junior colleges may create considerable difficulties. Many questions have surfaced: Can we be equal and excellent too? Can egalitarianism and meritocracy coexist? What happens to the value of the college degree when everyone has one? Is there some fixed concept of "college" that permits us to say who should attend?

Up to now there have been several ways to assist traditional students in becoming eligible for traditional higher education, but there is a real paucity in new and innovative forms of education to meet the needs of nontraditional students. Future enrollments in higher education cannot be increased under the present college mode without questionable rises in dropout rates, since the additional new students will be primarily those whose past performance at academic tasks has been rated as below average. Average and above average students have been successful in getting into college since the 1950s. The new source of students comes from the ranks of low achievers, who do not perform traditional educational tasks with competence. Contrary to what many educators may think, most of the low achievers currently seeking entry into higher education come from Caucasian families whose fathers are blue-collar workers (although a substantial number of these low achievers are members of minority ethnic groups). These potential students say their main reason for wanting to go to college, rather than their interest in learning, is to use education as a vehicle to acquire a better job and to lead a better life than their parents. One-fourth of these low achievement students have fathers who attended college. The heart of the dilemma is that traditional education cannot serve the privileged and disadvantaged equally well. Evidence shows that traditional education serves the privileged class very well and the disadvantaged very poorly.

Low achievement students grasp onto unrealistic aspirations as a strategy for meeting threats of failure. Many of them also display a lack of effort with regard to academic matters. Ways must be found to re-structure the learning situation so that these students will try again, and their efforts will be rewarded even if they don't succeed in the usual sense of the word. New students who come from the bottom third of their high school classes most often lack confidence in their own abilities, avoid risk situations whenever possible, and are more likely than others to be passive in their approaches to life and its demands.

Blue-collar youth have greater academic and vocational motivation than white-collar youth. (Blue-collar workers are the unskilled, semi-skilled, skilled, and service workers; white-collar workers are those in professions requiring a bachelors degree or more, or executive status. Middle level status, which includes salesmen, office workers, junior executives, and managers, is excluded from these two groupings [Comparative Guidance and Placement Program, 1969].)

There is some debate in educational circles as to whether community junior college curricula ought to be changed, or whether the colleges should attempt to modify the behavior of these traditionally unsuccessful students. In all probability there will have to be some modification in both.

Low achievement students spend their leisure time in nonacademic matters, while their high achievement counterparts devote more time to school-like activities. Only 30 percent of community junior college students (compared to 69 percent of university students) had high school averages or B or better. University students have the additional advantage of having higher levels of self-confidence. So in terms of traditional modes of education, the low achievement students have other factors working against them as well.

Ironically, schools have traditionally done a better job of preparing people for continuing in school than in preparing them for occupations. Most entering community junior college students hope their college experiences will enable them to engage in many activities, that their professors will help them understand their classwork, and that the campus will have a prevailing feeling of friendliness. Low achievement students indicate interest in preparing for a particular job or career and want to take courses which train them for their selected occupation. The college life of many low achievement students is further complicated by their having to work part-time in order to pay for their education or to support themselves while in school. Only a small percentage of high or low academic students selected as the most desirable college one which would be classified as a "fun college." It seems that community junior college students tend to be vocationally oriented.

There were more white-collar than blue-collar workers in the United States in the early 1970s. There has been a very rapid increase in white-collar workers since 1910, when they made up less than one-fourth of the work force. Today nearly half of all employed persons are white-collar workers. Workers in professional and technical occupations now have educational levels of more than sixteen years, and clerical and sales personnel have on the average more than a high school education. These data indicate that an increasingly larger portion of the work force is staying in school for longer periods of time.

A major reason for students' enrolling in community junior colleges (80 percent in 1970) is that they believe it will increase their earning power (Borow, 1964). Career preparation is one of the major motivations of persons enrolling in higher education, and this is especially true of the low achievement student.

Since career preparation is a high priority concern for community junior college students, we should have a knowledge of career development. There are four major dimensions relating to career development and the role of education in it: making career decisions, career aspirations, career preferences, and characteristics of the jobs rated as desirable. A brief examination of each follows.

Making Decisions. Decisions are easiest to make when there is a limited number of choices at hand. Low achievement students, probably because they consider many types of work above their abilities, make career choices by the time they enter college, and women are even more likely than men to feel confident about an early choice of occupation. Low achievement students recognize the necessity of making a career decision earlier than others. Only 11 percent of the students who enter community junior colleges indicate that they will probably change their career choices, which means the other 89 percent are pretty well convinced of what they want to become in the occupational world when they enroll in the community junior college.

Career Aspirations. Most community junior college students want to surpass their parents' level of education and also hope to qualify for higher status jobs than their fathers held. Most academically able high school seniors want to enter the professions or high status white-collar jobs (such as managers, executives, artists, or government officials). The lower achievement youngsters entering community junior colleges aspire to jobs that are higher than their fathers but lower than those selected by high achievement students. Many low achievement students would like to become social workers, teachers, and engineers. Over 40 percent of them aspire to do office work or enter sales or skilled crafts jobs. The career aspirations of low achievement youngsters are realistic for the most part and are closely related to their educational aspirations (which tend to be minimum).

Career Preferences. Low achievement students tend to make occupational choices that require little or no college education. Based on their aspirations and abilities, low achievement men and high achievement women appear to have the greatest chances of becoming dissatisfied with their occupations. Many low achievement males may be confronted with intellectual and technical demands that are beyond their interest or particular abilities. High ability women, on the other hand, may have interests and abilities that are most applicable in occupations that are not available to them.

Job Desirability. Low achievement students are more concerned with tangible job rewards, whereas the others value the less tangible job satisfaction variables. Both low and high achievement students rated the following job characteristics as essential or important: freedom to make one's own decisions (50 percent of the low achievers and 52 percent of the high achievers), opportunity for promotion and advancement in the long run (65 percent of the low achievers and 63 percent of the high achievers), meeting and working with sociable, friendly people (71 percent of the low achievers and 83 percent of the high achievers). These data are derived from the TALENT project.

The research cited in the preceding paragraphs indicates that the most important contribution community junior colleges can make is to prepare their students for the occupations most suitable for them in terms of their abilities and interests.

An important question for those interested in the cost of education is: What differential in the salary received five years after graduation does a post-secondary education make? In one study acquisition of the bachelors degree had more effect on salary than any of the other characteristics examined. It can be predicted that college graduates, regardless of ability or socioeconomic status, will earn higher salaries than those who have no post-secondary education. A comparison of baccalaureate degree graduates and high school graduates of comparable ability and background showed that 71 percent of the baccalaureate degree men were earning above average salaries, while only 48 percent of the men without degrees were earning above average salaries. Although socioeconomic status and ability may make some difference, the acquisition of a bachelors degree makes more difference than any other single factor. The percentage of income differential which may be directly due to schooling is probably somewhere between 67 and 82 percent (Hartnett, 1971).

Higher education is, in fact, an effective device for enhancing upward socioeconomic mobility. But would this be true if the number of people with baccalaureate degrees were to be greatly increased? If virtually everyone had a degree, it could not be used as a criterion for hiring or promotion. Such decisions would then have to be determined by other criteria. A substantial increase in the number of people having college degrees would probably elevate the standard of living for all, but the relative position in society of the low achievement graduates, as compared to high achievement classmates, would remain basically the same over the years (Levin, Guthrie, Kleindorfer, and Stout, 1971).

Students appear to be reasonably well satisfied with their education in terms of job preparation and its contribution to the general enrichment of their lives. Students feel higher education prepares them better for living a full life. A single purpose curriculum, in which training for a vocation is provided, is more satisfying for women than for men.

The assumption that more education will produce a happier citizenry and a better society is open to serious challenge. First, the relative economic value of the degree will likely decrease as the proportion of the population having the degree increases. Second, the basic tendency toward meritocracy will likely continue unabated. That is, college graduates with higher academic ability will be more likely to obtain jobs with higher salaries, will be better satisfied with their education, and will lead a more satisfying life than those with lower academic ability. Third, morale is apparently based on relative positions and not on absolute standards. That is, when fewer people are advanced, the promotions are appreciated more by everyone. Fourth, many people are probably already overeducated for their present jobs (Berg, 1970). The goal of community junior college education ought to be the development of individual talent with attention being paid to individual differences, the searching out of new techniques for fulfilling the students' potential, and a more careful matching of the worker's characteristics and job requirements.

Race continues to be a major barrier to higher education. Thirty percent of American Indians, 37 percent of Negroes, 42 percent of Spanish-Americans, 45 percent of those with mixed minority backgrounds, and 50 percent of Orientals go on to higher education from high school.

Most minority students want to obtain a higher education, and their parents support them in this desire. Like students from blue-collar families, they view college as their major vehicle for upward mobility. Sixty-three percent of high school students from minority groups and just under 40 percent of white low achievement youth expressed desires to enter college. The multiple handicaps of minority ethnic member-ship, low socioeconomic status, and low academic ability will probably continue to prevent many youngsters from ever becoming college stu-dents. One national study found that minority children fall further and further behind their white counterparts as they progress through the school system (Coleman et al., 1966). The initial handicaps of Negroes are not overcome in the public schools, nor is there any workable oppor-tunity to enable them to overcome these handicaps. The disadvantages of the minority groups are also seen in their SAT scores, which are acknowledged to be culture-bound tests (as are the schools themselves). The lowest two-fifths of an academic test found the following percent-ages of each ethnic group: Caucasian—29 percent; American Indian—54 percent; Orientals—62 percent; Mexican-American—63 percent; Negroes—71 percent. These findings were based on a CGP sample of junior college students from forty-five schools in a test of verbal and grammatical skills.

In view of all this, what is the prognosis for ethnic minorities in com-munity junior colleges? There has been an increase in the number of minority youth in community junior colleges lately. While the total col-lege enrollment increased 46 percent between the fall of 1964 and the fall of 1968, black enrollment for that same period increased 85 percent. Black enrollments increased 144 percent in white institutions, and only 30 percent in black colleges (*Higher Education and National Affairs,* 1970). The difference between median education levels of nonwhites and whites began to narrow in the mid-1960s—from 3.1 years in 1962 to 1.9 years in 1967. However, the actual proportion of minority students in college still remains well below their percentage of the population. Some claim that present efforts simply recruit from an existing pool of minority freshman (those that are encouraged to go to white colleges instead of black colleges which they would have gone to otherwise) (Astin, 1970). There are still black high school graduates with talent and interest who are being overlooked for college enrollment, particu-larly in the large cities (Knoell, 1970).

Obviously equality of educational opportunity demands more than mere equal access to post-secondary education such as community junior colleges. The college degree is declining in importance because its increased commonness renders it less useful as a device for selecting people for jobs. But this doesn't help the college dropout who will have an increasingly difficult time getting a job he considers satisfactory. Those who have been in the bottom third of their high school class will repeat that experience by being in the bottom third of their college class, with the result that there will be no overall change in their relative status. Many of the low achievement students' preferences have been identified. These students are attracted to vocations considered tangible and useful to them; they prefer an educational model that will teach them what they need to know in order to make a good living; they prefer watching television over reading; they would rather work with tools than numbers; they prefer to learn by accepting what others have said rather than participate in activities requiring intellectual questioning. Low achievement students are more pragmatic, less questioning, and have a more authoritarian system of values than high achievement students. Universities are probably the poorest place for low achievement students. New approaches to education still need to be devised that will increase maximum development of low achievement students' potential. A possible direction is to view vocations within the three basic categories of working with things, working with people, and working with data. The U.S. Department of Labor uses this approach in its *Dictionary of Occupational Titles*. Perhaps low achievement students can be examined to determine which of these three categories is most likely their strongest, and then a program of learning developed for them around that strength.

Garbin and Vaughn (1973) recently conducted a national study to identify demographic characteristics of community junior college students. They sent questionnaires to sixty community junior colleges throughout the country. The usable sample was just under 5,200 students, and the data dealt with demographic, socioeconomic, educational, and sociopsychological characteristics. As expected, some programs had higher proportions of females (home economics, health, and business-office curricula), and some were male-dominated (technical, trade and industry, and vocational/agricultural programs). Over half of the students were less than twenty years old, except in health occupations, where the average age was over twenty-four. More black students were found in business-office and health occupations, and greater percentages of whites were found in technical and vocational/agricultural programs. Eighty percent of the sample was single.

The socioeconomic data confirmed earlier findings. For example, more than one out of four students came from families whose head had a job in the craftsmen and foremen categories; about four out of ten had fathers with white-collar positions; and six out of ten were from blue-collar families. While the community junior colleges may provide opportunities for many youngsters who otherwise would not have gone on to college, students at the lower extremes of the socioeconomic structure are underrepresented in the community junior college occupational programs. Over 25 percent of the vocational students had B or better high school grades, over 90 percent C or better. Most of the sample had taken only a very few vocational courses in high school. One of the major conclusions of this study was that community junior college vocational students should not be viewed as a relatively homogeneous group, because there were considerable variations between occupational areas.

In 1967 the California Board for Community Colleges commissioned a study of special programs. The results showed the inadequacy of existing programs for recruitment and early identification of students needing special help (Knoell, 1973). The assumption that a tuition-free college doesn't cost anything to attend was disproved, and it was established that the cost to a student living at home ranged from $1,000 to $1,400 (not including the forgone income) at that time. The term "disadvantaged" was eliminated and replaced with "new student," probably because of the disparaging connotations of the former term. Twenty-two percent of the total day enrollment in the fall of 1970 in California community junior colleges was from the minorities (Knoell, 1973), which is significantly higher than the 8.5 percent reported for public two-year colleges in the American Council on Education normative report for the fall of 1971. California data for 1970 show the following percentages by ethnic groups: Mexican-American and Spanish surname students—8.1 percent, black students—7.6 percent, Oriental—2.6 percent, American Indians—1.2 percent, and unidentified minorities—1.4 percent. With increases in minority student representation in the community junior colleges, there has been an accelerated employment of minority faculty and staff in those colleges. Other changes that have accompanied the increased number of minority students are: (1) the development of career-counseling roles, (2) the use of tutors from the ranks of the new students themselves who possess similar characteristics, and (3) a move away from long-term intensive remedial programs for students with severe learning handicaps toward enrollment in degree credit courses with special help from tutors and/or special learning laboratories or in a limited program of developmental courses. Several new ethnic studies programs and courses are in evidence. Some educators now recognize that certain students do not want any general education course work but are willing and able to meet all the other requirements of an associate degree program. The inclusion of proprietary institutions as post-secondary schools, alongside of community junior colleges and technical institutes, is increasing the speed with which programs with reduced general education content are being introduced. There are several vocational fields where the student gets all his specialization in the first two years and then may proceed, if he so elects and is capable, to his junior and senior years where he takes general education courses at some cooperating university or senior college.

Major Organizational Variables

The average enrollment in all two-year colleges listed in *Community and Junior College Directory, 1975* has steadily increased over the years (750 in 1950, 950 in 1960, 2,300 in 1970, 2,927 in 1974). A major reason for the nearly 400 percent increase in average enrollment, along with the slightly greater than 200 percent increase in the number of two-year colleges during the same time period (597 in 1960, 678 in 1960, 1,091 in 1970, and 1,205 in 1974), is the establishment of these institutions in heavily populated urban areas in recent years. One can suspect that the internal characteristics of community junior colleges have changed during the past two decades from considerable concern with academic curriculums to vocational-practical types of programs, since these are more relevant for students with less than average secondary school academic achievement. Total enrollment for the 1973–1974 school year was 3.527 million.

The community junior colleges, like other higher education institutions, have expressed concern for the role of women in society. An example of this was the formation of a consortium of ten community junior colleges and the University of Maryland for the purpose of offering a series of workshops for women (Nordh, 1972). It was primarily geared to meet the needs of back-to-school mothers and other women seeking new careers, and it included counseling on job opportunities. The continuing education for women center at the Foothill Community College District is another illustration of interest in the women's movement. This program included a child care center, more than 100 course offerings in the day, evening, and summer school programs, along with guidance and counseling services for continuing education and vocational programs. The need for the development of programs geared to the new woman student has been expressed in the literature. Proponents of such programs believe the faculty and staff should be attuned to the different types of women students and their needs. The community junior college may not be as far behind as other colleges in employing and enrolling females, since 40 percent of the faculty and 40 percent of the students are women.

The community junior colleges are also concerned with minority groups, and many have given considerable thought to minimum ratios and their implementation via affirmative action programs. Pontua (1973) has proposed that well-developed affirmative action programs would establish six things: goals and timetables, a nondiscrimination policy, personnel policies and procedures, contract compliance policy, the role of the affirmative action office, and other ancillary academic services.

Some minority-group faculty members have expressed skepticism and negativism about career education and its impact upon minorities. One question raised is: "How can an educational system which has been programmed to serve people by race and economic resources guarantee that career education will not simply reinforce this tracking, sorting process, when, in fact, the total educational framework within which career education has been conceptualized has not itself been reconstructed?" (Love, 1973). Also, there appears to be a continued aversion to vocational education by minorities, which may be related to a history in which vocational education was used to keep them out of the professions (see Chapter 3). Many minorities feel preparation for the professions should be their goal.

Student involvement in institutional governance has been a subject of considerable concern in higher education since the student activism movement of the 1960s. Institutions where there is a long tradition of student participation usually succeed in attracting high quality students as office seekers, and the contributions these students make in their various committees is quite often useful. But this is apparently not the case in most American colleges (Ashby, 1971), and very likely not so in community junior colleges as a whole. College educators ought to define the constitutional status of college students more precisely, so that legitimate limits to student participation and conditions of partnership between faculty and students would thereby be established. Bringing student and faculty representation on the board of trustees beyond the mere tokenism level would be desirable. Ashby (1971) has proposed that self-perpetuating trustees yield some of their places to members nominated from outside the board room, and that trustees be elected by popular ballot. Although these recommendations are applicable for

American colleges in general, they are especially appropriate for community junior colleges.

The meaning of the term "faculty" has become shadowy during the last several decades (Rauh, 1969). The machinery of most colleges is established and functions as if the faculty were a unified body with a common voice and a purpose, which is not the case in most two-year colleges. Faculty members in some colleges are concerned with the extent to which they are involved with decision making. The American Association of University Professors in 1962 stated that faculty members should participate and exert influence in such areas as educational policies, faculty membership, administrative offices, and budgeting. Some educators believe the faculty–trustee and faculty–administrator relationships are becoming increasingly similar to the employer–employee relationship common in present-day industry. In some places the faculty has formed internal groups such as faculty senates and unionlike groups to protect their interests. The trustees of community junior colleges, based on one national study, take a conservative stance on this issue: 61 percent of them felt that collective bargaining has no place in a college (Rauh, 1969). Unionism is making progress in community junior colleges, however, and unions are trying to do several things: (1) replace merit with seniority in matters of salary and promotion, (2) alter working conditions, (3) eliminate limitations on academic freedom, particularly for church-related colleges, (3) and provide tenure after three years. Most of these issues strike at the traditional professional concepts of college teaching.

Many faculty members in urban community junior colleges are overly preoccupied with transfer programs or what is considered to be the more academically acceptable side of the institution (Palola and Oswald, 1972). This may be partially overcome by more careful recruitment of faculty for such institutions. Because of special problems encountered by urban schools, their budgetary approaches ought to be different from those of the other kinds of community junior colleges. Since students entering urban colleges are primarily low achievers, nontraditional programs should receive a maximum emphasis. The near absolute power of district boards, particularly their control over local groups and faculty unions, is open to question in terms of benefits to students, and struggles with regard to it will likely increase in severity in the future. The control structure of urban colleges must become more adaptive, and these colleges must seek to encourage participation by many persons and groups in the community. This calls for the development of new control structures that provide for temporary participation methods which can be easily changed to meet new situations.

With regard to furthering assistance to students, Collins (1967) has proposed several methods for improving student personnel policies, practices, and facilities in community colleges. For instance, all community junior colleges should make self-studies of their present status and map out plans for college development. They should communicate continuously with universities so as to be better enable the universities to improve their graduate programs for the preparation of professionals for junior college student personnel services, and cooperate with universities so the universities can provide short-term intensive in-service seminars for community college faculty; community junior colleges should establish regional demonstration centers for student personnel program models, and develop regional career information centers to collect, analyze, interpret, and disseminate current occupational information to community junior college counselors.

Because community junior college students commute daily and are on campus only at irregular hours of the day and/or evening, the claim has been made that they are partially deprived of free-going communication within the college community (Gibbs, 1972). According to one small survey, half the students view the student newspaper as their primary source of news about the college, whereas the administration thought the bulletin boards, commercial newspapers, radio and television, and president's talks provided that vehicle. There is some conflict about the role of the newspaper in some community junior colleges. The administration commonly views it as an official publication of the college and a public relations vehicle, whereas the students perceive it as a mechanism for expressing their own ideas and opinions. This very obvious contradiction leads to possibilities for confrontations. The AAUP, which is clearly oriented toward senior colleges and universities more than community junior colleges, has taken the position that student newspapers ought to be used in establishing and maintaining an atmosphere for discussion and intellectual explorations, which is probably not what community junior college students or administration have in mind. Some educators believe the college newspaper ought to be the mechanism for students to express their opinions, but also see the administration as responsible for establishing the journalistic framework and operational procedures and for demanding ethical and responsible action from those who operate the paper.

The degree of autonomy enjoyed by community junior colleges varies from complete state-local control in some places to very little such control in other places. Some states, such as Connecticut, Hawaii, Massachusetts, and Virginia, have a single board that serves for all the community junior colleges in the state. In such cases true financial control (and therefore actual decision-making authority on most major and many minor matters) rests with the state board and its executive officer. The leadership of each college functions more like that of a campus of a larger statewide community junior college. A major drawback of this variety of governance structure is the impotence of the local college leadership relative to making big decisions; on the other hand, there is a distinct advantage in that the college is free from the tyranny of local real estate taxation for college support. While the highly autonomous colleges (those with independent control, in particular) are able to make all decisions locally, they are, in many cases, severely handicapped by lack of adequate financial support. It appears that the price for autonomy is budgetary austerity, and the price for budgetary adequacy is the surrendering of considerable autonomy. It is highly unlikely that community junior college educators will ever have a high degree of institutional autonomy and adequate financial support simultaneously. The trend, particularly in view of the increased demands for accountability, appears to be in the direction of further reduction in local autonomy for community junior colleges.

The increase in the number of multi-campus urban community junior colleges has presented new college governance problems and several interesting approaches to them. One approach utilizes an executive committee, consisting of the campus presidents, for operation of the overall city system (Baxter and Corcoran, 1972). Each of the presidents serves as chairman of the executive committee on a rotation basis. The advantages of this format include the improvement of top management communications, a tendency for campus presidents to look at the entire district's welfare rather than at their individual campus, a broadened base for decision making, improvement of creditability for decisions made, and reduced cost of administration. Some of the drawbacks are that there is no overall district president, the executive committee confuses outsiders who seek action from the community junior college system, the committee imposes more responsibilities and work loads on the individual campus presidents, committee members tend to play one off against the other, and the committee approach may be screening many of the colleges' actual day-to-day problems from the board. The question still remains: Can a large multi-campus community junior college district find happiness under the governance of a three or more member committee instead of the more traditional single district president configuration? The approach needs to be tried out in several more urban settings.

No one solution or governance structure for community junior colleges can fit all fifty states, but there is consensus that the states have primary responsibility for post-secondary education (Millard, 1973). Increasing costs in these colleges and conflicting priorities with other state requirements have created funding difficulties. Adding to the complexity of the situation is the increasing pressure to find ways to aid private post-secondary institutions. Further reasons for requiring statewide planning and coordination include the reduction of duplications and overlap, increased efficiency and effectiveness, greater assurance of accountability and continuity of the educational process, increased guarantees for decision making at the state level that would strengthen the roles and functional autonomy of institutions. State level coordination can be an effective vehicle for encouraging community junior colleges to affirm that their primary roles are: (1) to provide vocational programs on a comprehensive basis, (2) to more effectively interact with secondary education, the business and industrial communities, appropriate health and social agencies, and other higher education institutions, (3) to enter into coordination and cooperation efforts with all other educational institutions, (4) to urge maximum flexibility and interpretation of legislation, and (5) to work positively and cooperatively with state and federal agencies.

Technological Complexity

Community junior colleges throughout the country have been relatively successful in obtaining funding for new campuses, including the erection of sophisticated buildings and purchase of modern and, in some cases, even exotic equipment to install within them. This has occurred even when the college originated in a makeshift arrangement such as a converted factory building, an abandoned elementary or secondary school, or as an after-hour college in a public school building. Clinton (1973) strongly recommends that governing boards be urged to allocate sufficient money for hardware and facilities to meet the needs of this sophisticated technological age. The following paragraphs provide examples of the most modern equipment, media, and other learning-related devices that are used in certain community junior colleges.

One of the more recent developments in new community junior colleges is the installation of learning resource centers (LRC), which are alternatives to the traditional type of libraries. The utilization of new resource centers, with one or more advanced technological devices in the facility, implies that the college has made a commitment to individualized instruction to some extent. Some colleges are even analyzing their entire institution so as to establish a systems approach to their overall teaching efforts. In such transition attempts it is important that teachers display positive attitudes toward individualization of instruction so that the students will accept it in the same positive vein. Implicit in the emergence of these new resources and the varied demands made upon faculty is a need for a new kind of training for community junior college teachers, along with new types of commitments by governing boards and administrators with regard to the newest concepts dealing with individualized instruction.

Some community junior college educators are experimenting in the use of microform materials, especially microfilm. The major advantages of using microform are: (1) reduced amounts of space required to store information, (2) reduced amount of time necessary to retrieve desired information, and (3) reduction in overall costs of handling the information (Gaddy, 1973). On the other hand, many educators who are responsible for operating learning resource centers haven't been convinced of the true advantages of microforms. Their passive resistance results in teachers not bringing these techniques into use in the learning resource centers. Several limited studies have indicated very little or no resistance to microforms on the part of the students. Furthermore, students who have utilized them have performed just as well scholastically as those who have not. What may be needed is more specific instruction for teachers and learning resource center personnel in methods for selection of appropriate microform equipment and materials, and how to teach students the manner in which microforms can be utilized. If the faculty members become familiar with this equipment, they may become secure enough about it to use microforms in their teaching. Converting selected printed materials to microform could save considerable funds. Although the use of microforms has been referred to in the community junior college literature, the faculties' resistance to this approach may retard its utilization.

The library commission of the American Association of Community and Junior Colleges and the Junior College section of the Association of College and Research Libraries conducted a survey to determine the nature and extent of the use of college libraries and learning resource centers as focal points in community junior college services. The study was limited to those institutions having libraries and learning resource centers considered outstanding by practitioners. Each college was sent a nominating blank, of which 232 were returned. Fifty-three of the colleges were nominated by three or more of the 232 respondents, and they were sent the survey form, of which forty were returned. The colleges sampled ranged from rather rural to completely urban and ranged in enrollment from less than 1,000 to nearly 10,000. Some of the results were as follows: (1) three out of four reporting colleges had integrated libraries and learning resource centers; (2) about three-fourths of the reporting colleges were involved in assisting a wide range of constituencies (rank order of emphasis were ethnic minorities, hospital staffs, high school students, high school faculties, elected civic leaders); (3) no territorial tension with other libraries in the institution was instigated by the presence of learning resource centers; (4) the usual pattern was to accept external requests and to provide whatever assistance possible; and (5) about six of the library/learning resource centers appeared to be moving into relatively sophisticated levels of community service programming (Raines, 1973).

A new modular system of instruction in mathematics has been described by Buzzard (1973). It employs a diagnostic approach which measures what students need to learn. A major claim is that it enables the advanced student to move ahead more quickly then he would in a traditional mode of instruction. When such a modular approach is fully developed, the entire mathematics program of the college can operate on a workshop basis. This would enable students to always work at their own levels with individually selected program material that would assist them in teaching themselves; a teacher would always be on hand for times when assistance is needed.

Another innovative instructional approach is the use of simulation games. In a limited student survey, Saxon (1973) found the use of simulation to be equal to or better than other teaching strategies, regardless of the discipline or particular learning objectives. Students who participated in this type of instruction scored one or two grade points higher in those courses than they normally did in traditional courses.

Another new approach is the dial access information retrieval (DAIR) system which can be used in educational media centers. The mechanical advantages and limitations of this system have been described by Konecny (1973).

There has been considerable discussion in the literature as to what ought to be included in a learning resource center. There appears to be some consensus that it should include library areas, audiovisual areas, learning systems, automation areas, computer areas, student areas, a faculty area, and a point of origin area (Humbert, 1972).

Some community junior colleges are leasing computer time from a service center or leasing a smaller computer, rather than own their own computer. The cost of leasing computer time is based on actual use, which could result in considerable savings. A further advantage is that computer service centers generally have large libraries of statistical and problem-solving programs, and this is not usually true of in-house computers in community junior colleges (Meyer, 1973). Such service centers afford a great amount of flexibility and easy access to the computer. Many of the benefits of the very best in computer technology can be obtained at a fraction of the actual computer cost by tying in with one of these centers.

Some community junior colleges have considered innovative structural designs. Buildings and rooms can now have malleable, rearrangeable structures which would allow the college to reallocate space from time to time (Green, 1973). The use of such malleable environments would likely introduce considerable complications, however, and needs much further study.

There are many proponents of individualized instruction in community junior colleges. Connolly and Sepe (1973) concluded that under individualized instruction 95 percent of the students can and want to achieve A's. There study was conducted in two stages. Stage 1 involved 377 community junior college students, who were provided with two models. One was an individualized approach to instruction, the other a traditional approach. About half of the respondents selected the individualized option. This came as a surprise because it was expected that most students would opt for the individualized instruction model. In stage 2 the two models were presented in a different way to a second sample of 388 community junior college students. The models were broken down into eight pairs of corresponding statements. In each pair one statement described the characteristics of individualized instruction, and the other described the corresponding characteristics of traditional instruction. The majority of the students selected seven of the eight individualized statements over their traditional counterparts. Of importance, however, is that the students expressed a desire for external control rather than learner control (which was included in that eighth statement, where they selected the traditional option). The implication is that students were not willing to assume responsibility for their learning, a factor that may be behind the failure of other attempts to implement individualized instruction. This is a serious obstacle, and new strategies which would require students to assume responsibility for their own learning need to be incorporated. The difficulty is that students would have to change their present learning style, which focuses on the teacher, to one in which the learner focuses primarily on himself.

Some community junior college faculties and administrators believe individualized instruction affords the student greater opportunity to assimilate course materials and interact with the instructor. On the other hand, one small study found that flexible scheduling in individualized instruction for sociology courses did not stimulate learning (Ioia, 1973). Surprisingly, the students said that it afforded them too much time, and they tended to delay doing their work. After the experience, the students asked that the course be more structured so as to coax them to learn. The implication here is that individualized instruction is likely to be a superior learning technique only for certain students.

Another innovative approach to learning is the maximized individualized learning laboratory (MILL) (Reedy, 1973). It was originally conceived as a communications laboratory but was then expanded to all disciplines and is best described as a service. The instructor diagnoses the student's problem, makes a recommendation based on the MILL catalog, and finally refers the student to MILL. All materials are programmed and developmental. The service provides an alternative learning technique that may very well be quite effective for certain types of students.

At least one community junior college has experimented with cable television. The goals of the endeavor were to provide a better variety of cultural programs to the community, training for students in the field of broadcasting and program production, interpretive local programming on community affairs, credit courses for people in the area, and area public schools time for programs (Beckes, 1972).

Another community junior college operates an educational television station (Watson and Luskin, 1972). When inaugurated, the station was going to cover five broad areas: community-oriented programs focusing on local problems, cultural events, and news documentary presentations; a municipal service telecasting for local city and county agencies, instructional programs for preschool, elementary age, junior high, and high school youngsters; general education programs; college level courses with and without academic credit. The plan has not been fully implemented.

There is a trend in some parts of the country for educational institutions to join television instruction consortiums (Wilbur, 1972). The advantages of such an arrangement are that it provides an additional means of instruction, reduces the transportation and facilities problems, provides coordination of teaching for particular courses, and can be economical in the long run. The effort has some drawbacks, however, including faculty subordination to a central control, a time lag, and the necessity for adequate funding for the entire endeavor prior to an assessment of its relative success or failure.

Community junior college educators have also been experimenting with videotape as a learning medium (Hernan, 1972). It was hoped that individual growth would be fostered by making faculty conscious of what teachers do inside the classroom and by sharing those experiences with other teachers. But, as expected, some of the teachers expressed considerable concern about outside observers and strange machines that might distort the nature of their classes. The results of the experiment indicated that faculty anxiety about having classes videotaped was considerable.

References

AACJC Directory: 1975. Washington, D.C.: American Association of Community and Junior Colleges, 1975.

Alden, V.R. "Making of College Presidents." *Saturday Review* 43, (20 February 1965).

Ashby, E. *Any Person, Any Study: An Essay on Higher Education in the United States.* New York: McGraw-Hill, 1971.

Astin, A. "Racial Considerations in Admissions," In D. Nichols and O. Mills, eds. *The Campus and the Racial Crisis.* Washington, D.C.: American Council on Education, 1970.

AVS Directory, 1975. Washington, D.C.: Department of Health, Education, and Welfare, Office of Education, 1975.

Baxter, C., Jr., and Corcoran, J. "Medusan Monster or Ingenous Model?" *Community and Junior College Journal* 43, 1 (1972).

Beckes, I.K. "Vincennes University: Pioneer in Cable TV." *Community and Junior College Journal* 43, 3 (1972).

Bender, L.W., and Hammons, J.O. "Adjunct Faculty: Forgotten and Neglected." *Community and Junior College Journal* 43, 2 (1972).

Berg, I. *Education and the Jobs: The Great Training Robbery.* Prepared for the Center of Urban Education. New York: Praeger, 1970.

Blake, L.J. "A Catalyst for Staff Development." *Community and Junior College Journal* 43, 2 (1972).

Bolman, F., and Wolfe, D. "How Will You Find a College President?" *Journal of Higher Education* 36 (1965).

Borow, H., ed. *Man in a World at Work.* Boston: Houghton Mifflin, 1964.

Brawer, F.B. *Personality Characteristics of the College and University Faculty: Implications for the Community College.* Washington, D.C.: American Association of Junior Colleges, 1968.

——, and Cohen, A.M. *Measuring Faculty Performance.* Washington, D.C.: American Association of Junior Colleges, 1969.

Brickman, W.W. "College Presidency." *School and Society* 89 (1961).

Buzzard, M. "Modular System at Kendall." *Community and Junior College Journal* 43, 9 (1973).

Clinton, R.L. "New Resources for Learning." *Community and Junior College Journal* 43, 1 (1973).

Cohen, A.M. "A Hierarchy of Disciplinarianism." Los Angeles: Graduate School of Education, University of California, 1970.

——, and Roueche, J.E. *Institutional Administrator or Educational Leader?* Washington, D.C.: American Association of Junior Colleges, 1969.

——, Brawer, E.R., and Brawer, F.B. *Confronting Identity: The Community College Instructor.* Englewood Cliffs, N.J.: Prentice-Hall, 1972.

——, et al. *A Constant Variable.* San Francisco: Jossey-Bass, 1971.

Coleman, J., et al. *Equality of Educational Opportunities.* Washington, D.C.: Government Printing Office, 1966.

Collins, C.C. *Junior College Student Personnel Programs: What They Are and What They Should Be.* Washington, D.C.: American Association of Junior Colleges, 1967.

Community Colleges and Occupational Education: NAM Public Policy Report. New York: Education Department of the National Association of Manufacturers, 1973.

Comparative Guidance and Placement Program, (CGP). *Interpretative Manual for Counselors, Administrators, and Faculty, 1969–1970.* New York: College Entrance Examination Board, 1969.

Connolly, J.J., and Sepe, T.D. "Individualized Instruction: Are Students Ready?" *Community and Junior College Journal* 43, 6 (1973).

Cross, K.P. *Beyond the Open Door.* San Francisco: Jossey-Bass, 1971.

Deegan, W.L. "Should Students Evaluate Faculty?" *Community and Junior College Journal* 43, 2 (1972).

Egerton, E.J. "Inflated Body Count." *Change* 4 (1970).

Evans, R.I., and Lippmann, P.K. *Resistance to Innovation in Higher Education: A Social Psychological Exploration Focuses on Television and the Establishment.* San Francisco: Jossey-Bass, 1967.

Folwell, W.W. *University Addresses.* New York: H.W. Wilson, 1909.

Friedman, Norman L. "The Subject Matterist's Orientation Toward Field of Academic Specialization." *The American Sociologist* 2 (1967).

Gaddy, D. "A Medium for Spies in Community Colleges." *Community and Junior College Journal* 43, 9 (1973).

Garbin, A.P., and Vaughn, D.D. "The Democratization of Higher Education." *Community and Junior College Journal* 43, 8 (1973).

Gibbs, A. "Insuring the Effectiveness of Student Newspapers." *Community and Junior College Journal* 43, 3 (1972).

Gilli, A.C., Sr. *A Study of Present and Former Two-Year College Presidents.* University Park: Department of Vocational Education, The Pennsylvania State University, 1976.

Gillie, A.C., Sr. *Essays: Occupational Education in the Two Year College.* University Park: Department of Vocational Education, The Pennsylvania State University, 1970.

———, *Principles of Post-Secondary Vocational Education.* Columbus, O.: Charles E. Merrill, 1973.

———, Leslie, L.L., and Bloom, K. *Goals and Ambivalence: Faculty Values and the Community College Philosophy.* University Park: The Center for the Study of Higher Education, The Pennsylvania State University, 1971.

Gleazer, E.J., Jr. "AACJC Approach." *Community and Junior College Journal* 43, 4 (1973a).

———, "AACJC Approach." *Community and Junior College Journal* 43, 6 (1973b).

———, "AACJC Approach." *Community and Junior College Journal* 43, 8 (1973c).

Green, A.C. "Places for Higher Learning: Some Ideas and Some Customs." *Community and Junior College Journal* 43, 7 (1973).

Gusfield, J., and Riesman, D. "Faculty Culture and Academic Careers." In K. Yamamoto, ed. *The College Student and His Culture: An Analysis.* Boston: Houghton Mifflin, 1968.

Hammel, R.E. "The Effects of Teachers in Four Year Colleges and Universities as Reference Groups for Teachers in Community Colleges." Unpublished doctoral dissertation, University of Oregon, 1967.

Hartnett, R.T. *Universal Higher Education: For Whose Benefit?* Paper prepared for the select education subcommittee of the Education and Labor Committee of the House of Representatives. Princeton, N.J.: Educational Testing Service, 1971.

Hernan, R.E. "Project Insight: Videotaping As a Learning Medium." *Community and Junior College Journal* 43, 3 (1972).

Higher Education and National Affairs. American Council on Education, 13 February 1970; 4 December 1970.

Hill, M.E. "History of Terminal Courses in California." *Junior College Journal* 12 (February 1942).

Hillway, T. "What Professors Want in a President." *School and Society* 20 (1959).

———, "How Trustees Judge a College President." *School and Society* 89 (1961).

Humbert, H.H. "What Does a Modern LRB Look Like?" *Community and Junior College Journal* 43, 3 (1972).

Ioia, J.J. "Individualized Instruction in Sociology: Myth and Fact." *Community and Junior College Journal* 43, 6 (1973).

The Public Community College 157

Johnson, B.L. *Starting a Community Junior College.* Washington, D.C.: American Association of Junior Colleges, 1964.
——, and Howe, Richard D. "Toward Change and Improvement." *Junior College Journal* 40, 4 (1970).
Kintzer, F.C., Jensen, A.M., and Hansen, J.S. *The Multi-Institution Junior College District.* Washington, D.C.: American Association of Junior Colleges, 1969.
Knoebel, R.M. From the Preface to Robert L. Sheppard, ed. *Pennsylvania Community Colleges: 1970–71: Open Doors to Learning.* Harrisburg, Pa: Bureau of Academic Services, Department of Education, 1970.
Knoell, D.M. *People Who Need College.* Washington, D.C.: American Association of Junior Colleges, 1970.
——, "The New Student in 1972." *Community and Junior College Journal* 43, 5 (1973).
Konecny, J. "An Innovation at Wesley." *Community and Junior College Journal* 43, 9 (1973).
Ladd, E., Jr., and Lipset, S.M. "Unionizing the Professoriate." *Change* 5 (1973).
Lange, A.F. "The Junior Colleges As an Integral Part of the Public School System." *School Review* 25 (1917).
Levin, H.M., Guthrie, J.W., Kleindorfer, G.B., and Stout, R.T. "School Achievement and Post-School Success: A Review." *Review of Educational Research* 41 (1971).
Lombardi, J. *Student Activism in Junior Colleges: An Administrator's Views.* Washington, D.C.: American Association of Junior Colleges, 1969.
Love, A. "As Soon As We Learn the Dance, You Change the Steps." *Community and Junior College Journal* 43, 8 (1973).
Medsker, L.L. *The Junior College: Progress and Prospects.* New York: McGraw-Hill, 1960.
——, and Tillery, D. *Breaking the Access Barrier: A Profile of Two Year Colleges.* New York: McGraw-Hill, 1971.
Meyer, D.F. "Yes, We Have No Computer!" *Community and Junior College Journal* 43, 9 (1973).
Millard, R.M. "The Need to Coordinate State and Federal Support." *Community and Junior College Journal* 43, 4 (1973).
Nelson, J.H. "Collective Bargaining: An Instrument for Staff Development." *Community and Junior College Journal* 43, 2 (1972).
Nordh, D.M. "The New Women and the New College." *Community and Junior College Journal* 43, 1 (1972).
O'Banion, T. "Staff Development: Priorities for the 70's." *Community and Junior College Journal* 43, 2 (1972).
Oppelt, M.L. "Attitude of Community College Instructors Toward Student Groups as a Function of Certain Teacher Characteristics." Unpublished doctoral dissertation, University of Washington, 1967.
Palola, E.G., and Oswald, A.R. *Urban Multi-Unit Community Colleges; Adaptation for the 70's.* Berkeley: Center for the Research and Development in Higher Education, The University of California, Berkeley, 1972.
Park, Y. "The Junior College Staff: Values and Institutional Perceptions." Unpublished doctoral dissertation, University of California at Los Angeles, 1970.
Pearce, F.C. *Basic Education of Teachers: Seven Needed Qualities.* Modesto, Calif.: Modesto Junior College, 1966.
Pontua, J.L., Jr. "Remedying Discrimination Through Affirmative Action." *Community and Junior College Journal* 43, 7 (1973).
Public Law 90-576. The Vocational Education Amendments of 1968.
Raines, M.R. "A Survey of Leading LVI/LRC's." *Community and Junior College Journal* 43, 9 (1973).
Rauh, M.A. *The Trusteeship of Colleges and Universities.* New York: McGraw-Hill, 1969.
Reedy, V. "Maximize Individualized Learning Laboratory." *Community and Junior College Journal* 43, 6 (1973).
"Report of the 1972 Assembly." *Community and Junior College Journal* 43, 6 (1973).
Richardson, R.C., Blocker, C.E., and Bender, L.W. *Governance for the Two Year College.* Englewood Cliffs, N.J.: Prentice-Hall, 1972.
Rodin, M.J. "Can Students Evaluate Good Teaching?" *Change* 5 (1973).
Roueche, J.E. *Salvage, Redirection, or Custody?* Washington, D.C.: American Association of Junior Colleges, 1968.
——, and Boggs, J.R. *Junior College Institutional Research: The State of the Art.* Washington, D.C.: American Association of Junior Colleges, 1968.

Saxon, T.J. "Simulation at Kalamazoo." *Community and Junior College Journal* 43, 9 (1973).

Schulman, B.R., and Trudell, J.W. "California's Guidelines for Teacher Evaluation." *Community and Junior College Journal* 43, 2 (1972).

Shannon, W.G. "The Community College President: A Study of the Role of the President of the Public Community College." Unpublished doctoral dissertation, Columbia University, 1962.

Simmons, H. "Priorities for Training Minority Staff." *Community and Junior College Journal* 43, 2 (1972).

Sims, D.M., and Bounds, G.L. "Some Perspectives on Staff Development: EPDA at a Community College." *Community and Junior College Journal* 43, 2 (1972).

Tappan, H.T. *University Education.* New York: Putnam's, 1851.

Taylor, H. "College President: Idea Man or Money Man?" *New York Times Magazine* (12 April 1959).

Watson, N.E., and Luskin, B.J. "Cables, Cassettes, and Computers at Cost." *Community and Junior College Journal* 43, 3 (1972).

Wilbur, L. "A Look at Televised Courses—Before Consorting." *Community and Junior College Journal* 43, 3 (1972).

Wilson, R.E. "Staff Development: An Urgent Priority." *Community and Junior College Journal* 43, 9 (1973).

Wolfe, D. *America's Resources of Specialized Talent.* Report of the Commission Resources and Advanced Training. New York: Harper, 1954.

9

The Private Junior College

Enrollments in privately controlled colleges have not kept pace with the overall rise in the number of college students. In 1930 about 52 percent of the total higher education enrollment of 1.101 million was found in privately controlled higher education institutions, and this decreased to 28 percent of the 7.136 million enrolled in 1970 (Lerner, 1973). The change in the distribution of enrollments in higher education was also reflected in distribution of funds allocated for capital expenditures, interests, and outlay or plant expansion. In 1930 the public expenditure for these items was $289 million, while the privately controlled colleges spent $341 million (54 percent of the total $630 million). Forty-three years later it was evident that the private sector was not maintaining its relative position. An estimated $32,500 million were spent in capital expenditure, interests, and outlay or plant expansion in 1973, of which about 33 percent was spent in private higher education.

The trend toward proportionate increases in public support for higher education has created serious problems for many of the less financially viable small private colleges (see Astin and Lee, 1972), and the privately controlled two-year colleges are caught in this dilemma as well. Evidence of this is seen in the increase in the number of public two-year colleges and their enrollments. There were 229 private junior colleges (about 42 percent of the total of 528 junior colleges) in 1950. Twenty-one years later this decreased to 221 (which was then about 26 percent of the total of 859 junior colleges). While total junior college enrollments increased from 0.217 million in 1950 to 1.725 million in 1971 (an eightfold increase), private junior college enrollments only doubled (from 50,000 to 103,000) during the same interval.

Some students are obviously pulled toward the community junior college sector and away from private junior colleges by the differential in tuition and other required fees. The estimated charges of this nature for the 1973–1974 academic year averaged $261 for public two-year colleges and $1,507 for private junior colleges (Lerner, 1973). Although it is very difficult to estimate the true cost of providing education in a two-year college, one can suspect that fundamental expenses are similar, regardless of whether the college is private or public. Also, one can assume that the differential in tuition and other charges between pri-

159

vate and public two-year colleges does not provide the private institution with a comparable financial base. From this, one can at least suspect that faculty salaries and financial allocations for facilities and equipment must be lower in the private two-year colleges. This has been indicated in the literature (see Astin and Lee, 1972; Medsker and Tillery, 1971; *AACJC Directory*, 1973).

A rough estimate of average student–faculty ratios for 1970 was twenty-four to one for the public community junior colleges and fourteen to one for the private two-year colleges. If a lower student–faculty ratio implies that a student may receive a greater amount of individual attention and assistance, this may be one of the private two-year colleges' major strengths. But, by the same token, if faculty salaries are significantly lower than those found in their public counterpart, one can question the colleges' ability to attract and retain the most qualified faculty, in spite of reduced class size. On the other hand, some two-year college educators have questioned the applicability of the traditional academic qualifications for two-year college faculty members, especially those teaching vocational subjects and nontraditional students (see Gillie, 1973). If the qualifications of present two-year college faculty are found to be inappropriate, the private two-year college faculty in the future will have to be more oriented toward vocational curricula than they presently are and the institutions will have to divest themselves of their primary concern for transfer-oriented students and programs (see Medsker and Tillery, 1971).

Various predictions have been made as to the future role of private two-year colleges in American education. Some of the more pessimistic ones predict that only sixty or seventy will have survived in 1980 (Garrison, 1969). Although private junior colleges will most likely never receive public financing at the level presently accorded the public community junior colleges, various schemes for providing student assistance have been initiated. These schemes would reduce, but not eliminate, the student cost differential between the two types of institutions. Should this approach be supported more strongly by the various states and/or by federal subvention of one variety or another, those private two-year colleges able to exert the most leadership and influence may survive. There is a general consensus among two-year college leaders that the private junior colleges should not be permitted to become extinct. The important question, which remains unanswered, is: How does society provide sufficient financial assistance to private two-year colleges while still enabling them to retain their autonomy without merely increasing public school tuition to match that of the private schools? One can suspect that the question will have many responses, but no true answer will emerge because of the basic contradiction between public funding and private control.

Objectives and Philosophy

The private junior colleges are similar to the public community junior colleges in many important respects but also maintain important differences. Up to now the private two-year colleges have favored curricula that were oriented more toward the transfer than the vocational student. This was a functional objective in the past, when higher education in general was aimed more toward serving the upper classes and the private two-year colleges could serve such clientele, but such an objective is not a viable one for the 1970s and 1980s. Virtually any academically capable individual can just as easily, and almost always more economically, gain entry into a public college or university. An increased emphasis on providing specialized education for college-bound aspirants who aren't yet "ready" for the traditional college bill of fare, and the offering of more vocational curricula, could help private two-year colleges to increase their enrollment. Furthermore, they do have the option of providing these kinds of studies in a new and different way, since they are more autonomous than the public counterparts. But the critical question is whether the private two-year colleges would be willing to change their objectives to stress specialized individualized instruction and vocational curricula.

The earlier philosophy of independent two-year colleges was elitist in that they sought to prepare carefully selected youngsters for entry into the third year of senior colleges. Also, more than half of the institutions are sectarian, with Roman Catholic and several Protestant groups predominating. One can suspect, therefore, that the philosophy of these schools includes the desire to transmit certain religious concepts and attitudes to the students. Parents who have a strong preference for religious-oriented education might elect to send their youngsters to such a school in spite of greater cost. The independent junior colleges are perceived as having four major advantages which reflect upon the philosophy and objectives of these institutions:

1. Because of small teacher–student ratios (see the preceding section for the actual ratios and a comparison with the public community junior colleges), they can provide individual assistance to students, extra instructional help, individual instruction when necessary, and counseling.

2. They have greater institutional autonomy, which provides them with greater flexibility to innovate, adjust to new demands, and exercise independence in their management.

3. They provide an interim college experience, thereby giving students the time and opportunity to either formulate their goals more clearly or prepare for entry into a senior college.

4. They provide a residential college experience for the student.

Giving these as the four advantages of private junior colleges does not necessarily make them a reality, however. While they may be perceived by some as the major advantages, one should recognize that the private two-year college may not be the best place for students to achieve their goals. One cannot help but express concern about the ability of private junior colleges to do any of the above to a significant extent in the face of continued financial austerity. One can point, with very little difficulty, to some public sector of higher education that can likely address itself to each of the four concerns listed with greater resources than are now available in private two-year colleges.

Perhaps the best reason for the continuation of private two-year colleges is the importance of maintaining a diversity in the kinds of higher education institutions available in the United States. Some observers have detected tendencies for higher education institutions to become increasingly similar to one another, and the demise of the private two-year college would certainly accentuate this unfortunate trend. Furthermore, the kinds of vocational curricula that can be offered within the rubric of private two-year colleges could provide opportunities for some experimentation.

The Students

Perhaps the best way to describe students who enroll in private junior colleges is to attempt to answer the question: Why do certain youngsters elect to attend private junior colleges in the face of the alternatives open to them? The question is a fair one, since private two-year colleges are more expensive for students (and/or their parents) and are among the least common delivery systems for freshmen-sophomore college education.

As the reader would suspect, there is no documentation as to why certain youngsters select this mode of college education. Some hints do emerge from behind the rhetoric, however. First, many of these schools have claimed in the past and continue to claim that they are institutions in which students receive extra individual attention and assistance (see Medsker and Tillery, 1971). These schools appear to be aimed at a particular student clientele, specifically those youngsters who aspire to a college education but have been academic underachievers in secondary school. Youngsters who have high and even average high school achievement records would not consider the possibility of getting individual attention and extra help of major importance. Youngsters who anticipate needing such services are the ones (often with direct encouragement from their parents) who might seek entry into a two-year college that advertises them. If this conjecture is true, private junior colleges must have a large proportion of youngsters with low academic achievements. The previous studies relating to student characteristics indicate that the intellectual predispositions and academic abilities of students in the nondenominational private two-year colleges generally are similar to those in the public community junior colleges. But many public community junior college students chose the junior college as a second or third choice (a common event in the 1950s and 1960s especially). The church-related two-year colleges, on the other hand, were apparently selected by students of higher academic ability than either of the above. Thus the conjecture made here remains unproven as far as the nonsectarian independent junior colleges are concerned, and appears to be untrue to at least some extent for students in the church-related two-year colleges.

Perhaps other factors, in addition to religious concerns, come into play when selecting a private two-year college and produce a masking of the importance of this element. Another factor that could encourage a youngster with low high school academic achievement to look toward a private two-year college is his ability to pay a higher tuition. That is, one may suspect that middle- and upper-class parents prefer to send their offspring to the most prestigious schools that will admit them. For the academic low achievers, the best choice is often a private two-year college.

Why are the students in denominational two-year colleges higher in academic ability than their counterparts in public community junior colleges and the private nondenominational two-year colleges? A conjecture is deemed appropriate here. Certain parents who are active participants in their religions may seek to place their more academically able youngsters in a church-based college. One reason may be that some parents and their youngsters feel that an education in a church-controlled private junior college will prepare them better for life and their role in society than the public-supported two-year college.

Possible reasons behind a youngster's final choice are varied and numerous. The particular factors affecting one youngster's decision are likely unique to him, and a slightly different set of factors probably influences every student. The quantitative data on demographic characteristics and academic abilities serve only as a broad guideline. A considerable number of personal and demographic factors enters into the decision-making process which determines where a particular youngster goes to college.

In general, however, students in the private junior colleges resemble those found in the public community junior colleges (whose characteristics are described in Chapter 8).

The Faculty

One of the most significant differences between private two-year college faculty members and their public community junior college counterparts is the difference in their salaries. Several sources (National Education Association, 1968; Garrison, 1969) indicate that the median salary of public two-year college faculty is $2,000 or more higher than that of private junior college faculty.

As would be expected, the chronic low salaries have created staffing problems in private junior colleges. Many private junior college presidents have encountered difficulty in recruiting and retaining competent faculty (see Medsker and Tillery, 1971). This may not be as severe a problem in the future, however, because of the surplus of college faculty in the 1970s and beyond. A "buyer's market" may very likely be in existence for the remainder of this century. With many colleges overextended in facilities and predictions of a reduced number of college age youngsters in the next several decades at least (see Lerner, 1973), a likelihood exists of there being several applicants for every college teaching position. As this condition becomes prevalent throughout higher education, the private two-year colleges will not encounter difficulties in attracting and holding competent faculty. Ironically, a reduction in the severity of the staffing dilemma is brought on by another problem which may force many private two-year colleges to close—a reduction in the number of college age youngsters. A scramble of sorts for students has ensued between the various higher education institutions in the country. It seems safe to predict that private two-year colleges may lose even more ground in retaining their share of the college age population.

Governance

Each private two-year college has a governance board, which is most often called the board of trustees. The private junior college's major problem, as stated several times, relates to finances. Various attempts have been and are being made to inject public funds into these institutions. The scholarship programs, both national and state, are such an attempt. The student must qualify for financial assistance (loan and/or scholarship), and he can then use it to enroll in whatever school he chooses. Also, there are attempts in many of the states to raise tuition at the public institutions so as to reduce the tuition gap between the private and public colleges, thereby creating a more competitive environment. This approach, as one would expect, has been endorsed by the private college sector and severely criticized by public college leaders. Public college tuition rose in the first half of the 1970s in many states, but signs of opposition to this trend have become evident. The American public may not permit additional equalization of public and private college tuitions by continued increases in public college tuitions. Regardless of the outcome, the two-year colleges are the most seriously troubled financially in the private college sector, and short of their being absorbed by the state or a regional school district, their problems will not be reduced sufficiently by this tuition trend to enable them to survive. Dire predictions for their future were alluded to in a previous section.

The board of trustees serves in the same basic capacity in these institutions as it does in public community junior colleges; that capacity is described in Chapter 8. The manner in which individuals become board members is obviously different (they are politically independent in most cases), with many of the boards being self-perpetuating.

The president's responsibilities are similar to those of his public community junior college counterpart, with the possible exception of his having to devote a greater fraction of his time to financial matters, particularly fund raising. The organizational chart of most private two-year colleges is also similar to that of the public community junior college. The pyramid organizational format prevails, with the president often playing a paternal-manager role rather than the role of educational leader. The academic dean quite often serves as the primary educational leader.

Although many of the private junior colleges offer some vocational programs, they have not (as a group) been most noteworthy in this effort. They have consistently sought recognition by providing a vehicle to help youngsters prepare for entry into the third year of senior colleges.

A reasonable prediction is that they will not substantially alter their present thrust, and vocational programs will not be a major consideration for those that do survive over the years.

References

American Association of Community and Junior Colleges, Directory: 1973. Washington, D.C.: American Association of Community and Junior Colleges, 1973.

Astin, A.W., and Lee, C.B.T. *The Invisible Colleges.* New York: McGraw-Hill, 1972.

Garrison, RH. "Private Junior Colleges: The Question of Survival." *Junior College Journal* 39, 6 (1969).

Gillie, A.C., Sr. *Principles of Post-Secondary Vocational Education.* Columbus, O.: Charles E. Merrill, 1973.

Lerner, W. *Statistical Abstract of the United States: 1973,* 94th annual ed. Washington, D.C.: Bureau of the Census, 1973.

Medsker, L.L., and Tillery, D. *Breaking the Access Barriers.* New York: McGraw-Hill, 1971.

National Educational Association. *Salaries in Higher Education, 1967–68.* Washington, D.C.: National Education Association, Higher Education Series Research Report, 1968-R-7.

Wade, G.H. *Fall Enrollment in Higher Education, 1970.* Washington, D.C.: National Center for Educational Statistics, 1971.

10

Technical Institutes and
Post-Secondary
Vocational Technical Schools

There is no universally accepted definition of a technical institute, but 306 post-secondary vocational institutions classified themselves as such in 1971. The governance structures of these were categorized in the following manner: public, 122; proprietary, 161; and independent nonprofit, 23. In addition, 119 of them were accredited by an agency approved by the U.S. Office of Education and 45 by a regional association. A total of 213 qualified for federally insured student loans, and 262 met minimum standards for veteran administration students (Kay, 1973). Table 10-1 gives the number of technical institutes by state and mode of control.

Enrollment figures were supplied by 113 of the technical institutes listed, and the total enrollment for these was just under 200,000 (Kay, 1973) with an average enrollment of slightly less than 1,700. The nonpublic technical institutes did not report their enrollments, as was also the case with other kinds of proprietary and independent vocational schools. No explanation is offered for this. Empirical observations lead one to suspect that their enrollments are much lower than those found in the public sector. Thus the average enrollment for all 305 technical institutes is probably much lower than reported here. Technical institutes seem to be concentrated in some states, with almost two-thirds found in eleven states. In descending order they are: Ohio (37), North Carolina (30), Indiana (22), Wisconsin (22), Pennsylvania (18), Texas (18), California (14), New Jersey (12), South Carolina (12), Massachusetts (10), and Missouri (10).

The schools listed in Table 10-1 classified themselves as technical institutes according to the description that each is an institution which offers instruction in one or more of the technologies at a level above the skilled trades and below the professional. Another institutional category of this general type is the post-secondary vocational school. These schools are similar to technical institutes in many respects and are also examined in this chapter. They have been defined as follows:

A school that exclusively or principally provides occupational education to persons who have completed or left high school and are available for full-time study. Special purpose schools that offer the following programs are included in this group: airline careers, auctioning, commercial art, adult grooming, fashion design, floristry, housekeeping, interior design, medical and dental assisting, mortuary science, practical nursing, sea diving, and travel. [Kay, 1973, p. xii]

A total of 1,027 institutions placed themselves in this category. They are listed by state and type of control in Table 10-2. As with the technical institutes, enrollments were not reported by the proprietary, independent, and religious schools. The average enrollment for those that did report it was 1,218. As with the technical institutes, this average is believed to be higher than is actually the case for the entire 1,027 schools. The total enrollment reported by 459 schools was just under 560,000.

TABLE 10-1 Technical Institutes[a]

State	All Types	Proprietary	Independent	Public	Enrollment[b]
Alabama	5	3	—	2	524
Arkansas	2	1	—	1	11,312
Indiana	22	9	—	13	5,427
Kansas	2	1	—	1	176
Kentucky	4	3	—	1	863
Louisiana	3	2	—	1	1,963
Maine	2	—	—	2	1,128
Massachusetts	10	1	4	5	899
Missouri	10	7	1	2	620
Nebraska	3	1	—	2	1,234
Nevada	2	1	—	1	131
New Hampshire	2	—	1	1	840
North Carolina	30	—	—	30	79,581
Ohio	37	16	4	17	9,006
South Carolina	12	2	—	10	9,148
Tennessee	8	5	—	3	3,231
Texas	18	14	—	4	2,189
Utah	3	—	—	3	11,159
Vermont	1	—	—	1	562
Washington	9	6	—	3	13,465
Wisconsin	22	4	—	18	35,557
Guam	—	—	—	1	410
Other states[c]	78	85	12	—	—
Totals	305	162	22	122	189,425

[a] Most proprietary technical institutes and independent technical institutes did not report enrollment.
[b] Total reporting enrollment: 113; average enrollment for reporting schools: 1,676. States reporting fewer than the total number of schools as follows: Massachusetts, enrollment reported for 3; Missouri, 1; Nebraska, 1; North Carolina, 29; Utah, 2; Washington, 2; Wisconsin, 16.
[c] States and territories with no reported enrollment are included in last item.

Source: Extracted from data presented in Kay (1973).

TABLE 10-2 Post-Secondary Vocational Technical Schools

State	Number	Public	Enroll- ment[a]	Pro- pri- etary	Inde- pen- dent	Reli- gious
Alabama	29	26	13,106	3	—	—
Arkansas	14	14	26,272	—	—	—
Colorado	22	5	31,234	17	—	—
Florida	34	26	77,785	7	1	—
Georgia	37	25	107,413	12	—	—
Iowa	6	5	6,421	—	1	—
Kentucky	16	13	26,354	3	—	—
Louisiana	26	25	32,224	1	—	—
Massachusetts	34	18	6,689	12	4	—
Minnesota	45	34	17,693	8	3	—
Missouri	43	27	23,893	16	—	—
Nebraska	12	11	18,075	1	—	—
Nevada	8	7	9,467	1	—	—
New Mexico	8	4	9,482	3	1	—
North Carolina	10	8	26,772	2	—	—
Ohio	71	45	40,850	24	2	—
Oklahoma	31	28	7,572	3	—	—
South Carolina	10	7	6,409	2	1	—
Tennessee	53	41	19,753	10	2	0
Washington	14	4	15,472	9	1	—
Wisconsin	24	16	6,004	6	1	1
Other states[b]	481	171	30,392	282	24	3
Totals	1,027	560	559,332	422	41	4

[a] Total institutions reporting enrollment: 459; average enrollment per reporting institution: 1,218. Proprietary, independent, and religious schools did not report enrollment, and 101 public institutions did not report enrollment.

[b] States and territories with enrollments below 5,000 are included in the last category.

Source: Extracted from data presented in Kay (1973).

Over half of these schools were concentrated in ten states. They were (in descending order): California (114), Ohio (71), New York (67), Tennessee (53), Minnesota (45), Pennsylvania (44), Missouri (43), Georgia (37), Florida (34), and Massachusetts (34).

High among the problems of technical schools of this type is accreditation. Some aspects of the problem include difficulties in: (1) preparing personnel so they are knowledgeable enough to fairly evaluate the vocational programs, (2) determining acceptable general educational requirements, (3) identifying the place of general education in the vocational programs, and (4) recruiting faculty members who are able to relate general and technical education in their instruction (Davis, 1966).

Gartland and Carmody (1970) sought to obtain information about guidance and research programs in these institutions. They included just over 350 vocational technical schools that offered no transfer programs in their investigation and also sent a modified version of the questionnaire used to 689 community colleges that offered both transfer and vocational programs. The results show that vocational schools tended to use more extensive standardized data to select students, whereas community junior colleges appeared to provide and rely more upon comprehensive counseling. The limited research conducted by community colleges was most often oriented toward demographic studies, whereas the vocational schools' research efforts were, for the most part, related to matters such as student satisfaction and success (both in school and after graduation). It was found that vocational school students were less likely to transfer after completing their course of study and also had lower dropout rates. Also indicated was that community colleges and vocational technical schools differ in structure, function, and purpose, although the effect and true meaning of these differences are purely speculative at this time.

As one would expect, several technical educators have attempted to define the technical institute. Graney (1967) viewed the technical institute as a school offering an education that has direct application to life. In his view such an education is post-secondary, is essentially terminal in that students enter employment upon completion of their programs, is related to the broad fields of science and technology, provides intensive instruction in a brief span of time, and emphasizes practical applications and is less theoretically oriented than professional curricula. Graney takes the position that technical institutes are at an educational level between the high school and the professional schools. The technical institute was described in a similar manner by Henninger (1959). Another definition was offered by Smith and Lipsett (1956), who identified it as a post-secondary school whose curricula are one to three years in duration, are technological in character, and emphasize the understanding and application of scientific principles more than manual skills. They listed the salient characteristics of the technical institute as follows: (1) It is a post-secondary school distinct in character from colleges or universities; (2) its major purpose is to train people for occupations categorized as being between the skilled crafts and the higher scientific professions; (3) it caters to persons who through previous or collateral experiences in industry have found the occupation they want to enter and desire intensive preparation for that occupation; (4) its offerings include technical training concerned with operation and maintenance; (5) its courses are of short duration and essentially terminal in nature rather than being preparatory for further study; (6) its requirements for admission and graduation tend to be less formal than those for other college level institutions; (7) its staff often use direct methods of teaching with strong emphasis on doing; (8) teachers are primarily recruited on the basis of their practical experience, which may take precedence over their professional teacher preparation; and (9) a common instructional mode is to replicate actual approaches used in industry.

Some states (e.g., Connecticut, North Carolina, Tennessee, and South Carolina), probably because of technical educators' strong leadership, have attempted to establish separate systems for technical institutes in close cooperation with state and regional boards. In some places such an approach was coordinated with efforts to attract industry to the state. A good example of this is the South Carolina experience. In 1961 that state established an advisory technical-training group to:

1. [Inaugurate] a crash program coordinated with industrial expansion which would provide immediate training for established . . . and . . . particular industries.

2. Increase emphasis on industrial arts programs and basic industrial vocational programs within existing high school curricula.

3. [Inaugurate] technical-training programs . . . primarily designed to train high school graduates as technicians for initial employment in industry.

4. Provide trade extension courses . . . [for] persons who desire employment, [for] industry, and also . . . [for] those presently employed who wish to improve their skills (McDougle, 1973).

This committee was further charged with setting forth requirements for the establishment of technical education centers, with provision for joint local and state control. The initial legislation was modified ten years later, from which emerged a joint committee that produced the basis for a new bill creating the State Board for Technical and Comprehensive Education in South Carolina (passed by the State Legislature in 1972). This legislation provided the two-year institutions in the state with three options for expanding their offerings: (1) add first- and second-year college academic curricula thereby converting the technical education centers to comprehensive institutions, (2) merge two or more two-year institutions, or (3) obtain permission for university branches or centers to expand into comprehensive institutions under the direction of the State Board for Technical and Comprehensive Education. This legislation, in effect, established a comprehensive community college technical institute system in that state, with the technical education centers as an important focal point. While continuing to place the primary emphasis and focus upon technical training, that legislation permitted (and encouraged) the technical education centers to become comprehensive institutions by adding the traditional freshmen and sophomore offerings. There appears to be some movement in this direction in several other places; that is, some single purpose technical institutions seem to be expanding their offerings and becoming more like the community junior colleges described in Chapter 8.

Many of the public technical institutes (such as the technical education centers of South Carolina) have modern facilities and curricula. Also, the design of these facilities is similar to that found in community junior colleges (Barton, 1973).

Technical institutes are one of the least common types of vocational school described and analyzed in this book. The number of broad-based post-secondary vocational technical schools will likely increase, however, and enrollments may grow. This type of institution may also offer a more comprehensive selection of curricula in both vocational and non-vocational areas in the future. Should this take place, they (like the technical institutes) will take on an appearance more like the community junior colleges. It is not certain, at this point, whether such a trend will continue.

Objectives and Philosophy

Technical institutes have been the elites among vocational institutions, especially before the wave of community junior college growth in the 1960s. This is evident from the frequent use of such descriptions as "post-secondary" and "the technician is the link between the craftsman and the professional" in the literature on technical institutes (see Smith and Lipsett, 1956; Henninger, 1959; Graney, 1967). During the earlier years of the technical institute movement, the bulk of the institutes' curricula dealt with the preparation of technicians for the engineering-related professions. Later (sometimes in attempts to bolster sagging enrollments), some of them expanded their offerings to include curricula in the health, business, and social worker fields. Others, for varied reasons, elected to restrict their curricula to the engineering-related areas, and the result often was reduced enrollments and accompanying financial difficulties (most serious with the private technical institutes). Since these schools were elitist in their views to begin with, it is no surprise to find that they were among the first to offer baccalaureate degrees for vocationally oriented programs. The drift in this direction resulted in the creation of technology programs. Since that time such four-year programs have gained much popularity and have had considerable effect upon vocational programs in general, as described elsewhere in this book.

As with all educational institutions, the underlying philosophy of the technical institute is reflected in the curricula and teaching methods employed in these schools. Up to the time that public community junior colleges began to make serious inroads upon enrollments in technical education, the technical institutes' curricula had the following characteristics: (1) The two-year associate degree program, which requires sixty semester hours of credit for completion in other post-secondary institutions, sometimes required as many as seventy or more credit hours. (2) The proportion of the total curricula allotted to general education courses was often restricted to 20 percent or less, whereas other post-secondary institutions allotted up to 50 percent of the program to such offerings. (3) The academic level of the support and specialty courses was higher than that of similar programs in community colleges. In the engineering-related technologies, for example, the level of mathematics required for graduation often included some working knowledge of calculus. (4) Although a considerable amount of time was spent in laboratories, laboratory instruction included experimentation with the broad principles behind a specialty, and relatively little time was earmarked for practice in specific skills.

From the end of World War II through the 1950s the technical institutes were able to maintain their uniqueness and elitelike characteristics. This may have been due to the abundance of youngsters and veterans seeking socioeconomic mobility through education at a time when there was a general lack of other types of vocational education institutions. Community colleges were hardly beginning their phenomenal growth at that time and did not achieve their maximum momentum until the 1960s (both in terms of number of colleges and total enrollments).

The public community junior college movement, with its rapid growth of free or low-tuition curricula offerings, was probably the major catalyst for the changes that took place in technical institutes in the 1960s. While the public community junior colleges were growing rapidly, the technical institutes were either holding their own or experiencing considerable reductions in enrollment. Those that did have increased enrollments were, for the most part, the public-supported institutes which could compete with the community colleges in terms of tuition and other costs. But even then, the students tended to gravitate toward the more glamorous public community junior colleges, and the differences in the content of the technical curricula may have had an effect. Many of the community colleges began offering programs that were similar in title to those offered in technical institutes, with an associate degree awarded for fewer academic credits (sixty semester hours, while many technical institutes' requirements ranged from sixty-seven to as much as seventy-two semester hours for the same degree). The opening of a public community junior college in the 1960s would almost always be accompanied by a surge of youngsters seeking admission, and in many instances there was a corresponding reduction in enrollments at proprietary and independent vocational schools in that region. Often the presence of a new community junior college not only encouraged persons who would not have enrolled elsewhere to enroll, but also attracted students who would have gone to the technical institutes.

Historians and students of vocational education may wonder why many of the technical institutes failed to maintain their former position in vocational education. Many were bypassed, and several general reasons can be offered: (1) the tuition cost differential between private-proprietary technical institutes and public community junior colleges was considerable; (2) the expressed differences between the philosophies of these two types of school were great, and that of the community junior college became the most widely accepted; (3) the overall image projected by the community college as serving many needs of the region was viewed more favorably by most people; (4) some people viewed the offerings in technical institutes as being too restrictive, terminal, and dead-end; (5) the differences between comprehensive and single or special purpose institutions were considerable, with technical institutes suffering in popularity because of it; (6) the status of vocational education, never as high as that of other forms of post-secondary education, affected the attractiveness of technical institutions, since the community junior colleges offered the prospect of enrolling in transfer-oriented curricula.

Independent and proprietary technical institutes were never able to compete successfully with the public community junior colleges. Although the most ostensible reason is the difference in tuition and other costs, there were other important philosophic and prestige factors.

The expressed philosophy of the public community colleges, especially during the 1950s and 1960s, was aimed at drawing favorable attention to these schools so they would be more strongly supported by their communities and legislative bodies. Much of the rhetoric was highly idealistic and based on the "something for everyone" approach, and it was believed by many. Guidance counselors and parents were encouraged to direct youngsters into the nondefinitive liberal arts programs, which were often merely carbon copies of college freshman and sophomore courses. In many instances such programs had dropout rates exceeding 50 percent (see Chapter 8). Nevertheless, the technical institutes could not, in most cases, attract their proportionate share of students. The public community colleges undeniably offered greater flexibility for students by providing a greater number of curricula, so important to youngsters who felt they had to dabble in several programs before making a final selection (although such experimentation is often accompanied by student frustration and loss of time). The technical institutes were the choice of only a few youngsters, particularly those who had decided on an occupation before enrolling. A sizable number of public-supported technical institutes converted themselves into technical colleges or community junior colleges during the 1960s, and they became more like the community junior colleges as a result. This is an example of changed institutional goals in response to external demands. While all this was going on, some of the proprietary and independent schools went out of business. The overall result was a sharp reduction in the number of technical institutes, with many of the remaining ones being the nonpublic variety (see Table 10-1).

As community junior colleges became more popular, they became increasingly more intent on providing truly comprehensive offerings, and vocational curricula became more commonplace in them. A recent survey indicated that 40 percent of community junior college students are enrolled in vocational curricula (Gillie, 1973), and a considerable portion of these curricula are technical programs. With the tapering off of higher education enrollments, which began in the early 1970s, community junior colleges will likely become more vocationally oriented so as to attract their share of students. The role of the technical institutes may well be merged with that of the community junior colleges as they seek to become more vocational and less academically oriented. There is some evidence of this occurring in some states (e.g., see McDougle, 1973; Barton, 1973).

The continuance of such merging doesn't necessarily bode well for vocational students. Vocational educators have some serious reservations about offering vocational programs alongside of academic ones. Although the content of vocational programs can probably be offered just as effectively in a comprehensive community junior college as in a single purpose institution, the effects of unfavorable comparisons among students would be minimized in single purpose schools (Ashby,

1971; Gillie, 1973; Kaufman, 1967). As evidence supporting one side or the other of this question mounts, a new trend may develop in the mid- and late 1970s. Community junior colleges may become more vocationally oriented, possibly through cooperative or coordinated programs with the area vocational schools (as described in Chapter 6) and other types of schools. Should this occur, the technical institute philosophy could reemerge in a modified and modernized fashion within the rubric of a new institutional form, such as the "universal college" (Gillie, 1973).

In summary, the technical institutes of the 1950s and 1960s have undergone an evolutionary change in philosophy and have therefore modified their objectives to some extent in order to provide better middle level preparation for occupations in the health, business, social, and engineering areas. Many of the public-supported ones have taken on objectives more like those of the community junior colleges. Some community colleges are, in fact, converted technical institutes. If technical institutes remain at all, they are likely to be private proprietary institutions which make direct attempts to be different from the public community colleges. Such attempts will be an essential ingredient in their continued survival. Indications are, however, that technical institutes will gradually become more like comprehensive post-secondary vocational schools (listed in Table 10-2) or community junior colleges. It will become increasingly difficult to separate these types of institutions in the years ahead.

Administration

Some characteristics of the administration of technical institutes and post-secondary vocational technical schools are similar to those of the two-year colleges. Most notable is the utilization of the pyramid-shaped governance structure. Like many two-year college presidents, the chief administrator (commonly used titles include president and director) governs in a manner that can be loosely described as paternalistic or authoritarian. In many of these schools the chief administrator has firm control over curricula as well as finances and facilities, and in many cases he has at least partial control over the content of courses.

This mode of leadership may be the result of other factors as well as the type of institution. There is reason to suspect that paternalistic-authoritarian leadership is commonly found in educational institutions with small enrollments, since it is possible for the chief administrator to have considerable personal contact with most of the students and all faculty members. The paternalistic authoritarian leadership found in small schools includes the tendency for the head administrator to intervene frequently.

Although no nationwide documentation is available at this time, it appears that many chief administrators in technical institutes and post-secondary vocational schools are oriented toward industry and commerce to a substantial degree. Many (if not a majority) of them have a considerable number of years of experience in industrial or commercial employment, and entered the field of education later in their lives as a mid-career change. There are both advantages and disadvantages to having such individuals lead these institutions. One major advantage is that educators with such backgrounds are sometimes most helpful in establishing liaison with businesses and industries. This can be of great value in keeping curricula modern and in placing graduates in good jobs. Also, some believe such administrators tend to use business and industrial practices in the institution's operation, which can enhance their school's efficiency. The other side of the coin, however, finds that persons with such backgrounds and little or no professional education preparation can become automaton-like and impersonal in the conduct of their teaching and administration duties. In their attempts to apply the procedures and policies of industry and commerce to the educational institution, such administrators may forget the humanistic aspects of vocational education (i.e., assisting each student in dealing with the realities of the labor market and in finding an occupation that he considers worthwhile and is within the range of his abilities and interests). Most educators agree that the humanistic aspect of vocational education must be given primary attention, even at the expense of reduced institutional efficiency and effectiveness. The hazards of drawing upon business and industry for vocational school leaders can be minimized, however, if not completely overcome, by requiring such individuals to join a good professional vocational administrator-training program.

In view of the source of administrators, it is not surprising that a smaller percentage of technical institute and post-secondary vocational school administrators have earned doctorates than found in the community junior colleges. It appears, however, that an increasing number of such administrators will have a doctoral degree in the future.

The duties of technical institute administrators are similar to those of their community junior college counterparts, who devote most of their time to the nonacademic aspects of their school and do not usually serve as true educational leaders. The technical institute administrator's overall relationships, both inside and outside the institution, are also quite similar to those of the community junior college president. (See Chapter 8 for details on this matter.)

The Faculty

No definitive study of all kinds of technical institute and post-secondary vocational technical school faculty has been made. But the employment and experiential characteristics of two-year college teachers of science, engineering, and technology have been examined (National Science Foundation, 1969). Since these faculty types are commonly found in technical institutes and post-secondary vocational technical schools, as well as in many community junior colleges, the most significant findings are reported in the following paragraphs.

Junior college teachers of science, engineering, and technology hold academic degrees as follows: doctorate, 9 percent; professional, 3 percent; no degree, 3 percent; bachelor's only, 11 percent; master's, 74 percent. These percentages are not unlike those found in all types of two-year colleges, but the degree level is likely higher than the average for technical institutes and post-secondary vocational technical schools. Of those holding doctorates 60 percent have ten or more years teaching experience, while slightly less than 50 percent of the master's degree holders and 25 percent of the bachelor's degree holders have that much teaching experience. Instructors holding the lowest academic degrees were most frequently found among those whose teaching experience averaged less than five years. Another 16 percent of the teachers said they had been admitted to candidacy for the doctorate. This may be indicative of those who are in search of professional advancement. Also, another 65 percent indicated that they had taken additional study beyond their last earned degree. Just under 60 percent of all of the courses were taught by teachers having more than five years experience. Seventy-five percent of the faculty sampled had taken part in a National Science Foundation institute or accepted a fellowship or a traineeship since 1960. (This survey was conducted in 1967.) With regard to work experience other than teaching, the teachers of more than one-half of the courses indicated that they had had nonteaching work experiences twelve years or more before the survey. About 14 percent of the teachers had research experience. This is a considerably higher proportion of teachers having research experience than is found in other two-year college areas and is an important difference between the two types of teachers. Instructors with research experience are likely to have considerably less antipathy toward research than is found among the average two-year college faculty members.

Other faculty characteristics are as follows: 16 percent of the teachers were appointed to their current teaching assignments in 1955 or earlier (indicating a tenure of over ten years in their present position); 44 percent had taught only in that one institution; and about 66 percent had begun their teaching careers since 1955. Nearly 25 percent of the faculty included in this survey had held high school positions prior to their present job; 16 percent had taught in other junior colleges, and 4 percent had been senior college faculty members. A few reported having had teaching experiences in elementary schools and nonteaching-related jobs.

The work week of the typical junior college science teacher was found to break down as follows: classroom duties, 73 percent; administrative duties, 11 percent; outside professional activities, 4 percent; other duties, 12 percent.

Specializations in which teachers received their training were as follows: mathematics, 24 percent; biological science, 14 percent; social sciences, 14 percent; technology, 13 percent; chemistry, 19 percent; psychology, 6 percent; physics, 5 percent; engineering, 4 percent; other sciences, 11 percent.

A few aspects of these teachers' self-perceptions were examined. About 61 percent regarded themselves as "quite successful" teachers; 37 percent considered themselves "moderately successful"; and 2 percent considered themselves "barely adequate" in their role as teachers.

When queried about their future intentions, just over 60 percent of the teachers indicated that they hoped to either stay in teaching or combine teaching and research as a career, and the remaining 38 percent indicated an interest in administration, in research only, or in some other nonteaching activity. About 56 percent said they were very satisfied with teaching as a career; 36 percent said they were satisfied; 3 percent were indifferent; and 5 percent were either dissatisfied or very dissatisfied. Again, the comparatively high regard for research is noteworthy.

Considerable concern has been expressed over the years about the need for special professional training for technical institute teachers, particularly for those who do not enter the profession via the traditional teacher-training institutions. There seems to be some consensus that professional training for such instructors should produce teachers who: (1) have a clear and realistic understanding of the philosophy and purposes of technical institutes, (2) have the ability to implement the above in their teaching activities, (3) have functional ability to deal with the complex factors of human growth and development, (4) have a broad, general mastery of their special field of knowledge, and (5) have developed the ability to initiate new curricular patterns and to bring to the entire undertaking an objective evaluative point of view (Jarvie, 1948).

The Students

The characteristics of students in technical institutes and post-secondary vocational technical schools are similar in most respects to those of vocational students found in the community junior colleges. Considerable attention has been devoted to this topic in Chapter 8, and the reader is urged to return to that chapter for a review of these characteristics. It is sufficient to state here that these students, as a group, are low academic achievers and view their post-secondary schooling as a vehicle for obtaining good jobs.

References

Ashby, E. *Any Person, Any Study. An Essay on Higher Education in the United States.* New York: McGraw-Hill, 1971.

Barton, T.E., Jr. "Greenville TEC: A Decade of Progress." *Community and Junior College Journal* 43, 8 (1973).

Davis, R.H. "Accrediting Technical Vocational Programs." *The North-central Association Quarterly* 40 (1966).

Gartland, T.G., and Carmody, J.F. *Practices and Outcomes of Vocational Technical Education in Technical and Community Colleges.* Iowa City: American College Testing Program, Research and Development Division, 1970.

Gillie, A.C., Sr. *Principles of Post-Secondary Vocational Education.* Columbus, O.: Charles E. Merrill, 1973.

Graney, M.R. *The Technical Institute.* New York: Center for Applied Research Education, 1967.

Henninger, G.R. *The Technical Institute in America.* New York: McGraw-Hill, 1959.

Jarvie, L. L. "Preparation of Technical Institute Instructors." *Technical Education News* (March 1948). New York: McGraw-Hill, 1948.

Kaufman, J., et al. *The Role of Secondary Schools in the Preparation of Youth for Employment.* University Park: Institute for Research on Human Resources, The Pennsylvania State University, 1967.

Kay, E.R. *Directory of Post-Secondary Schools with Occupational Programs: 1971: Public and Private*. Washington, D.C.: Government Printing Office, 1973.

McDougle, L. G. "TEC in South Carolina." *Community and Junior College Journal* 43, 8 (1973).

National Science Foundation, *Junior College Teachers of Science, Engineering and Technology, 1967: Experience and Employment Characteristics*. Washington, D.C.: National Science Foundation, 1969.

Smith, L. F., and Lipsett, L. *The Technical Institute*. New York: McGraw-Hill, 1956.

11

Proprietary Schools

A significant component in the vocational education delivery system is the proprietary school. In 1971 there were 1,000 nonaffiliated, nonpublic secondary schools (Lerner, 1973), a number of which were proprietary. There were 185,000 students enrolled in these non-affiliated, nonpublic secondary schools, and they employed 17,000 teachers (Lerner, 1973). This categorization includes independent non-profit, nonsectarian as well as the profit-making, or proprietary, variety. On the basis of these figures, the overall student–teacher ratio was about 11 to 1, and the average enrollment per institution was 185 students. These data show that the average secondary proprietary school is a small institution.

A closer approximation of the actual number of secondary proprietary schools is given in Table 11-1, which lists by state the number of non-public "other" institutions offering occupational programs. A total of 209 secondary schools were categorized in this manner in 1971 (Osso, 1973).

The major thrust of proprietary vocational schools is made by those considered to be at the post-secondary level. Of the almost 8,200 post-secondary vocational institutions identified, over 5,000 were classified as proprietary (Kay, 1973). More than 1,900 of them (38 percent of the total) were found in six states. They are, in descending order: California (678), Texas (288), New York (259), Illinois (236), Pennsylvania (234), and Ohio (231). The distribution of post-secondary proprietary schools by state is given in Table 11-2, and the distribution by type of instruction is given in Table 11.3. The greatest concentration of post-secondary proprietary schools fell in the vocational areas of cosmetology (1,475) and flight (1,332), which together account for about 58 percent of all such schools. Of incidental interest is that private independent and religious vocational schools tend to offer "hospital school" occupational programs. The vocational programs in public post-secondary schools, on the other hand, are distributed such that 1,756 of them offer "hospital school" curricula, of which about 37 percent are found in community junior colleges, 32 percent in technical vocational schools, and 12 percent in senior colleges.

A term which is satisfactory to all concerned and adequately depicts

TABLE 11-1 Number of Nonpublic "Other" Secondary Schools Offering
Occupational Curricula by State or Other Area: Aggregate
United States, Fall 1971

State or Area	Number of Schools	State or Area	Number of Schools
Alabama	1	New Hampshire	5
Alaska	—	New Jersey	8
Arizona	5	New Mexico	—
Arkansas	—	New York	60
California	3	North Carolina	—
Colorado	—	North Dakota	—
Connecticut	15	Ohio	8
Delaware	—	Oklahoma	—
Dist. of Columbia	1	Oregon	—
Florida	—	Pennsylvania	12
Georgia	—	Rhode Island	1
Hawaii	1	South Carolina	—
Idaho	—	South Dakota	—
Illinois	30	Tennessee	1
Indiana	2	Texas	—
Iowa	—	Utah	—
Kansas	—	Vermont	5
Kentucky	4	Virginia	2
Louisiana	—	Washington	—
Maine	—	West Virginia	—
Maryland	4	Wisconsin	6
Massachusetts	4	Wyoming	—
Michigan	3	Canal Zone	—
Minnesota	5	Guam	—
Mississippi	—	Puerto Rico	19
Missouri	3	Trust Territory of the Pacific Islands	1
Montana	—	Virgin Islands	—
Nebraska	—	Total	209
Nevada	—		

Source: Extracted from Osso (1973).

the wide spectrum of activities in proprietary schools has not been
coined. The term "specialty school" has been suggested (Clark and
Sloan, 1966), but there are no clear indications that it is being widely
used. One authority has estimated that more than 35,000 specialty (vocational and avocational) schools were serving more than 5 million persons in the United States in 1968 (Fulton, 1969). This same authority
stated that 3.3 million people were enrolled in proprietary vocational
programs (Fulton, 1973).

One aspect of all such schools is that they prepare students for specific
vocations. They are truly specialized in their approach. Many of them
elect to leave out most or all of the general education courses frequently
associated with vocational education programs in public schools. A sec-

TABLE 11-2   Number of Post-Secondary Proprietary Schools:
Aggregate United States, 1971

State	Number of Schools	State	Number of Schools
Alabama	65	New Hampshire	19
Alaska	17	New Jersey	118
Arizona	70	New Mexico	41
Arkansas	60	New York	259
California	678	North Carolina	102
Colorado	86	North Dakota	34
Connecticut	75	Ohio	231
Delaware	11	Oklahoma	124
Dist. of Columbia	27	Oregon	100
Florida	138	Pennsylvania	234
Georgia	101	Rhode Island	23
Hawaii	14	South Carolina	57
Idaho	29	South Dakota	18
Illinois	236	Tennessee	126
Indiana	130	Texas	288
Iowa	69	Utah	41
Kansas	69	Vermont	10
Kentucky	63	Virginia	84
Louisiana	81	Washington	150
Maine	30	West Virginia	41
Maryland	83	Wisconsin	79
Massachusetts	116	Wyoming	18
Michigan	179	American Samoa	0
Minnesota	95	Guam	0
Mississippi	50	Puerto Rico	37
Missouri	121	Trust Territory of the	0
Montana	37	Pacific Islands	
Nebraska	58	Virgin Islands	0
Nevada	14	Total	5,036

Source: Data extracted from Kay (1973).

ond commonality is that most proprietary schools classify themselves as
post-secondary level institutions.

Until the early 1970s the public vocational education sector largely
ignored its proprietary school neighbors, and sometimes viewed them
as a near nonrespectable mode of education. But a trend toward including proprietary schools as a viable component in the overall vocational
education delivery system has been observed in recent years, after some
urging of such a movement on the part of a few leading educators (see
Hoyt, 1967; Venn, 1966). Since many of these institutions have curricula that cover virtually the entire gamut of vocational education
and most of them have been suffering from underenrollments, some
national and state legislators have attempted to discover ways to
bring them into cooperative arrangements with public vocational
institutions.

TABLE 11-3 Number of Proprietary Schools:
Aggregate United States, 1971

Type of School	Number of Schools
Technical-vocational	423
Technical institute	161
Business-commercial	940
Cosmetology school	1,475
Flight school	1,332
Trade school	509
Correspondence school	112
Hospital school	47
Junior community college	12
College	5
Other	20
Total	5,036

Source: Data obtained from Kay (1973).

The first proprietary school in the United States, Foster's Commercial School, was established in 1827 in Boston (Reigner, 1963). This school, incidentally, provided a special class for women. About twenty similar institutions were founded between 1827 and 1852 in the Midwest and the East. Just before the turn of the twentieth century, when only 6,000 students were enrolled in the commercial courses of universities and colleges, the proprietary business schools boasted of having 71,000 students (James, 1900).

During these years the debate between vocational education and the traditional curriculum was a heated one in American education. One offshoot of this prolonged educational quarrel was a rapid growth in the number of vocational schools, many of which are proprietary trade, technical, and business schools.

Philosophy and Objectives

As with other educational institutions, the philosophy of these schools determines their goals, and these in turn are manifested in their programs. A major claim made by proprietary school leaders is that these institutions have great flexibility in establishing curricula, no matter how unusual. As pointed out in previous chapters, a considerable amount of time is required to make program changes at public institutions. At many proprietary schools, particularly the small ones (and many of them are small), hardly more than a decision from the chief administrator is necessary to initiate program changes. Furthermore, these schools are most apt to tailor the length of each program to fit the objectives of the particular curriculum; thus programs may range from short ones of several weeks to two-year associate degree programs. But these claims may well be muted with time because of two significant changes. First, more and more proprietary schools are seeking "respectability" by granting the associate degree, which in turn generally introduces more stringent state controls, including such requirements as earmarking a significant portion of the program for general education courses. Second, proprietary schools are being bought out and becoming components of large business-industrial conglomerates, which removes much of their decision-making authority. One can suspect that in such cases the process of starting, terminating, or changing programs is almost as cumbersome as that found in the public sector. Thus the proprietary schools may inadvertently become more and more like the public vocational institutions and lose some of their individuality in the process.

A major (and indeed crucial) objective of proprietary schools is "to make a profit." Much stigma has been associated with this fact, as evidenced by the special licensing (i.e., permit to operate) required by state departments of education in many states. Such licensing is in addition to certification of curriculum, staff, and facilities, which public and private secondary institutions alike are subjected to everywhere and in some states post-secondary institutions are subjected to as well. At least one-third of the states have licensing and certification requirements specifically aimed at proprietary schools (Miller, 1964). The public tends to view these licensing and certification laws as some measure of protection against "fly by night" and "fast buck" schools. Despite these fears, there is evidence that by and large proprietary schools have served their constituency well (see Podesta, 1966; Hoyt, 1965).

As would be expected, there has been considerable rhetoric emphasizing the legitimacy of the proprietary school. Fulton (1972) describes all educational institutions as either (1) tax-paying institutions (i.e., the proprietary schools), (2) tax-avoiding institutions (i.e., the private non-profit schools), or (3) tax-consuming institutions (i.e., the tax-supported schools such as area vocational schools, community junior colleges, and state colleges and universities). One can suspect that such carefully devised comparisons are attempts to improve the status level of profit-making educational institutions.

The proprietary schools have sought ways to benefit from public education funds, and some have had limited success. Federal grants and subsidies are still limited to public and nonprofit private schools. But proprietary institutions are now able to receive federal funds via student aid and contract-training programs. There are several federal programs dealing with financial loans, grants, and tax benefits for which students in proprietary schools can qualify. Federal contract-training programs have included areas such as vocational rehabilitation and The Manpower Development and Training Act programs (Fulton, 1969). Many proprietary schools may be able to obtain funds for vocational-training activities through the Comprehensive Employment and Training Act of 1973 (CETA).

Proprietary schools have also established institutional associations in order to obtain greater acceptance by the public. The major associations include the Association of Independent Colleges and Schools, the National Association of Trade and Technical Schools, the National Association of Schools of Cosmetology, and the National Home Study Council.

The Association of Independent Colleges and Schools has as its constituency about 500 business schools, junior colleges of business, and senior colleges of business. They are defined as follows:

> The commission classifies institutions that have accredited business schools, junior colleges of business, or senior colleges of business.
> A business school is generally a specialized institution which states its objectives in terms of vocational competence, sets skill goals for completion of courses, emphasizes placement as the educational objective, and offers programs which usually do not exceed one academic year in length.
> A junior college of business is a two-year college devoted primarily to education for business at the college level and confers upon its graduates an appropriate diploma or degree.
> A senior college of business is a four-year collegiate institution devoted primarily to professional business administration at the college level. [AICS, 1973, p. 4]

The National Association of Trade and Technical Schools describes itself as follows:

> NATTS is a voluntary organization of accredited private residence schools offering job oriented specialty training in trade and technical occupations.
> As the standard setting agency for private schools, NATTS admits those which give evidence of subscribing to quality educational and administrative standards and ethical practices. [NATTS, 1973, inside cover]

The other two associations serve the same general purposes for their special constituencies.

Thus the proprietary schools are aggressively seeking to demonstrate that their mode of education is quality education in its own right. Proprietary school leaders seek greater public acceptance, both to increase enrollments and to qualify for additional public funds.

The Students

Proprietary school students are similar in some respects to the low achievement students found in the public post-secondary vocational schools and community junior colleges. There are contradictions in the literature relative to the characteristics of proprietary school students, but this may merely be the result of examining students in different kinds of proprietary school settings. Schools with the proprietary form of governance can be divided into four basic groups: business, trade and industrial, cosmetology, and correspondence. Total enrollment figures in some of these groups are indeed difficult to come by because of incomplete or lack of reporting. Fulton (1972), an authority in the area of business schools, has stated:

> There's about 125,000 full-time students in schools accredited by the accrediting commission for business schools . . . some . . . are nonprofit . . . so it comes down to about 100,000 students in accredited proprietary business schools. The median school has somewhere between 151 and 200 students out of the 436 schools in a 1971 study. [P. 9]

Complete enrollment breakdowns in the other three areas are not available, and there are discrepancies in the estimates. One estimate is that proprietary vocational schools enrolled 3.2 million students during 1973 (Wilms, 1973), although one can suspect that this figure includes all who have been enrolled in one of these institutions and may well be a distortion of actual student enrollment.

Students who seek out or are recruited by proprietary schools appear to be among those who feel least comfortable in the more common setting found in comprehensive high schools or even secondary vocational schools. These students tend to have poor verbal skills, as compared to the national norms. They are more likely to come from an ethnic minority than students in the public vocational schools, who are usually Caucasians. A greater percentage of proprietary school students than of students in public post-secondary programs were previously enrolled in low status general or vocational secondary school programs. An additional disadvantage is that proprietary school students are *not* more highly motivated than public school students (although contrary but unsubstantiated claims regarding this have been made). Perhaps a suitable summary statement is that proprietary school students are largely youngsters who didn't "fit" in public educational institutions at either the secondary or the post-secondary level.

Since there are numerous similarities among the various kinds of public vocational schools, it is understandable that a youngster who finds one of them unsuitable for his interests and needs would find the same true of others. It appears that the existing operational mode of public vocational schools is not the best learning-training environment for many "nonacademic" students. Proprietary school proponents use this point as a rationale for urging the public to come to their support. Although there seems to be some merit to the statement that proprietary schools offer the best vocational education environment for certain kinds of persons, the claim does need to be more carefully examined in a longitudinal manner. One must ask why the public vocational education delivery systems do the least (comparatively speaking) for individuals with nonacademic abilities and interests. Why should the training and education of low achievers be a unique feature of the proprietary school? Or is it? Much still needs to be learned about this component in the education system. Could it simply be that proprietary schools have adjusted their institutional goals to a student market that is realistic and have thereby come to accept persons who are more or less cast off by the public schools? In the examination of the basic characteristics of organizations (Chapter 1), it was pointed out that institutions will sometimes adjust their objectives to fit the changing realities of a situation in order to remain viable. This is not intended to be a cynical explanation for the heavy concentration of low achievement students in these institutions, but merely an attempt to explain *why* proprietary schools have moved in this direction to such an extent. It does appear that as the number of public vocational institutions grew after World War II, proprietary schools were forced to find a new student clientele—one for which the public secondary schools and colleges would not actively compete. In view of the continuing concern over academic achievement by most public institutions, it comes as no great surprise that proprietary schools fell heir to the low achiever and dropout variety of student. Ironically, many of the proprietary schools, as pointed out earlier, are now seeking to cloak themselves with the accouterments of the two-year colleges. In attempting to achieve greater "academic respectability," they pay the price of surrendering some of those elements that made them unique in the first place.

The actions of many public area vocational schools and public community colleges indicate they are beginning to catch up with their rhetoric and are becoming more interested in taking on tasks that a few years ago were left (more by neglect than by design) to the proprietary schools. One major motivating factor behind this trend may be the simple fact that fewer students will be available for these institutions in the late 1970s and 1980s. Along with the reduction in the number of potential students is the present tendency for many proprietary schools to become similar to area vocational schools and community colleges, and as a result these sectors of vocational education compete for certain public funds and students. If this trend is not carefully watched and monitored by some authorative power, the result could be the weeding out of low achievement students from proprietary as well as public schools, and these students would then have to fend for themselves. They would have to obtain assistance through on-the-job training, or some other institutional mechanisms would have to be provided so they could receive the vocational training they need. Such new ventures may indeed be fostered by the Comprehensive Employment and Training Act of 1973 and similar subsequent legislation.

The Faculty

Several studies report some demographic characteristics of proprietary school faculty. One of these, limited to Santa Clara County in the San Francisco Bay Area, found considerable variations in the academic background and related employment experiences of proprietary school teachers (Podesta, 1966). Teachers in the trade and technical areas were found to have little college education (even less than one year in many cases). The number of years of occupational experience plus years of teaching in their specialty area averaged from six to ten. An earlier study of 900 proprietary school teachers found that 55 percent of them held the bachelor's degree (and 23 percent had advanced degrees). From this it can be deduced that 45 percent were without baccalaureate degrees (Fulton, 1963). In 1967, in an apparent attempt to upgrade professional requirements, the accrediting commission for business schools required that at least half the faculty teaching second-year courses possess a master's degree or an equivalent professional degree. The academic background for teachers in the trade and technical schools, according to one source (Johnson, 1967), did not include baccalaureate degrees for the most part; 62 percent had one or more years of college, with a relatively low proportion actually holding a baccalaureate degree.

Proprietary school teachers are usually recruited directly from business or industry. There are some unknown factors involved in the schools' ability to do this, since proprietary school faculty salaries are generally lower than those offered to faculty members with comparable experience who teach similar subjects in public schools. Research needs to be done in this area, since no concrete comparative data are available. One suspects that soliciting data and information for studying proprietary school faculty would be most difficult. Many of these schools are loath to release information concerning operation of the school, including information about salaries. Querying proprietary school teachers about their self-concepts, their perceptions of their previous work experiences, and their present teaching duties, in a non-threatening but quantifiable manner, may be very difficult.

Although there is no research to substantiate it, some educators suspect that many proprietary school teachers left their previous work environments in order to escape from noncreative work providing low self-satisfaction. Their entry into teaching was, in effect, a mid-career occupational change. When research is conducted in this important area, one hypothesis worthy of testing is that teachers from such backgrounds are more highly motivated to assist students in acquiring vocational knowledge and skills than those vocational faculty with a more usual background. Such an inquiry would be confronted with many measurement difficulties, but the hypothesis is an extremely important one and is worthy of early consideration.

The characteristics of proprietary school faculty vary according to the instructional level. Those institutions that have some of the trappings of a "college" environment employ faculty with characteristics similar to two-year college faculty in the same specialty areas. In many cases a change in this direction can create a serious financial dilemma for the institution, since it results in higher salaries, while operational and capital costs continue to be paid by student tuition only. The other proprietary schools, those who elect to maintain an atmosphere of "direct training for jobs," employ faculty members primarily on the basis of employment experiences related to the jobs for which students are to be prepared. Such faculty members, in many if not most schools of this type, establish themselves as "trainer" models rather than as traditional teachers. The educational background of such models is deemed not to be of primary relevance. Not only do proprietary school teachers feel that traditional teaching modes are unimportant, but they also feel that way about professional teacher preparation. While proprietary school teachers feel this way, professional vocational teacher educators believe these "trainers" could become more proficient if they were required to complete a series of professional teacher-training courses and a period of closely supervised practice or internship teaching.

One can suspect that proprietary school management resists the idea of introducing a systematic training program for their teachers. The ostensible reason is that the faculty members have a rich background in related work experiences and therefore should not be required to participate in a professional teacher preparation program. But the real (and clandestine) reason is that proprietary school leaders chronically fear losing their teachers to the public schools. One way to minimize such a possibility is to discourage their faculty members from acquiring the prerequisites that would enable them to qualify as vocational teachers in the public vocational institutions. The severity of this problem may be greatly reduced by the late 1970s and 1980s, because a sizable teacher surplus in most areas of vocational education is anticipated by them. If that should happen, the job market for vocational faculty may become sluggish enough so proprietary school leaders will not be concerned about losing faculty to the public vocational schools.

Governance

Proprietary schools are conducted as business enterprises, and their management can take on the characteristics of sole proprietorships, partnerships, business corporations, or subsidiaries of large publicly held corporations.

As already indicated, proprietary schools have small enrollments and limited capital investment. In most proprietary schools, the organizational chart is pyramidal, and the leadership is authoritarian. Financial austerity is an everyday state of affairs for the typical profit-making educational institution, and this is commonly reflected in facilities and equipment, which are generally older, more heavily used, and in poorer condition than those found in most public vocational institutions.

Many smaller proprietary schools are owned by one person or a family, and in some instances the ownership has been passed on down to the third generation (Fulton, 1972). Such schools have considerable difficulty attracting and holding administrators for middle management positions. Added to this difficulty is that some proprietary school teachers who take an interest in becoming middle managers in such an institution start their own school rather than serve as someone else's manager. This has been most true with business schools, where the investment in capital equipment is comparatively low.

Proprietary school managers consistently emphasize that the school's major goal is to train people for jobs (Fulton, 1972). They stress this in their student recruitment drives, which can be very intensive. Student recruitment is indeed a serious business with the proprietary schools, and many hire a professional recruiting firm on a royalty basis—so many dollars for each student who enrolls and appears in class the first day. Recruitment techniques, for the most part, utilize mail, telephone, and direct contacts with potential students and their families.

According to some proprietary school authorities, the only way for proprietary schools to remain in business is to single out the market they serve best and then do it better than any other school (Fulton, 1972). A successful proprietary school chief administrator commonly has a background that combines experiences in both business-industry and education. He must be both a successful entrepreneur and a competent educator. Many of these administrators are self-trained and are localites in orientation (i.e., their roots are in the region in which the school is located). The chief administrators of subsidiary proprietary schools of large conglomerates, on the other hand, are cosmopolites, since they may have been promoted by that company, may come from another region of the country, and may have a stronger orientation to the profession.

If one were to itemize the three major concerns of proprietary school head officers, they would probably be finances, student recruitment, and accreditation. Since the reduced national birth rate will have its strongest effect on post-secondary education in the late 1970s and 1980s, it might well be that the proprietary schools have yet to enter into their most difficult times. Indications are that many of them will disappear from the educational scene by 1980.

References

AICS, *The Compass (October, 1973)*. Edited by R.A. Fulton. Washington, D.C.: Association of Independent Colleges and Schools, 1973.

Clark, H.F., and Sloan, H.S. *Classrooms on Main Street*. New York: Teachers College, Columbia University, 1966.

Fulton, R.A. "Proprietary Schools." In Robert Ebel, ed. *Encyclopedia of Educational Research*, 4th ed. Toronto, Canada: Macmillan, 1969.

———, *Proprietary Education Systems*. Speech given at the Fourth National Invitational Seminar on Higher Education Management, held in Washington, D.C., 17 October 1972. Mimeographed.

———. *Unpublished Survey*. Washington, D.C.: United Business School Association, 1963.

Hoyt, K.B. *Statement on Higher Education Act of 1965 to U.S. Senate Subcommittee on Education*. Washington, D.C.: Government Printing Office, 1965.

———, "The Vanishing American." *Delta Pi Epislon Journal.* St. Peter, Minn.: Gustavus Adolphus College, 1967.

James, E.J. "Commercial Education." In Nicholas Murray Butler, ed. *Monographs on Education in the United States,* No. 3. New York: Lion Press, Fayie Publishing Company, 1900.

Johnson, E.L. "A Descriptive Survey of Teachers of Private Trade and Technical Schools Associated with the National Association of Trade and Technical Schools." Doctoral dissertation, George Washington University, 1967.

Kay, E.R. *Directory of Post-Secondary Schools with Occupational Programs: 1971 Public and Private.* Washington, D.C.: National Center for Educational Statistics, 1973.

Lerner, W. *Statistical Abstract of the United States: 1973,* 94th annual ed. Washington, D.C.: Department of Commerce, 1973.

Miller, J.W. *The Independent Business School in American Education.* New York: McGraw-Hill, 1964.

National Association of Trade and Technical Schools: 1973. Washington, D.C.: National Association of Trade and Technical Schools, 1973.

Osso, N.A. *Directory of Secondary Schools with Occupational Curriculums: Public and Non-Public, 1971.* Washington, D.C.: National Center for Educational Statistics, 1973.

Podesta, E.A. *Supply and Demand Factors Affecting Vocational Education Planning.* Stanford, Calif.: Stanford Research Institute, 1966.

Reigner, C.G. *Beginnings of the Business School.* Baltimore, Md.: H.M. Rowe, 1963.

Venn, G. *Man, Education, and Work.* Washington, D.C.: American Council on Education, 1966.

Wilms, W. W. "Study of Comparative Effectiveness of Proprietary Schools and Other Educational Institutions." Abstract of a research study at the Center of Research and Development in Higher Education, University of California at Berkeley. 1973. Mimeographed.

12

Senior Colleges
and Universities

In recent years about 25 percent of all associate degrees have been granted by institutions classified as other than public two-year colleges. More than 50,000 of the 207,000 associate degrees awarded in 1969–1970, for example, were conferred by schools that were not two-year public colleges (Hooper, 1973). These institutions were senior colleges and universities, public and private. The figures include all associate degrees, of which 108,000 (52 percent of the total) were awarded for successful completion of vocationally oriented programs. Better than a third (38 percent) of the associate degrees granted for graduating from vocationally oriented programs were conferred by senior colleges and universities, even though this same group awarded only 25 percent of all associate degrees (vocational and pre-professional).

These figures indicate that those senior colleges and universities that offer associate degrees tend to do so for occupationally oriented curricula. This is verified by examining the 1969–1970 associate degree award figures: Almost 80 percent of the associate degrees awarded by senior colleges and universities in that year were in vocational curricula, whereas just under half (48 percent) of the associate degrees awarded by two-year colleges were for completion of vocational programs. The senior colleges and universities clearly view the associate degree chiefly as an award for occupationally oriented programs, rather than as an award for completion of the first two years of a pre-professional or general academic program. This is logical in that senior college and university graduates of other than vocational curricula would be expected to move into the third college year with no interruption or institutional transfer. Table 12-1 lists associate degrees awarded by institutional control and type.

An interesting question is: Why did senior colleges and universities get into the business of awarding associate degrees in the first place? One suspects there are as many specific reasons as there are senior institutions of higher education offering such curricula. In some instances a two-year college evolved into a four-year college, maintained its associate degree programs while establishing new baccalaureate offerings, and then never bothered to discontinue them. In other cases economics played a major

TABLE 12-1 Associate Degrees, Diplomas, and Other Awards Based on Less Than Four Years of Work Beyond High School in Institutions of Higher Education, by Length and Type of Curriculum, Sex of Student, and Control and Level of Institution: Aggregate United States, 1969–1970

| | Based on at Least 2 but Less Than 4 Years | | | | | | Based on at Least 1 but Less Than 2 Years, Programs Designed Chiefly for Occupational Competence | | |
| | Associate Degree Programs[a] | | | Programs Designed Chiefly for Occupational Competence | | | | | |
Control and Level of Institution	Total	Men	Women	Total	Men	Women	Total	Men	Women
Publicly and privately controlled	206,753	117,657	89,096	107,908	62,600	45,308	27,005	9,671	17,334
Four-year institutions	26,056	14,523	11,533	20,576	11,550	9,026	4,028	1,850	2,178
Universities	11,889	7,502	4,387	9,421	5,478	3,943	1,266	408	858
Other four-year and over	14,167	7,021	7,146	11,155	6,072	5,083	2,762	1,442	1,320
Two-year institutions	180,697	103,134	77,563	87,332	51,050	36,282	22,977	7,821	15,156
Publicly controlled	171,278	101,274	70,004	88,481	53,311	35,170	23,247	8,127	15,120
Four-year institutions	14,638	8,846	5,792	13,113	7,665	5,448	1,971	566	1,405
Universities	10,322	6,543	3,779	8,014	4,751	3,263	873	325	548
Other four-year and over	4,316	2,303	2,013	5,099	2,914	2,185	1,098	241	857
Two-year institutions	156,640	92,428	64,212	75,368	45,646	29,722	21,276	7,561	13,715
Privately controlled	35,475	16,383	19,092	19,427	9,289	10,138	3,758	1,544	2,214
Four-year institutions	11,418	5,677	5,741	7,463	3,885	3,578	2,057	1,284	773
Universities	1,567	959	608	1,407	727	680	393	83	310
Other four-year and over	9,851	4,718	5,133	6,056	3,158	2,898	1,664	1,201	463
Two-year institutions	24,057	10,706	13,351	11,964	5,404	6,560	1,701	260	1,441

[a] Some awards designated as associate degrees and reported in columns 5–7 are also reported in columns 2–4.

Source: Extracted from Hooper (1973).

role: Some private senior colleges considered associate degree programs crucial for maintaining high enrollment and a stable tuition income. We can conjecture about the long-term indirect effects of the Morrill Act of 1862 upon those land-grant universities which offer vocationally oriented programs today. For example, one historian described The Pennsylvania State University's experience as follows:

> To found new institutions motivated by radically different concepts of education and as serving a different constituency, it was felt that the emphasis should be changed from the classics to the natural and physical sciences for at least the latter should be recognized as no less important and should be given equal rank in curriculum. This concept leads to a new movement in technical training and vocational education, aiming not only to democratize higher education, but also to broaden its scope. It was a revolt against existing education standards, and was to go far towards revolutionizing those standards in harmony with the new political, economic, and social democracy then in process of developing. [Dunaway, 1946, p. 2]

In order to carry out the mandate extracted from the land-grant concept, many state universities established networks of branch campuses throughout the state. This way, they felt, a maximum number of citizens could avail themselves of the university offerings. The Pennsylvania State University, for example, established such centers during the economic depression of the 1930s, and these centers had expanded into eighteen branch campuses by the 1960s. At the end of World War II some impetus was added to this movement by a demand for technical training for returning veterans (Smith and Lipsett, 1956). During their early history such university programs were one year in length, and the award upon completion was a certificate. During the late 1940s and 1950s, many of these curricula were lengthened to two years, and the award was upgraded to the associate degree. At The Pennsylvania State University campuses, for example, associate degree programs were initiated in 1953, and the degree "was to be conferred on graduates of occupationally-oriented programs . . ." (Glenn, 1973, p. 5).

The community college movement, then beginning to catch hold nationally, provided impetus for universities that, at least in the early days of the movement, perceived themselves as fulfilling the role of a community college as well as other roles to expand their two-year programs. Those were the days when some of the larger state universities were toying with the idea of serving their states with an even greater multitude of services and programs. Some community college educators viewed this as an attempted takeover, and very bitter battles were fought in some states. Much of the tension was neutralized in the late 1960s and 1970s, however, by the introduction of coordination and cooperative programs, voluntarily in some places, by state legislative bodies in others. Today the public and most state legislators take a dim view of educational institutions that indulge in fighting for preservation of their "turf." Such battles, prevalent in the 1950s and 1960s, are now not much more than quaint notes in the histories of these institutions.

Does this mean that senior colleges and universities will play a reduced role in offering associate degree vocational programs in the future? It is reasonable to assume that they will—the likelihood that this responsibility will be taken on by the community junior colleges and area vocational schools is great in most states. If the two-year colleges do become vocationally oriented institutions, they, along with the area vocational schools, will likely relieve the senior colleges and universities of the need to offer such programs, as statewide coordination efforts attempt to assign responsibility for certain kinds of programs to certain types of institutions. Thus this aspect of the land-grant tradition may be relinquished by the great state universities as they sharpen their expertise and services in other areas, most notably in research and in the preparation of professionals.

Objectives and Philosophy

Many of the senior institutions involved in sub-baccalaureate vocationally oriented programs are land-grant colleges and universities. Although the term "vocational" was not used during the era when the Morrill Act was inaugurated, there was a belief that higher education should do more than acquaint persons with the arts and letters. The term coined to label this "other" kind of education was the "mechanical and practical arts." The subjects that these "arts" were meant to include were, indeed, well within the rubric of the present-day term "vocational education." Thus an important part of the philosophy of many state universities was to prepare and educate the citizenry for the mechanical and practical arts (i.e., vocational education).

The implementation of this philosophy brought about many of the present schools of agriculture and engineering in the land-grant universities. In the beginning these curricula were both pragmatic and practical, with a substantial dose of the show-and-tell element in them. Gradually, an increased concern for the cognitive elements underlying the practical arts resulted in the lengthening of the programs, and there was a corresponding increase in the intellectual rigor demanded for successful completion.

As time went on, most of these programs became "professional" and led to baccalaureate, master's, and even doctoral degrees. But this change was at the expense of the practical aspects of the curricula. An outcome of the trend was a drift away from the short-term practical type of curricula. Gradually, this void was filled by vocational programs in some secondary schools, which were introduced at about the time high schools began to be viewed as institutions for all youngsters, not just those preparing to go on to college. Certain secondary education leaders, with the help of pressure from some vocational educators, came to realize that a practical form of education (i.e., work preparation) was an appropriate alternative for those who were likely to seek entry into the job market after completing secondary school. But agreement was far from unanimous, and a long and acrimonious battle developed. One result was that vocational education was not successfully integrated into the mainstream of secondary education, and ironically, this was happening at about the time vocational education was being eased out of the senior colleges and state universities. Through the persistent efforts of some vocational educators and others over a long period of time, federal legislation was brought to bear on the situation, and this may well have been the major factor that enabled vocational education to remain viable.

A renaissance of interest in sub-baccalaureate vocational programs in senior colleges and universities began at the end of World War II and was part of the great surge toward universalization of higher education which gained momentum at that time. A major thrust was provided by the millions of returning war veterans who wanted to better themselves and viewed education as an important vehicle in their quest. For many of them, higher education became a reality primarily because of the financial benefits provided by the historic GI Bill of Rights. This epic-making legislation proved to be a major catalyst in American society by providing the mechanism for greatly increasing the number of persons who were able to acquire some form of additional education or training. The senior colleges and universities responded to the demand to serve this clientele which threatened to inundate the nation's educational facilities and quickly established curricula (often in makeshift facilities). Within the demand to serve this clientele was the perceived need for a new kind of trained individual, who came to be known as a technician or paraprofessional. Those who addressed themselves to this need agreed that the technician, or paraprofessional, would be one whose vocational expertise was better than the high school graduate's but less than the baccalaureate degree holder's and whose occupational status was between the skilled worker's and the professional's. In many places such programs were considered a part of the state universities' desire to serve their clienteles on a statewide basis. It was during this era, as briefly alluded to earlier, that many state universities blanketed their states with two-year campuses. These satellite campuses were often comprehensive institutions in that both pre-professional and vocational curricula were offered (usually with the most emphasis on the pre-professional). Shortly thereafter the community junior colleges became a part of the mainstream of higher education, and in many places they assumed the local two-year program functions of the universities.

Some senior colleges and universities, however, persisted in serving those functions, and in a few states they have continued to do so into the mid-1970s, although there are indications they may gradually relinquish their two-year programs (especially the vocational ones) and permit the more locally oriented community junior colleges and area vocational schools to take up the slack. Indeed, this would likely have happened at a faster rate than it actually has in many places if the public community junior colleges were really willing to take on all of the vocational preparation tasks (see Chapter 8).

The universities may be shifting philosophically in that they may decide to leave all two-year vocational programs to other kinds of institutions. But this trend is muted and muddled by the simultaneous drift toward expansion of some vocational curricula from two years (associate degree) to four (baccalaureate degree). Freshman and sophomore years are less costly to colleges than the junior and senior years. Therefore, if the senior institutions are to offer the third and fourth years, some probably will seek to retain all elements of the four-year program. Since the trend toward inaugurating baccalaureate vocational programs is still only partially developed, its impact upon both two-year colleges and universities will not be clear until the late 1970s. Baccalaureate degrees are likely to remain within the exclusive province of senior colleges and universities, and in view of the downturn in higher education enrollments, attempts by two-year colleges to expand into four-year institutions will encounter resistance from the public and legislators.

The Students

In many respects the characteristics of students in the vocational programs in senior colleges and universities are similar to those of their counterparts in the public community junior colleges, as an examination of their demographic and intellective characteristics verifies (Gillie,

1973). Also, many of the difficulties encountered by students in public two-year colleges are equally evident in senior institutions. In many instances vocational and pre-professional students are close enough together to encourage unfavorable comparisons and the establishment of informal prestige hierarchies among students.

As indicated in other chapters, such arrangements for the coexistence of the two types of students may not be in the best interest of vocational students in the long run. There are indications, although no solid documentation, that students prefer to enroll in vocational programs in a university rather than a two-year college because enrolling in a university is perceived as more prestigious (even though the programs being offered are similar in level and content). But one wonders if, after arriving on the university scene, the student ends up suffering more from unfavorable comparisons than he or she would at a community junior college or area vocational school, where there are few academic students and, therefore, less chance of unfavorable comparisons. Because of the lack of data on this point, one can only conjecture about it.

The Faculty

Faculty members teaching vocational programs hold the least desirable teaching positions in the university, of course. This fact must be obvious to them, and the perceived reduced prestige must certainly generate some difficulties, both within themselves and in their relationships with other faculty (Gilli, 1975). The present love–hate relationship will probably continue, for they are happy and proud to be associated with the university, although they deeply resent being the least prestigious faculty members in the school. For external purposes these faculty members appreciate being associated with a university as opposed to a community junior college or area vocational school, but the internal relationships place them in positions that are more unfavorable than the positions they would hold in a community junior college or area vocational school. The dilemma extends to faculty promotion and evaluation problems. The university professor is traditionally evaluated not only by the amount and perceived quality of his teaching, but also by his productivity in research, publications, and related scholarly work. On the other hand, the university vocational faculty member, like his counterpart in the two-year college, is not likely to hold the doctoral degree and probably has very little expertise and experience in matters of research, publications, and other scholarly activities. Yet these faculty members desire the same academic ranks accorded the traditional research-oriented faculty. Considerable difficulty has been encountered in dealing with this problem. In some schools virtually all the vocational faculty members are limited to academic ranks of instructor and assistant professor. Only a very few achieve associate professor after many years of service, and a full professor without a doctorate is indeed a rarity. This is the most common result when publication, research, scholarship, and doctorate degree are used as criteria for determining the academic advancement of vocational faculty.

The real dilemma, of course, lies in the fact that the vocational faculty member is essentially a different breed of instructor from the theoretically oriented university professor. He is a member of the teaching faculty and not a scholar in a true sense. One side claims faculty evaluation should be based on common criteria used for all faculty (the position taken by the scholarly type of university professor), while the other side claims there should be a special set of evaluation criteria for vocational faculty. This, of course, is a more pronounced version of the undergraduate–graduate faculty dilemma relative to salary and promotions. No obvious solution is at hand, and the dilemma may persist as long as universities have vocational programs. While the university vocational faculty members may extract some comfort from teaching in the university setting, they may in the long run be more alienated from other faculty than they would be if they were working in a community junior college or area vocational school, where teachers who are not scholarly oriented are found in plentiful quantities. At any rate, the according of less prestige to vocational faculty is at least as evident (and probably more so) within the university setting as it is in the other kinds of institutions.

Governance

Governance of vocational programs in universities can take several forms. Some places have established schools of vocational studies (under various titles) which include all sub-baccalaureate programs (and sometimes baccalaureate programs) of occupational orientation. Such schools have the same degree of autonomy as the other schools within the university. The chief administrator often has the title of dean, and his administrative staff follows the chain-of-command format adopted by other schools within that university. Funding comes to the school through the central administration of the university, which is governed by a board of trustees under the leadership of the university president. Thus in such an administrative arrangement, the vocational programs function under the direction of the college dean, who in turn reports to the central administration. Financial decisions, which determine the long-term operation of the vocational curricula, are ultimately made by university authorities, who most frequently have only a passing acquaintance with vocational education, its programs, and objectives. However, the fact that such a school exists within the university framework is of itself a manifestation that vocational education is accepted (even if not completely understood) as a legitimate component within the university.

Another approach to governance of vocational programs is through the related departments in the university. In this arrangement an associate degree electronics curriculum, for example, would be under direct control of the electronics department within the College of Engineering. Such an arrangement is fraught with difficulties. It is questionable (at least in many cases) whether professional specialists at the university level are the ones who should design and teach courses in paraprofessional programs. Although electronics technicians, for example, are apt to work with and for electronics engineers after they graduate, the level and nature of technicians' work is very different from that of the engineer. One would suspect there is a real danger of the engineer-oriented teacher's attempting to fashion his students into truncated or budding engineers. Similar hazards exist in all paraprofessional curricula.

In conclusion, the governance of vocational programs in universities, regardless of the approach used, is less autonomous in some ways than the governance in other institutions. Wide variations are found within the two governance configurations examined here.

Conclusions

The universities are still very much in the business of granting associate degrees, but primarily for completion of vocationally oriented curricula. It isn't clear whether the earlier trend of turning such programs over to the community junior colleges and area vocational schools will continue. With the introduction of third and fourth years (and the baccalaureate degree) for many programs that were once "job entry" vocational curricula, the earlier trend may slow down or stop. There are no basic conflicts between the universities and two year colleges, however, relative to these matters because of the coordination (voluntary in some places and legislated in others) that exists. The love–hate relationship between vocational faculty and the university appears to escape remediation, and may become even more severe as competition for university faculty positions increases. Also, there is no evidence to indicate that vocational students are better off in the university setting, and they may indeed be in an environment that is less conducive to their well-being than they would be in a vocationally oriented community junior college or area vocational school.

The future role of the senior institutions in offering associate degree vocational curricula is unclear, and there are conflicting indicators. It seems that we'll have to wait until the late 1970s to see what other intervening factors provide impetus in one direction or the other.

References

Dunaway, Wayland Fuller. *History of the Pennsylvania State College*. University Park: Pennsylvania State College, 1946.

Gilli, Angelo C. "Vocational Associate Degrees: Their Place in the Universities," *Community and Junior College Journal* 45, 5 (1975).

Gillie, A.C., Sr. *Principles of Post-Secondary Vocational Education*. Columbus, O.: Charles E. Merrill, 1973.

Glenn, John W., Jr. *A Study to Determine Relationships Between Geographic and Job Mobility Characteristics of Selected Associate Degree Graduates*. University Park: The Department of Vocational Education, The Pennsylvania State University, 1973.

Hooper, M.E. *Associate Degrees and Other Formal Awards Below the Baccalaureate, 1969–70*. Washington, D.C.: Government Printing Office, 1973.

Smith, Leo F., and Lipsett, Lawrence. *The Technical Institute*. New York: McGraw-Hill, 1956.

13

Federal Manpower Programs

Several job assistance and training programs have been funded in the past by the federal government through the Department of Labor. These include institutional training under the Manpower Development and Training Act (MDTA), Job Opportunities in the Business Sector (JOBS) Program, on-the-job training under the Manpower Development and Training Act, neighborhood Youth Corps, Operation Mainstream, Public Service Careers (PSC), Concentrated Employment Program (CEP), Job Corps, Work Incentive Program (WIN), Public Employment Program (PEP), Veterans Programs, Vocational Rehabilitation, and other programs. The proliferation of different types of programs was in response to perceived training needs of particular sectors of the adult population. New enrollments in these federally supported programs increased from 278,000 in 1964 to an estimated 2.35 million in 1973 (see Table 13-1), which is an increase of more than 800 percent in the first nine years such support was provided. These efforts have become substantial elements within the overall vocational curricula in the nation. In 1973 legislation was enacted in which all such funding was consolidated in order to reduce fragmentation, duplication, redundancies, and other undesirable proliferation. The result was the passage and funding by Congress of the Comprehensive Employment and Training Act of 1973 (PL 93-203).

New enrollment and funding estimates by program for 1974 are displayed in Table 13-2. One important trend that can be seen from the figures in Tables 13-1 and 13-2 is the role of institutional training (i.e., training subcontracted to the public schools) under MDTA had decreased from about 25 percent of the total enrollments in federally assisted work and training programs in 1964 to just under 6 percent in the 1973 (estimated) enrollments. In 1974, 38 percent of the total enrollments were trained in institutions, using 22 percent of the total funds (see Table 13-2). The 1974 enrollments were inflated by the large numbers in social service training. These figures underscore the dilemma discussed elsewhere: There is a pronounced trend afoot to dichotomize vocational education.

Table 13-3 gives the completion and job placement rates for Labor Department-sponsored programs. Enrollees represented by these figures were generally from among those who would have had considerable

TABLE 13-1 New Enrollments in Federally Assisted Work and Training Programs, Fiscal Years 1964 and 1973

Program	Fiscal Year	
	1964	1973 (estimated)
Institutional training under the MDTA[a]	69,000	140,000
JOBS (federally financed) and other OJT[b]	9,000	167,000
Neighborhood Youth Corps		
In-school and summer		145,000
Out-of-school		60,000
Operation Mainstream		27,000
Public Service Careers		37,000
Concentrated Employment Program		58,000
Job Corps		49,000
Work Incentive Program		120,000
Public Employment Program		97,000
Veterans Programs	—[c]	79,000
Vocational rehabilitation	179,000	533,000
Other programs[d]	21,000	837,000
Total[e]	278,000	2,350,000

[a] Generally larger than the number of training or work opportunities programmed because turnover or short-term training results in more than one individual in a given enrollment opportunity. Persons served by more than one program are counted only once.

[b] Includes the MDTA-OJT (On-the-Job Training) program which ended with fiscal 1970 (except for national contracts) and the JOBS-Optional Program which began with fiscal 1971; also Construction Outreach, with 68,900 enrollees in fiscal 1972.

[c] Included with "other programs."

[d] Includes a wide variety of programs, some quite small—for example, Foster Grandparents and vocational training for Indians provided by the Department of the Interior. Data for some programs are estimated. Substantial revision of 1971 figure relates to Social Services Training for public assistance recipients, funded under grants to states by the Social Rehabilitation Services Administration in the Department of Health, Education, and Welfare.

[e] Detail may not add up to totals because of rounding.

Source: Office of Management and Budget, Special Analyses, Budget of the United States Government, Fiscal Year 1974.

difficulty in preparing for and finding employment anyway. Blacks accounted for 45 percent of all enrollments in the Manpower programs, 60 percent in CET and Job Corps, 23 percent in PEP, and from 19 to 53 percent in the other programs listed. Since blacks made up 23 percent of the national unemployment rate in 1971, most of these programs enrolled a proportionately higher percentage of blacks. The same skewness is found for Spanish-Americans, who, while representing 5 percent of the nation's population, comprise 13 percent of these program enrollments. Although these proportions in program enrollment are high compared with national averages, they do correspond to the racial-ethnic breakdown of sixty low

TABLE 13-2 Estimated Outlays and New Enrollments in Federal Manpower Programs, Fiscal Year 1974

Activity	Expenditures (millions)	New Enrollees (thousands)
Institutional training[a]	$771	981
Manpower revenue sharing	303	162
Job Corps (national program)	111	38
Work Incentive Program	164	61
Social service training	120	692
Other	73	29
On-the-job training[a]	566	371
Manpower revenue sharing	159	120
JOBS (basic)	96	117
Work Incentive Program	97	56
OJT for veterans	203	69
Other	11	9
Vocational rehabilitation[a]	824	573
Vocational rehabilitation	707	560
Veterans rehabilitation	117	13
Work support[a]	1,285	632
Manpower revenue sharing	481	464
Emergency employment assistance	574	14
Work Incentive Program	102	27
High school work-study	9	57
Other	119	71

[a] Detail may not add up to totals because of rounding.

Source: Office of Management and Budget, *Special Analyses, Budget of the United States Government, Fiscal Year 1974.*

TABLE 13-3 Completion and Placement Rates for Federal Manpower Program Trainees

Program	Terminations	Employed Completers	Employment Rate
All programs	751,400	336,800	45%
MDTA—institutional	153,800	81,500	53
JOBS	91,300	44,200	48
MDTA—JOBS—optional	50,600	28,000	55
MDTA—OJT (national contract)	29,200	23,300	80
PSC	68,500	26,200	38
CEP	88,000	39,300	45
Job Corps	48,600	35,000[a]	72
WIN	110,200	33,300	30
PEP	57,400	17,800	31
Construction Outreach	53,800	8,200	15

[a] Job Corps obtains follow-up placement data on both completers and non-completers.

Source: Extracted from Lerner (1974).

TABLE 13-4 Hourly Earnings of Federal Manpower Program Trainees

	Hourly Earnings			
	MDTA			
Characteristic	Institutional	On-the-Job	CEP	WIN
All trainees	$2.49	$3.16	$2.24	$2.46
Sex				
Men	2.75	3.44	2.38	2.92
Women	2.23	2.12	2.03	2.14
Race or ethnic group				
White	2.55	3.27	2.14	2.59
Black	2.32	2.71	2.28	2.26
Spanish-speaking	2.25	2.96	2.23	2.48
Age				
Under 22 years	2.27	2.77	2.15	2.22
22 to 44 years	2.57	3.26	2.31	2.49
45 years and over	2.71	3.41	2.15	2.66

Source: Extracted from Lerner (1974).

income areas surveyed by the Bureau of Census in 1970–1971 (*Manpower Report of the President*, 1973).

The average rate of employment for the total manpower programs effort (listed in Table 13-3) was about 45 percent in 1972.

The usual biases in the American work force were found for these graduates as well. Whites earned more than blacks graduating from the same programs, and men earned more than women. These relationships, in terms of hourly earnings, are given in Table 13-4.

Characteristics of Graduates

As indicated in Chapter 3, the traditional vocational education institutions draw their clientele from the upper, lower, and middle classes. On the other hand, enrollees in the Federal Manpower Training programs are largely from those sections of the population commonly identified as the disadvantaged, the minorities, and the difficult to employ.

About 70 percent of MDTA clients in 1972 were under twenty-two years of age. Women were underrepresented in the JOBS, PEP, and Job Corps programs. The distribution of minority groups was described in the preceding section. The overall characteristics of enrollees are given in Table 13-5.

The chief differences between these enrollees and those found in the

TABLE 13-5 Characteristics of Enrollees in Federally Assisted Work and Training Programs, Fiscal Year 1972

Program	Percentage of Total Enrollees			Age		Years of School Completed		On Public Assistance[b]
	Women	Blacks[a]	Spanish-Speaking	Under 22 Years	45 Years and Over	8 Years or Less	9 to 11 Years	
Institutional training under the MDTA	37	33	12	38	8	10	32	15
JOBS (federally financed) and other OJT	27	34	18	38	7	15	35	12
Neighborhood Youth Corps:								
In-school and summer	43	53	12[c]	100		19	77	30
Out-of-school	50	43	16[c]	94	3	25	72	38
Operation Mainstream	31	19	10[c]	4	44	42	29	24
Public Service Careers	65	45	16	21	18	7	23	20
Concentrated Employment Program	41	61	20	45	5	16	42	14
Job Corps	26	62	10	100		30	61	39
Work Incentive Program	60	36	19	28	5	17	41	99
Public Employment Program	28	23	7	14	16	9	16	11

[a] Substantially all the remaining enrollees were white, except in Operation Mainstream, JOBS, and Job Corps. In these programs, 4 to 15 percent were American Indians, Eskimos, or Orientals.

[b] The definition of "public assistance" used for these figures varies somewhat among programs (e.g., it may or may not include receipt of food stamps and in-kind benefits). In the New York City program, it may relate to enrollees' families as well as enrollees themselves.

[c] Includes Mexican-Americans and Puerto Ricans only; data on other Spanish-speaking Americans are not available.

Source: Extracted from Lerner (1974).

vocational schools (the public ones in particular) is that a very sizable portion of them completed less than eleven years of prior schooling, and a disproportionately large number of them receive public welfare assistance. These characteristics clearly indicate that persons served by federal training programs have, at least up to the mid-1970s, come from the group that has not profited from traditional public school vocational programs in the past. It is conceivable, and quite probable, that efforts through the prime sponsors established by CETA of 1973 will result in an increased involvement of adults with more traditional backgrounds in the late 1970s. Should this happen, the overall profile of the graduates will change.

Revenue Sharing in Vocational Education and Training

The federal legislation of 1962 and 1963 (i.e., Manpower Development and Training Act [P.L. 87-415] and the Vocational Education

Act of 1963 [P.L. 88-210]) was the watershed of vocational education and training for the 1960s. It reaffirmed an earlier trend toward the dichotomizing of the vocational education delivery system whereby state systems comprised one type of delivery, and the training programs initiated by the United States Department of Labor in several labor market areas comprised the other type. In many places the custodians of the two sources of vocational funding and training refused to enter into ventures that would enhance possibilities of mutual utilization of all available training and educational resources. One result was a reduced delivery of vocational services to persons most in need of it. Included in the difficulty was the gradual fragmentation of efforts under the Manpower Development and Training Act of 1962. (See the variety of program types listed in Table 13-2.)

In response to these and other perceived needs, the Comprehensive Employment and Training Act of 1973 (P.L. 93-203) was brought into being. It brought, among other things, the concept of prime sponsors into the governance mechanism. Possible prime sponsors were identified as follows (P.L. 93-203):

> . . . a prime sponsor shall be—(1) a state; (2) a unit of general local government which has a population of 100,000 or more persons on the basis of the most satisfactory current data available to the secretary; (3) any combination of units of general local government which includes any unit of general local government qualifying under paragraph (2) of this subsection; (4) any unit of general local government or any combination of such units, without regard to population, which, in exceptional circumstances is determined by the Secretary of Labor—(A) (i) to serve a substantial portion of a functioning labor market area or (ii) to be a rural area having a high level of unemployment; and (B) to have demonstrated (i) that it has the capability for adequately carrying out programs under this Act, and (ii) that there is a special need for services within the area to be served, and (iii) that it will carry out such programs and services in such areas as effectively as the state; or (iv) a limited number of existing concentrated employment program grantees serving rural areas having a high level of unemployment which the secretary determined have demonstrated special capabilities for carrying out programs in such areas designated by him for that purpose.

The distribution of jurisdictions with a population of 100,000 or more that are eligible as prime sponsor applicants under the Comprehensive Employment and Training Act of 1973 is given in Table 13-6. The table also gives the number of prime sponsors actually in operation in each state in mid-1974. There was a total of 390 in operation.

The CETA legislation calls for planning, participation, and cooperation among the constituents in the vocational education and training delivery systems (P.L. 93-203):

. . . provide for the cooperation and participation of all state agencies providing manpower and manpower related services in the implementation of comprehensive manpower services planned by prime sponsors in accordance with the provision of this act; . . . set forth an overall state plan for the development and the sharing of resources and facilities needed to conduct manpower programs under its direct sponsorship without unnecessary duplication and otherwise in the most efficient and economical manner . . . set forth arrangements, if any, which the state may desire to provide for planning areas to serve geographical regions within the state; . . . make adequate provision for the coordination of manpower and related services to be provided by the

TABLE 13-6 CETA Prime Sponsors

State	Number Eligible[a]	Number Established[b]	State	Number Eligible[a]	Number Established[b]
Alabama	9	6	New Jersey	23	23
Alaska	2	3	New Mexico	2	2
Arizona	4	3	New York	36	26
Arkansas	3	3	North Carolina	13	10
California	46	36	North Dakota	1	1
Colorado	9	6	Ohio	29	14
Connecticut	6	6	Oklahoma	5	5
Delaware	2	1	Oregon	7	6
Dist. of Columbia	1	1	Pennsylvania	33	28
Florida	22	17	Puerto Rico	5	6[c]
Georgia	9	9	Rhode Island	2	2
Hawaii	2	2	South Carolina	7	1
Idaho	2	1	South Dakota	1	1
Illinois	19	20[c]	Tennessee	8	7
Indiana	16	15	Texas	23	21
Iowa	6	6	Utah	5	1
Kansas	5	4	Vermont	1	1
Kentucky	5	4	Virginia	12	10
Louisiana	9	9	Washington	11	8
Maine	1	1	West Virginia	3	3
Maryland	8	5	Wisconsin	12	8
Massachusetts	6	7[c]	Wyoming	1	1
Michigan	26	22	Virgin Islands	1	0
Minnesota	9	7	American Somoa	1	0
Mississippi	3	2	Guam	1	0
Missouri	7	6	Trust Territory of Pacific Islands	1	0
Montana	1	1	Totals	494	390
Nebraska	3	3			
Nevada	4	3			
New Hampshire	1	3[c]			

[a] Jurisdictions with a population of 100,000 or more. Each state contains one such jurisdiction intended to encompass the areas not covered by other prime sponsors listed for that state. Extracted from Department of Labor publication 61:2003 MIS-RF-95 (January 1974).
[b] Department of Labor figures as of May 1974.
[c] The CETA legislation does permit jurisdictions of under 100,000 to establish a prime sponsor region.

state and areas to be served by prime sponsors other than the state, and that provision has been made for the establishment of mechanisms to (A) provide for the exchange of information between states and local governments on state, intrastate, and regional planning in areas such as economic development, human resource development, education, and such other areas that may be relevant to manpower training; and (b) promote the coordination of all manpower plans in the state so as to eliminate conflict, duplication, and overlapping between manpower services.

The call for cooperative planning and participation in the provision of vocational education services and training didn't stop with the CETA legislation. A general administration office study of the impact of federal funds (i.e., the Vocational Education Act of 1963 and the Vocational Education Amendments of 1968) on vocational education sounded the same call (*Report to the Congress*, 1974):

> GAO recommendations to the secretary, HEW. [The] HEW should: —expand its efforts to have state and local education agencies establish working partnerships among all institutions providing occupational training at all levels—secondary, post-secondary, adult . . . . [The] HEW should: —clarify the roles of various organizational entities within HEW involved in occupational training and implement some mechanism by which these jurisdictions can engage in coordinated, comprehensive planning . . . . [The] HEW should: —require that LEA's [Local Education Agency] in their application to SEA's [State Education Agency] describe and document the nature and extent of their cooperative efforts with other sources of training and employment . . . work with states to increase flexibility in vocational training arrangements, through such mechanisms as expansion of the present school day, week or year; inclusion of transportation costs to make better use of existing facilities; and a provision of vocational training and nonpublic facilities so that more people can be trained in more occupational categories . . . . [The] HEW should: —work with states to identify statutes and administrative procedures which may prevent schools from utilizing other community training resources, and implement plans to remove these obstacles, including encouraging state agencies to make recommendations to appropriate legislative bodies.

The CETA legislation also authorizes several ways in which comprehensive manpower programs are to be established under Title I (Comprehensive Manpower Services):

> . . . shall include the development and creation of job opportunities and training, education, and other services needed to enable individuals to secure and retain employment at their maximum capacity . . . [Programs and activities can include] . . . outreach to make persons aware of the availability of manpower services . . . assessment of the individual's needs, interests, and potential . . . orientation, counseling, education, and institutional skill

training . . . training on the job . . . payments or other inducements to public or private employers to expand the job opportunities
. . . and providing supportive services for low income persons and
those regularly employed . . . services to individuals to enable them
to retain employment . . . payment of allowances to persons in training for which they received no remuneration . . . supportive services
to enable individuals to take advantage of employment opportunities
. . . development of information concerning the labor market and
activities . . . manpower training, employment opportunities, and related services conducted by community based organizations,
. . . transitional public service employment programs, and . . .
[other] programs authorized by [other sections of the bill].

And Title II of that Act provides:

> . . . unemployed and underemployed persons with transitional
> employment in jobs providing needed public services in areas of sub-
> stantial unemployment and wherever feasible, related training and
> manpower services to enable such persons to move into employment or
> training not supported under this title.

The third title of CETA authorizes funds to provide assistance to special manpower target groups:

> . . . to provide additional manpower services as authorized under Ti-
> tles I and II to segments of the population that are in particular need of
> such services, including youth, offenders, persons of limited English
> speaking ability, older workers, and other persons.

The CETA legislation (Title III, Part B) also provide funds for research, training, and evaluation in the area of manpower education and
training, which can include the following:

> . . . a comprehensive program of manpower research utilizing the
> methods, techniques, and the knowledge of the behavioral and social
> sciences and such other methods, techniques, and knowledge as will
> aid in the solution of the nation's manpower problems . . . shall es-
> tablish a program of experimental developmental, demonstration and
> pilot projects, through grants to or contracts with public or private non-
> profit organizations, or through contracts with other private organiza-
> tions, for the purpose of improving techniques and demonstrating the
> effectiveness of specialized methods in meeting the manpower,
> employment, and the training problems . . . to conduct, either di-
> rectly or by way of contract, grant, or other arrangement, a thorough
> evaluation of all programs and all activities conducted pursuant to this
> act to determine the effectiveness of such programs and activities in
> meeting the special needs of disadvantaged, chronically unemployed,
> and low income persons for meaningful employment opportunities and
> supportive services to continue or resume their education and employ-
> ment and to become more responsible and productive citizens
> . . . shall develop a comprehensive system of labor market informa-

tion on a national, state, local, or other appropriate basis, which shall be made publically available in a timely fashion . . . shall develop reliable methods, including the use of selected sample surveys, to produce more statistically accurate data on unemployment, underemployment and labor demand by state, local, and poverty areas . . . shall develop preliminary data for an annual statistical measure of labor market related economic hardship in the nation.

And in terms of evaluation, the act has provisions for the

> . . . continuing evaluation of all programs and activities conducted pursuant to this act including their cost in relation to their effectiveness in achieving stated goals, their impact on communities and participants, their implications for related programs, the extent to which they meet the needs of persons of various ages, and the adequacy of a mechanism for the delivery of services . . . periodic reports . . . shall contain data which shall include information on . . . enrollment characteristics . . . duration in training and employment situations . . . total dollar cost per training.

Another concern addressed to in the legislation is the removal of artificial barriers to employment and advancement:

> . . . conduct a continuing study of the extent to which artificial barriers to employment and occupational advancement [exist] . . . shall develop and promulgate guide lines . . . designed to encourage career employment and occupational advancement.

CETA (Title IV) provides for establishment and conduct of a Job Corps. The purpose is to establish

> . . . a job corps for low income disadvantaged young men and women . . . to assist young persons who need and can benefit from an unusually intensive program, operated in a group setting, to become more responsive, employable, and productive citizens.

Title V of the Comprehensive Employment and Training Act authorized the establishing of a national commission for manpower policy. Reasons offered, as stated in the act, are as follows:

> . . . the responsibility for the development, administration, and coordination of programs of training and manpower development generally is so diffused and fragmented at all levels of government that it has been impossible to develop rational priorities in these fields, with the result that even good programs have proved to be far less effective than could reasonably be expected. The Congress further finds that the lack of a coherent, flexible, national manpower policy reduces our prospects of solving economic and social problems which threaten fundamental interests and objectives.

> . . . accordingly the purposes of this title is to establish a national commission for manpower policy which will have the responsibility for

examining these issues, for suggesting ways and means of dealing with them, and for advising the secretary on national manpower issues . . . there is established a national commission for manpower policy . . . which shall consist of 17 members.

Public Law 93-203, through these five titles (and a sixth not alluded to here), provides for comprehensive manpower services; public employment programs; funds for special manpower target groups, research, training, and evaluation of manpower education and training; establishment and conduct of a Job Corps; and authorization of establishment of a national commission for manpower policy. This effort should have a major impact in the late 1970s and 1980s.

The CETA legislation, in conjunction with the recommendations made by the general administration office (Report to the Congress, 1974), will likely result in closer cooperation between CETA prime sponsors and public school vocational education leaders. Furthermore, it is highly likely that some modification of present federal legislation (particularly that represented by the Vocational Education Amendments of 1968) will be inaugurated in order to assure better that such cooperation does indeed take place. It appears that the prime sponsor approach to vocational education and training will increase in popularity, and may be viewed as a new approach for all vocational education and training efforts in the years ahead. Two major results of such a change will likely be a new kind of input into the vocational organizations and a transfer of the major governance function from the state to the prime sponsors.

References

Lerner, William. *Statistical Abstracts of the United States: 1973*. 94th annual ed. Washington, D.C.: Government Printing Office, 1974.
Manpower Report of the President: 1973. Washington, D.C.: Department of Labor, 1973.
Public Law 93-203. Comprehensive Employment and Training Act of 1973.
Report to the Congress: What Is the Role of Federal Assistance for Vocational Education? Washington, D.C.: Controller General of the United States, 1974.

14

Other Vocational Education Delivery Systems

The major vocational education delivery systems outside the vocational education institutions are the federally supported job assistance and training programs (see Chapter 13) and those endeavors categorized as contract learning or performance contracting. Performance contracting began as an attempt to meet specific needs of industry and government, especially those of the United States Department of Defense under the leadership of Secretary of Defense Robert McNamara. There are important differences between performance contracting in education and that found in industry and government. In order to understand these differences, we must understand the structure of performance contracting programs, including their essential elements and the manner in which these elements interact with one another and with other components in the learning situation. Up to the mid-1970s very few school systems have attempted to ascertain circumstances which favor going into performance contracting for certain aspects of their educational endeavors and, even more importantly, to identify elements and circumstances within the educational system that would preclude or interfere with performance contracting.

Problems Associated with Performance Contracting in Education

---

The most important difficulty associated with performance contracting in education relates to the measurement, testing, and evaluation of what goes on in the educational process. Since performance must be evaluated in order to determine the timing and amount of contract payments, evaluation is probably the most crucial requirement. The validity of the tools used in measurement, testing, and evaluation lies at the core of the problem, and there are four major criticisms of these tools (Levine, 1972):

1. Standardized tests are frequently used in order to determine the contractor's payment. In many instances these tests are inappropriate to the program.

2. The pupils' scores on the individual achievement tests, also used to help in computing payments, reflect things other than actual achievement.

3. Using grade level increases as a basis for comparison or comparative internal evaluation is considered totally inadequate.

4. Criterion reference tests also have serious defects when used in contracting performance.

Certain curriculum elements lend themselves better to performance contracting than others. Some educators claim that the vocational education curriculum is best suited for performance contracting because it is heavily involved with training activities. According to this argument, the objectives of vocational programs and like endeavors can be more readily stated in concrete behavioral terms. Many proponents of this approach believe that verbal and quantitative skills are the least difficult to assess in performance contracting. Many consider those curriculum elements which are highly normative or affective in content to be inappropriate for inclusion in performance contracting.

Most of the early performance contracting attempts involved groups of disadvantaged students. Perhaps this is because school systems are more apt to resort to exotic approaches, such as performance contracting, when students fail to respond to traditional methods of education. Furthermore, disadvantaged students often seem to have clear-cut academic and behavioral problems. If we assume this is true and recognize that if the target group is fairly homogeneous the likelihood of successfully achieving specific objectives is increased, then it appears that disadvantaged student groups may be among the most suitable for experimental performance contracting programs. Also, according to the advocates of performance contracting, disadvantaged groups seem to be motivated in certain performance-oriented programs which offer a wide range of extrinsic and intrinsic rewards to the learner. Many educators, however, have seriously questioned the affective by-products of such approaches to learning.

Levine (1972) indicated that performance contracting is probably best suited for a student population that (1) has not showed satisfactory achievement gains in response to the usual school system efforts, (2) has relatively specific problems and characteristics, and (3) has consistently low achievement.

A critical element in determining the feasibility of profitably utilizing performance contracting in a school system is the teacher's feelings about such endeavors. It appears that the entrepreneurial type of teacher with a high degree of flexibility, inventiveness, and adaptability is most likely to respond constructively to performance contracting programs. In schools where conformity ranks high, there is much risk aversion and avoidance of conflict, teachers are concerned with accommodating themselves to the bureaucracy and are primarily motivated by job security, the environment is considered to be poor for performance contracting programs. In some situations the faculty may even aggressively resist performance contracting.

The two extremes described here do not, of course, characterize any particular school system. Actual organizational climates and faculty attitudes in secondary and post-secondary schools fall between the two antipodes, with most of the schools probably residing closest to the conformity end of the spectrum.

In some places teachers' unions and professional associations have demonstrated strong and militant resistance to performance contracting. Such high resistance can limit the value of performance contracting to only marginal gains, even when it is negotiated into a school system.

The structure, personalities, and procedures that determine classroom operation also affect the feasibility of using performance contracting in a school. To examine these factors, one would have to answer the following questions: Are the school's testing procedures informative enough to be used as a basis for selecting potential students for the contracted program? Is the school sufficiently flexible to adapt to the program and take advantage of it after the original attempt is completed? Is the school sufficiently aware of its own educational goals, objectives, and programs to see how a performance contracting program might increase its productivity?

Performance contracting has several disadvantages—primarily, its complexity and its narrowness. Further, it may aggravate old management problems and create legal and other difficulties with teachers' unions. Performance contracting has two rather important advantages, however: It can facilitate radical changes because those outside the system are freer to implement change under the guise of an experiment, and it can produce an increased emphasis on accountability. Some educational experts, however, question whether an undue emphasis on accountability can be more of a disadvantage than an asset. The role of performance contracting as a helpful change agent may be its major strength. But whether performance contracting will have any lasting benefits for students, a school system, or any aspect of vocational education is up for debate. One thing appears certain: The measuring instruments that are so critically needed for successful performance contracting are still in a relatively primitive state.

Assessment of performance contracting can be a very serious problem. Many educators believe that the cultivation of knowledge should be the major focal point of school curricula, including vocational programs (at least to some extent). Such an approach, if seriously endorsed, would mean that very large domains in the educational field would not lend themselves to performance contracting. Contrary to earlier thoughts, criterion reference tests do not appear to offer any real promise for substantial improvements in educational performance contracting. Many classroom teachers and administrators also oppose performance contracts because testing of performance is done by outsiders rather than the teachers, and they oppose this on the grounds that: (1) external evaluation of achievement will eventually lead to external control of the curriculum; (2) externally produced tests cannot be completely relevant to the local instructional situation; (3) teachers, threatened by possible unfavorable evaluations, will likely attempt to teach for the tests through rote learning and drill rather than incorporate the more effective pupil-oriented teaching techniques being used in some performance contracting demonstrations; and (4) external tests place too much emphasis on easily measured goals and too little (if any) on less measurable outcomes. There is both truth and error in these defenses. Proponents of performance contracting believe that when external assessment is carefully controlled and prespecified, it shouldn't be harmful to the educational process or the institution, or threatening to the teachers. These advocates emphasize their belief that teachers cannot escape accountability, to students, parents, and taxpayers, for their performance. In response to the criticism that teachers may teach for the tests, some performance contracting proponents warn teachers to avoid this, and also advise students of the undesirability of such teaching and encourage them to report it when it occurs in their classroom. This is indeed threatening—for even the most secure teacher! Another hazard, which is a threat, lies in the determination of a satisfactory performance level. There is an almost infinite number of variables than can enter into such a determination, and many of them are not directly attributable to the teacher or even the actual school environment.

In conclusion, performance contracting does not appear to have a truly viable future as an alternative delivery system for vocational education as of the mid-1970s.

Reference

Levine, Donald M., ed. *Performance Contracting in Education–An Appraisal*. Englewood Cliffs, N.J.: Educational Technology Publications, 1972.

III

Quo Vadis

15

State of the Art:
A Status Report

A Brief Look Backward

Vocational education enters the last quarter of the twentieth century as a remarkably humanistic endeavor, perhaps even more so than traditional classical and liberal arts forms of education. But this is a recent turn of events.

More than any other element in education, vocational education has benefited from federal financing, and this has been going on for over a hundred years (see Chapter 3). When vocational education was first supported by federal legislation in the 1860s, such assistance from the national level was viewed as a necessary *addition* to the nation's educational effort—a mechanism to prepare sons (and perhaps an occasional daughter) of the populace for occupations in the mechanical and agricultural arts. Although not explicitly stated in the legislation or in any of the associated rhetoric, it was implicitly understood that this variety of education was aimed at providing opportunities for the offspring of the new middle class and perhaps a few carefully selected sons of families from lower-class backgrounds. In its time, one could identify it as a part of the trend of turning away from elitism and toward equalitarianism in American education. But the movement was undeniably sparked by a need, perceived by certain educators and political leaders, for trained workers who could not be brought into the work force through the traditional routes of education or apprenticeships. So the movement, while possessing some characteristics of equalitarianism, was essentially pragmatic, since it was an attempt to meet the manpower needs of society, which was moving from being an almost exclusively agricultural society to one of greater industrial orientation. Within its inner core, then, we find that the initial federal funding of vocational education was primarily geared toward the concerns of the work society. Vocational education was basically devoid of humanistic characteristics in that the intention was to mold persons (via training) so that they had the behaviors necessary to perform the occupational skills needed in the work force at that time. People did not believe at

223

that time that society was supposed to exist for them, nor did they even give the thought any serious consideration. Instead, every person was to find his or her place in society and submit to the needs of society.

Since education is a service-oriented endeavor, it has been traditionally subservient to the dominant philosophical mood of contemporary society. More often than not, society views its institutions (including education) as major mechanisms for the achievement of its perceived needs. This phenomenon has resulted in education traditionally assuming the role of a follower, and rarely has it taken a leadership position relative to new directions in our society. Vocational education is similar in this regard to the rest of education. Leaders in education are those individuals who are first to perceive societal changes that will call for a modification of re- sponses from the nation's educational delivery system. (Chapter 2 examines leadership concepts in more detail.) Because of the complexity and diversity of American society, true trends are sometimes difficult to distinguish from the many fads and panaceas, usually accompanied by self-defeating jargon, that seem to plague American education.

Enter Career Education

Unfortunately, vocational education has not been spared. During the mid-1960s and early 1970s, vocational education was virtually over- whelmed with "career education." During this time some vocational educators were quietly working toward development of a broad kind of vocational education espoused by the Vocational Education Act of 1963. It was indeed a career-oriented form of education, and was in progress long before the term "career education" was adopted by national education authorities. Its espousal at that level, and the resulting publicity it re- ceived before solid conceptualization of career education could take place, produced a rash of efforts throughout the nation to inaugurate career education programs, many of which were abortive. Many, if not most of these efforts were so ill conceived that failure was virtually assured at their onset. In many places vocational funds were diverted into endeavors that were identified as career education programs but in fact were nothing more than slight modifications of what these institutions had been doing previously. The "game" was to change the names of programs to fit the latest jargon. While this was not true in some places, it most certainly was in many. In the meantime new vocational education modes were quietly conceptualized and implemented, with resulting improvements in vocational education. As the term "career education" gradually began to fade, the real conceptualizers in vocational education continued to work with a minimum of fanfare toward true career education curricula. Many of their programs will likely appear under other names, however, since the term "career education" (like previous slogans) has lost much of its public attractiveness.

And Then, Competency-Based Vocational Teacher Education

Competency-based vocational education, for both students and teachers, gained some impetus in the early 1970s as career education began moving toward its nadir. This trend was a response to a number of perceived needs, most notable among them being a demand for increased accountability in education. Associated with the plateauing of spending for education in the 1970s was increased competition for funds, and competency-based education was viewed by some as a basis upon which funding decisions could be made. Its thrust in vocational teacher education is indicative of the entire competency-based vocational education movement.

Vocational education is deeply involved with competency-based teacher education. As was the case with career education, considerable effort had been expended by a number of reputable vocational educators before the slogan was drawn to the attention of the public at large. About 71 percent of 783 teacher education institutions had become involved with competency-based teacher education by 1973 (Massanari, 1973), and some forty states had begun some activity related to competency-based certification for vocational teachers by that same year. The predicted future role of competency-based teacher education is provided in Chapter 17.

An indication of the present status of competency-based teacher education is the position taken by the American Vocational Association when it went on record as encouraging various vocational services "to investigate the potential of competency testing to validate the occupational qualifications of vocational students and teachers" (AVA House of Delegates, 1973). Advocates of competency-based vocational teaching believe its incorporation into the profession would be a major step toward increased professionalization of vocational teachers. Should such validation be possible, it indeed would be a boon to vocational education. But there are negative factors to be considered as well, most important of which is the impossibility of validation (see Chapter 17).

Competency-based validation is being included in vocational teacher education in some states and they are moving toward adapting some new certification mechanisms that may end up being inferior to the present ones. In those places preservice and in-service vocational teacher education may become politicized and deprofessionalized (a result opposite to original expectations).

Further, many researchers believe that validating teacher competencies is beyond the state of the art (Barro, 1972), at least at the present time.

Also, many (if not most) teachers strongly dislike competency-based teaching and are fearful of how it will be used in evaluating their practices. This of itself is sufficient reason to insist that we move very slowly indeed and ever so intelligently into this very difficult area of inquiry.

Vocational education is still wrangling with competency-based education in the mid-1970s. Where this movement might end up and its possible overall effect on vocational education are examined in Chapters 16 and 17. A most important concern relative to competency-based vocational education is the possibility of its damaging the teaching profession. As stated earlier, teachers feel considerably threatened by this movement and are resisting its entry into their schools. The teaching profession is already preventing its adoption on a large-scale basis in many places, and there are moves afoot in some places to stop it entirely. In other places it is being altered such that the threat to teachers will be minimized. In short, the profession appears to be successfully resisting the full-fledged entry of competency-based efforts into vocational programs during the mid-1970s.

The Dual Vocational Education System

As was explained in Chapter 3, the nation already has a de facto dual vocational education delivery system.

One part of the duality consists of a large conglomeration of vocational institutions (with considerable diversity within it), which are described in Chapters 5–12. This conglomeration represents a considerable effort with a total enrollment of almost 10.5 million students in 1971 and total expenditures of about $2.07 billion ($317 million from federal sources and the remaining $1.75 billion from state and local funds) (Lerner, 1973). Table 15-1 gives state enrollments and expenditures by state. These statistics indicate only the magnitude of the public vocational school involvement. Enrollment and expenditure figures for the proprietary schools (described in Chapter 11) are not available, but would almost certainly increase the total number of vocational students by at least an additional 1 or 2 million.

The other side of this duality is the delivery system provided through federal funding. The major vehicle has been the Manpower Development and Training Act Program, and will now be the Comprehensive Employment and Training Act of 1973 and subsequent legislation. Enrollment in MDTA programs, shown in Table 15-2, totaled about 233,000 in 1972. About 133,000 enrollers found post-training employment. In view of the fact that a large proportion of MDTA enrollees are disadvantaged and hard to train and employ, an employment record of about 57 percent of the starters is a commendable one. In recent years these efforts have expanded beyond the original MDTA efforts and include other programs, which are listed in Table 15-3.

The total enrollment opportunities rose to almost 1.6 million in 1972, with about 2.7 billion federal dollars committed to the effort (see Table 15.3). It is clear that the federal government has invested heavily in this aspect of vocational education—that is, the part referred to as "work and training programs" under the direction of the Department of Labor. Why are the federal funds spent in this effort more than the total amount spent by state, local, and federal sources for the other "vocational programs"? Although there is no direct answer, we can find an implicit one by examining the enrollee characteristics given in Table 15-4.

The most obvious enrollee characteristics, as alluded to in Chapter 13 and shown in Table 15-4, are the high proportion of non-Caucasians and of persons whose educational level is below high school completion. The number of enrollees age 45 and older is disappointingly low, however. (More is said relative to trends in this regard in Chapters 16 and 17.) These characteristics indicate that the work and training programs examined above have been aimed at the disadvantaged and hard-to-employ sectors of the labor force. Since appropriations have been substantial, it seems safe to assume that Congress has felt the high cost per enrollee would be "worth the money" in the long run.

One can expect such efforts to continue, and they may expand as well, particularly via legislative vehicles such as the Comprehensive Employment and Training Act. This apparently is a *fait accompli:* The

TABLE 15-1 Vocational Programs—Enrollment and Expenditures, States and Other Areas: 1971 (For year ending June 30)

State or Other Area	Enrollment (1,000) Total[a]	Consumer and Home-making	Office Occu-pations	Trades and Indus-try	Agri-cul-ture	Expenditures ($1,000) Total	Federal	State and Local
Alabama	154	41	14	34	47	30,983	7,424	23,559
Alaska	13	2	5	2	—	2,766	422	2,344
Arizona	89	31	17	17	4	10,849	3,070	7,780
Arkansas	109	38	8	24	21	10,411	4,004	6,407
California	1,218	210	420	275	49	160,578	24,086	136,492
Colorado	108	33	20	19	4	21,237	3,515	17,722
Connecticut	134	35	46	28	2	29,370	3,435	25,934
Delaware	36	10	16	4	1	6,444	657	5,788
Dist. of Columbia	11	2	1	3	(z)	2,864	1,039	1,825
Florida	462	158	78	95	26	63,357	9,397	53,960
Georgia	272	77	86	37	39	38,895	9,248	29,647
Hawaii	45	19	12	7	3	6,003	1,132	4,872
Idaho	30	12	6	5	5	4,726	1,301	3,425
Illinois	1,228	32	237	177	24	163,756	13,361	150,395
Indiana	131	50	20	28	21	20,940	7,776	13,165
Iowa	128	40	10	26	29	28,378	4,012	24,366
Kansas	97	26	10	39	9	14,198	3,717	10,481
Kentucky	145	50	20	36	19	23,341	5,217	18,124
Louisiana	174	53	60	24	20	18,323	7,480	10,843
Maine	23	2	9	7	1	8,735	1,722	7,013
Maryland	163	59	53	28	3	46,329	5,157	41,172
Massachusetts	122	5	71	34	1	116,675	8,324	108,351
Michigan	320	83	61	84	14	46,065	11,803	34,262
Minnesota	286	136	29	51	32	42,078	6,092	35,986
Mississippi	107	33	7	22	22	17,399	4,583	12,815
Missouri	150	64	18	26	17	30,862	7,675	23,187
Montana	27	9	5	7	4	5,520	1,348	4,173
Nebraska	65	27	7	15	8	9,123	2,217	6,906
Nevada	19	4	5	5	1	3,140	541	2,600
New Hampshire	44	27	10	4	1	4,796	1,114	3,682
New Jersey	330	117	116	51	2	34,792	9,652	25,141
New Mexico	53	18	19	7	4	6,597	2,038	4,559
New York	832	356	218	126	13	272,634	25,106	247,528
North Carolina	416	114	31	124	31	79,099	10,732	68,366
North Dakota	26	10	4	4	5	4,303	1,258	3,045
Ohio	417	137	41	95	30	166,953	17,029	149,924
Oklahoma	105	34	9	24	24	23,250	4,559	18,692
Oregon	112	50	23	19	4	21,622	3,223	18,400
Pennsylvania	338	52	102	76	14	147,005	16,263	130,742
Rhode Island	18	9	1	5	1	5,586	799	4,787
South Carolina	102	34	11	19	23	19,552	6,099	13,452
South Dakota	25	13	2	3	5	3,309	1,234	2,075
Tennessee	144	48	16	38	22	26,707	6,866	19,841
Texas	608	229	42	95	147	81,738	17,572	64,166
Utah	109	36	27	18	7	14,368	1,922	12,446
Vermont	13	5	1	4	1	9,784	830	8,953
Virginia	302	91	60	65	29	31,868	8,088	23,780
Washington	231	74	56	46	16	37,488	5,654	31,834
West Virginia	59	20	10	19	5	9,555	3,533	6,022

TABLE 15-1 (continued)

| State or Other Area | Enrollment (1,000) | | | | | Expenditures ($1,000) | | |
	Total[a]	Con- sumer and Home- mak- ing	Office Occu- pations	Trades and Indus- try	Agri- cul- ture	Total	Federal	State and Local
Wisconsin	190	43	49	49	25	60,174	6,680	53,494
Wyoming	17	6	6	1	2	3,637	557	3,080
Puerto Rico	127	65	18	21	6	15,460	5,959	9,501
American Samoa	2	(z)[b]	1	(z)	(z)	82	82	—
Guam	3	(z)	(z)	1	—	655	267	388
Trust Territory of the Pacific Islands	3	1	(z)	1	(z)	1,403	128	1,275
Virgin Islands	3	1	(z)	(z)	(z)	679	89	590
Total	10,495	2,932	2,227	2,075	845	2,066,439	317,083	1,749,356

[a] Includes programs not shown separately.
[b] Z, Less than 500 persons.
[c] — Represents zero.
Source: U.S. Office of Education, Vocational and Technical Education, annual.

TABLE 15-2 Manpower Development and Training Act Program—
Enrollments, Completions, and Employment:
1963 to 1972

(In thousands. For years ending June 30. Excludes Construction Outreach Program. Fiscal years 1963–69 survey data based on three follow-ups, the third occurring one year after completion of training. Beginning November 1969, survey data based on two follow-ups, the second occurring six months after completion of training. Post-training employment includes persons employed at time of most recent follow-up)

Item	Total, 1963–1972	1964	1965	1966	1967	1968	1969	1970	1971	1972
Enrollments	1,887.5	77.6	156.9	235.8	265.0	241.0	220.0	221.0	203.4	232.7
Completions[a]	1,267.0	51.3	96.3	155.7	192.6	164.2	160.0	147.0	117.1	162.7
Post-training employment	995.1	39.4	73.4	124.0	153.7	127.5	124.0	115.3	88.9	132.8

[a] Excludes dropouts.
Source: U.S. Manpower Administration, Manpower Report of the President, 1973.

hard-to-deal-with vocational students have been moved into special programs that fall outside the rubric of the vocational institutions described in Chapters 5–12. In actuality, this isn't a case of vocational schools "losing" some of their clientele—they never addressed themselves to any large extent to the kinds of people enrolled in the Department of Labor's work and training programs. But many public vocational school leaders view the trend with some alarm, perhaps because

TABLE 15-3 Work and Training Programs—Enrollment and Federal Obligations, by Program: 1970 to 1972

(For years ending June 30. Covers programs administered by the U.S. Department of Labor)

Program	Enrollment Opportunities[a] (1,000)			First-time Enrollment[b] (1,000)			Federal Obligations (mil. dol.)		
	1970	1971	1972	1970	1971	1972	1970	1971	1972
Manpower Development and Training Act	211	214	229	221	255	302	337	336	425
Institutional training	137	145	[c]139	[?]130	[c]156	[c]151	277	275	[c]356
Jobs optional program/on-the-job training[d]	64	69	91	91	99	151	50	60	69
Part-time and other training	10	—[c]	—[c]	—[c]	—[c]	—[c]	10	12	—[c]
Neighborhood Youth Corps	600	699	363	482	740	1,011	357	426	517
In school	97	79	102	74	120	186	59	58	75
Out of school	45	40	42	46	53	65	98	115	122
Summer	458	580	720	362	567	760	199	253	320
Operation Mainstream	18	23	22	13	22	31	51	72	85
Public Service Careers[e]	35	42	21	4	47	66	89	92	58
Concentrated Employment Program	—[f]	—[f]	—[f]	110	94	85	188	167	155
JOBS (federally financed)	60	88	61	87	93	83	149	169	118
Work Incentive Program	66	61	150	93	112	121	79	64	175
Job Corps	22	22	24	43	50	49	170	160	202
Public Employment Program[g]	(x)[h]	(x)[h]	193	(x)[h]	(x)[h]	226	(x)[h]	(x)[h]	962
Total	1,011	1,250	1,562	1,051	1,413	1,973	1,419	1,485	2,697

[a] Refers to number of training positions provided for by funding.
[b] Refers to new enrollees; their number per fiscal year is generally larger than the number of enrollment opportunities (slots) programmed, as a slot may be used by more than one individual during the year because of turnover or short-term training. If openings are unfilled, the number of first-time enrollments may be smaller than the number of enrollment opportunities.
[c] Part-time and other training included with institutional training.
[d] Includes the Jobs-Optional Program (JOP) which began in fiscal 1971 and the MDTA (OJT) which ended in fiscal 1970 except for national contracts. Also includes Apprenticeship Outreach.
[e] Includes new careers.
[f] Data not meaningful because an individual may be enrolled in one or more program components.
[g] Program initiated August 1971.
[h] Not applicable.

Source: U.S. Manpower Administration, *Manpower Report of the President,* 1973.

they fear it may be expanded to include traditional kinds of vocational students. On the other hand, some observers of vocational education do not perceive this as the intention of the Department of Labor or the federal government and therefore see no cause for such concern. There is some reason to suspect, however, that dissatisfaction with the way traditional vocational institutions have responded to nontraditional problems may have encouraged the passage of special legislation like MDTA of 1962 and CETA of 1973. Perhaps if both elements in the dual system make greater attempts to understand more completely what the other is about, the tendency for each to be suspicious and concerned about the other will be eased. The fact is both elements of the duality

TABLE 15-4 Work and Training Programs—Selected Characteristics of Enrollees: 1970 and 1972
(For years ending June 30. Covers work and training programs administered by the U.S. Department of Labor)

				Percentage					
	Total Enroll-ees (1,000)	Male	Negro and Other Races (excl. White)	Age in Years			Education, by Grade		
Year and Program				Under 22	22–44	45 and Over	Less Than 9th	9th–11th	12th and Over
1970									
Manpower Development and Training Program:									
Institutional	130	59	41	37	54	9	15	38	47
Jobs optional program/on-the-job trainingᵃ	91	66	33	35	54	11	17	37	46
Neighborhood Youth Corps:									
In school (enrolled Sept.–May)	74	50	46	100	—ᵇ	—	17	82	1
Out of school	46	48	50	98	2	—	32	66	2
Summer (enrolled June–Aug.)	362	54	56	100	—	—	21	78	1
Operation Mainstream	13	71	38	4	46	51	52	28	20
Public Service Careersᶜ	4	23	68	21	72	7	13	42	45
Concentrated Employment Program	110	59	74	41	51	8	20	45	35
JOBS Programᵈ	87	69	78	47	49	4	15	50	35
Work Incentive Program	93	29	48	23	71	6	24	44	32
Job Corps	43	74	74	100	—	—	37	56	7
1972									
Manpower Development and Training Program:									
Institutional	151	63	39	38	54	8	10	32	58
Jobs optional program/on-the-job trainingᵃ	151	78	27	32	59	9	12	30	58
Neighborhood Youth Corps:									
In schoolᶜ	946	57	60	100	—	—	19	77	4
Out of school	65	50	52	94	3	3	25	72	3
Operation Mainstream	31	69	33	4	52	44	42	29	29
Concentrated Employment Program	85	59	71	45	50	5	16	42	42
JOBS Programᵈ	83	69	54	43	52	5	17	40	43
Work Incentive Program	121	40	40	28	67	5	17	41	42
Job Corps	49	74	66	100	—	—	30	61	9
Public Employment Program	226	72	31	15	69	16	9	16	75

ᵃ Includes the Jobs-Optional Program (JOP) which began in fiscal 1971 and the MDTA (OJT) which ended in fiscal 1970 except for national contracts. Also includes Apprenticeship Outreach.
ᵇ — Represents zero.
ᶜ Includes new careers programs.
ᵈ Job opportunities in the business sector.
ᵉ Includes enrollees in summer programs.

Source: U.S. Manpower Administration, *Manpower Report of the President,* 1973.

are very much in evidence and remain an integral part of the delivery system, and direct attempts to serve the vocational and training needs of the population in an optimum manner (mutually in some cases, separately in others) should take precedence over all other concerns.

Varieties of Vocational Organizations

One of the purposes of this book is to examine the kinds of organizations found in the vocational educational delivery system. Chapters 5–14 are devoted to this endeavor, and it is obvious that the system is blessed with considerable diversity. These organizations can be categorized in a number of ways; the most frequent are type of control, level of instruction, and kind of institution. If one so desires, other rationales can be used for categorization of these organizations with very little difficulty, but these appear to be the most common.

Identifying vocational organizations by type of control results in a trichotomy: (1) public, (2) private nonprofit, and (3) proprietary. The public element is by far the most important, both in terms of its impact upon society and in terms of the financial investment in its activities. The private nonprofit and proprietary components are experiencing funding and enrollment difficulties, ranging in severity from impending bankruptcy, on one hand, to a year-to-year bare-bones kind of survival, on the other. In spite of much rhetoric and some attempts to find ways to funnel public funds into such vocational organizations, not many public dollars (comparatively speaking) have gone into their treasuries, and the financial condition of these schools was clearly worse in the mid-1970s than it had been in the previous decade.

The categorization of vocational organizations according to instructional level also results in a trichotomy: (1) secondary, (2) post-secondary, and (3) adult and continuing education. During the decade from the mid-1960s to the mid-1970s, enrollments in vocational programs at all of these levels increased at faster rates than corresponding enrollments in other forms of education (i.e., general and academic). Post-secondary growth gained considerable impetus through the community colleges and area vocational schools, as there was a sharp increase in the number of these institutions. The relatively silent component in the trichotomy is adult and continuing education. Actually, it is not entirely appropriate to consider this as a level of education, since offerings within the rubric of adult and continuing education range in level from the basic to the most advanced. Earlier chapters point to the very great need to provide reasonably easy career-changing opportunities for large segmer.ts of the work force. No concerted effort on a widespread basis has ever been made in this direction, and up to now many persons have had to bungle their way out of one career into another without benefit of public or institutional assistance. The need for professional help in making career transitions is greater now than ten years ago, and will reach almost crisis proportions in the next decade. Society can no longer afford to ignore this phenomenon. No one has taken a major initiative to date, and it will be interesting to see if any of the public schools examined in this book will respond to this vital need. It appears most likely that the Department of Labor will perceive these services as an extension of their present efforts in employment and training.

When vocational organizations are categorized by institutional type, they can be broken down into the kinds described in Chapters 5–14. Using this approach for an analysis of vocational organizations permits convenient clustering of schools into such categories. Furthermore, they are most often identified in this manner for funding purposes. Much of the discussion in Chapters 16 and 17 is directed at the continued use of this kind of categorization for coordination and cooperation as well as funding purposes.

Sources of Leaders in Vocational Education

No large nationwide study of vocational education leadership has been made up to the mid-1970s, and some ambitious, carefully planned inquiries into this subject should be instituted soon. Some major questions now beg for answers: (1) Do the traditional requirements relating to certification affect the kind of leadership available in vocational education? Do they indeed keep out only the "incompetent," or do they also prevent certain types of leaders from coming into vocational education at all? Furthermore, do they even keep out the incompetent? (2) How well are the vocational teachers–administrators training institutions preparing leaders? (3) What are the backgrounds of the most significant leaders in vocational education? A biographical study of fifty recognized vocational leaders could provide a rich base of data and information from which vocational leadership could be studied intensively and ultimately better understood.

Many more questions can be posed, but the central ones are those listed. Answers to them would enlighten the field of vocational education in this most critical matter of leadership. All too often, leadership positions are vested with persons who have learned to "toe the line" and to conform to the traditional constructs of vocational education. A preponderance of such individuals and the absence of maverick types in leadership positions will ensure high levels of traditionalism in the profession and bankrupt leadership (in terms of innovative ideas and approaches).

References

AVA House of Delegates. Atlanta, Georgia, 5 December 1973. Resolution No. 15.

Barro, S. M. "A Review of the Power of Competency-Based Teacher Education." Paper prepared for a committee on National Program Priorities in Teacher Education, City University of New York, May 1972.

Lerner, W. *Statistical Abstract of the United States: 1973*, 94th annual ed. Washington, D.C.: Bureau of the Census, 1973.

Massanari, K. "Performance-Based Teacher Education." *Journal of Teaching Education* 24 (Fall 1973). Washington, D.C.: American Association of Colleges for Teacher Education, 1973.

16

Models for the Future:
The Ideal

A projection of what utopian vocational education might be like is worthwhile for several reasons. First, such a venture is a refreshing departure from continuously dealing with the hear-and-now realities in vocational education. Second, an exercise in utopianizing vocational education, contrary to being a mere waste of time and energy, may indeed be a helpful catalyst in the generating of new ideas. Third, a view of the "perfect" situation can be of great value in assessing the condition of vocational education, for we can use this view to ascertain the distance of vocational education from that ideal configuration. In view, then, of the possible benefits that could be derived from an excursion into utopian vocational education, a short chapter devoted to such an endeavor should be worthwhile.

The Students

Perhaps 95 percent of all persons would be vocational education students at least once in their lifetime. For the person whose occupation is destined to be other than a profession, his or her first contact with vocational education would occur during adolescence, as an integral part of his or her secondary school education. For one group of students the initial exposure would occur in very early adolescence as part of a meaningful transition from a well-conducted prevocational experience in the pre-high school grades to initial occupational preparation in early high school years. A second group of students would continue the prevocational-exploratory type of educational experiences until the student and the educators associated with him perceive that the time is right for him to move into an occupational area of study. A third group of students would enter institutions that are presently identified as post-secondary (i.e., grades 13 and 14), where they would decide on an occupation and begin to prepare for it. And finally, a fourth (and very small) group, consisting largely of the most intellectual persons in the secondary schools, would be guided into the preparatory phases of carefully selected professions. Most of what has just been described should seem familiar to the reader, because it has been a part of the rhetoric in education for many years. The fact is, however, that such guiding and sorting of individuals into occupations has only been taking place for a very small number of persons—those going into training for the professions. And even then, the final determination of successful entry into a profession depends heavily upon situational factors having little to do with personal ability (such as proximity of a suitable school and an adequate source of income while preparing for a profession). In our utopian vocational education delivery system, geographic, physical, and financial factors would be partialed out of the actual situation so that a person's entry into a course of study for an occupation would be determined solely by his desires and abilities.

Virtually all youngsters, then, would be enrolled for at least a part of the time they are attending high school. Specific preparatory studies would be provided for some students, while others would be limited to exploratory studies of the place of occupations in society. Students in the former group would be separated away from the other students and placed into job placement preparation via the universal college model (examined in several early chapters and Chapter 17). Gone would be the present two- and three-year high school vocational programs, where the trainee enters the program without having been placed in a job which he has accepted ahead of time. The present mode, where occupational preparation is provided first and then followed by job procurement, would be considered archaic and dysfunctional.

Students identified as being the most suitable for early preparation for entry into a profession would not be exempted from vocational education experiences. They would enroll in courses from which they would develop certain broad vocational skills considered important for living in modern society. These skills would be clearly distinguished from the general education component of the school curricula. Included would be skills in home-apartment maintenance and management, maintenance and use of motor vehicles, roles and functions of business and industry in modern society, and roles and functions of the various worker categories in our society (i.e., blue collar, white collar, paraprofessional, professional, etc.).

Thus most students would be involved with vocational education at some time in their secondary school years. In addition, the majority of post-secondary students (perhaps 70 to 80 percent) would be enrolled in vocationally oriented curricula, and only 20 to 30 percent would be in pre-professional preparatory programs. This ideal system would permit easy and frequent entry into and exiting from vocational curricula.

Faculty

Faculty in the ideal vocational education system would be perfectly distributed along sexual lines in all of the vocational areas. Half of the trade and industrial area vocational teachers, for example, would be women, and half of the home economics faculty members would be men.

The backgrounds of faculty members would be more diversified throughout the profession as a whole than they are presently, and there would be a preponderance of teachers who acquired their competencies in specially designed and controlled laboratory-shop-clinic environments (of the variety proposed in the universal college idea elsewhere in this book). Such a method for specialty preparation would provide considerable assurance that each teacher would enter the classroom for the first time with a broad, yet intensive, group of experiences in that particular occupational area. Drawing vocational teachers with this type of training and background into the profession would result in increased professionalization of vocational teaching, especially in those specialty areas where college degrees are not presently considered as important as on-the-job experience. Using this approach as the major entry into vocational teaching would result in better trained teachers in the classroom and ancillary staff throughout the school, because they would have completed at least the baccalaureate and, in many instances, a master's degree. The experiences involved in acquiring such degrees would socialize professionals to the field of education in general and vocational education particularly. These professionals would possess a more favorable attitude toward intellectualism and education, which they would in turn transmit to their vocational students. This new professional preparation, besides increasing professionalism of vocational teachers, would result in a marked improvement in the quality of teaching skills currently found in vocational faculty. One of the most pronounced improvements would be that every vocational teacher would be a polished speaker able to write capably in his or her occupational specialty.

The ideal faculty member would view research in vocational education in a positive manner. Furthermore, he or she would always seek to incorporate research findings throughout his curricula and teaching practices, and would provide for such efforts in his routine faculty responsibilities. Associated with this would be an ongoing and fruitful relationship between vocational teachers and researchers so that bidirectional feedback between these two groups would be continuous and nonthreatening.

The ideal faculty member would be in frequent touch with his specialty subject matter and experts in the field, as well as with vocational educators in general. Common vehicles used by faculty for keeping up-to-date with the state of the art in their occupational field and in vocational education would be workshops and seminars organized and sponsored by universities and senior colleges. Each faculty member and administrator would spend about 10 percent of his or her professional life in such renewal, updating, and professional improvement activities. The school in which the person is employed would provide financial support and required time so that such functions would be incorporated into his routine professional time, and not be an "extra-on-your-own-time" type of effort.

The ideal faculty would have teachers ranging in age from the early twenties to the seventies, with an even distribution in each of the vocational areas. The younger faculty members would have as many of the attractive teaching posts as the older teachers, and the less attractive teaching tasks would be rotated among all faculty members in the institution, regardless of age and/or length of employment.

In conclusion, the ideal vocational faculty member would be professionally oriented, would thoroughly enjoy teaching, would like people, and would have a well-rounded up-to-date perception of his or her occupational specialty and vocational education as a whole.

Administration-Governance

The ideal governance mechanism would be one in which the sundry needs of the several elements in the system would be quickly and accurately communicated to decision makers. Governance of the ideal vocational education system would appear to be benign but basically authoritarian, with decisions for system-wide actions emanating from a regionalized administrative group. But closer examination of the governance structure would reveal that decisions made by leaders at upper levels of the administrative hierarchy were formed from other decisions made at lower levels. Each institution in the system would have sufficient autonomy to determine its own regular and routine activities along with the manner in which these are constructed and scheduled. The regional-governance center would provide the parameters within which each school would be required to operate. These parameters would include such matters as curricula, enrollment ceilings, level of programs (i.e., secondary or post-secondary), and total annual budget appropriations.

In the utopian scene each level of governance would have clear-cut prerogatives in terms of rendering certain decisions, accompanied by equally clear-cut requirements which each element within the system must observe. While a superficial view of such an arrangement shows it to be authoritarian-like, a closer examination shows that it has much room for individuals at every level from the classroom to the top regional office administrator to become involved in decision making. This idealized amalgam of localized decision making coexisting with region-wide regulatory authority contains the virtues of both forms of leadership (authoritarian and democratic), while simultaneously minimizing the weaknesses associated with each.

The ideal governance configuration would hold all professionals in vocational education responsible for decision making at their particular level of involvement, and in this regard they would have no option as to whether or not they would become involved. Every faculty member, for example, would be required to make decisions relative to the conduct of his or her teaching, so that his or her performance could be carefully coordinated with other faculty and teaching activities. The local school administrators, in turn, would have to render decisions relative to overall conduct of that school's vocational education affairs, but within the context of a constellation of decisions made by faculty, on one hand, and regional administrators, on the other. Such a governance mode would attain maximum effectiveness with the inauguration of easy bidirectional communications between faculty and the regional government unit. The time to be fully involved in such a form of communication would be provided within the context of the normal everyday operation of these schools and the regional administrative units.

The ideal administrative unit would be viewed by faculty as the major advocate of those vocational education activities perceived to be of maximum benefit to students and the profession as a whole. The spirit of confrontation, so common in many places today, would be absent, and faculty and administrators would have implicit trust in each other. Since the relationships established between these two groups would be constructive, trusting, and agreeable, faculty unions would disappear from the professional scene. Furthermore, regional governance units would be viewed positively by the institutional level administrators, and tension between these levels would be kept down to a constructive level. The regional administrative centers would be the real focal point of governance, even though many of the funds within their jurisdiction would originate from a state source. The state level element within the administrative structure would be service-oriented, and the amount and kind of control it exercised over the regional governance units and the institutions would be limited to routine administrative affairs.

Provisions would be made in the governance structure for funding of exemplary programs and for conduct of considerable research in vocational education. Financial support for these two important efforts would be as much as 5 percent of the total budget each year. These efforts would be the cutting edge of vocational education. They would be sufficiently insulated from routine demands to ensure freedom to truly experiment in programs and the conduct of research, but enough contact would be maintained to permit those involved in such efforts to remain apprised of what is going on in the profession and out in the field.

Institutions

In the utopian situation there would be fewer types of institutions (instead of the existing array of comprehensive high schools, area vocational schools, other special purpose public-supported vocational schools, community junior colleges, senior colleges and universities, proprietary schools, and independent nonprofit schools). The ideal would be limited to only two institutional types.

The fundamental institution for delivery of vocational services would be the universal college configuration (alluded to in several earlier chapters and Chapter 17), where specific vocational training is delayed until the student has accepted a specific job with a particular industrial or business concern. This ideal arrangement permits maximum flexibility to all concerned (students, business-industry, and the vocational institution itself). The universal college approach is centered upon the concerns and needs of students and their potential relationships with the occupational world and society at large. This configuration would be a radical departure, in many respects, from the manner in which vocational education and services are now provided. The major change would be from job preparation in anticipation of entering the world of work to the new approach of helping students obtain jobs most congruent with their interests and abilities, after which they would be provided with training to develop the specific skills needed for that job.

In the utopian situation two universal colleges would be in operation simultaneously, conceivably on the same campus but each with sufficient autonomy to remain independent of the other. The first of these would serve adolescents who have had no previous full-time work experiences of any consequence. This college would include those activities described in Chapter 17, where programs ranging in length from a few weeks to a four-year in-school sequence for certain students would be available. The last two years of secondary schools, area vocational schools, special purpose vocational schools, proprietary schools, and the community junior colleges would be replaced by this configuration.

The second universal college configuration, while similar to the first one, would be specially devised to serve adults requiring mid-career changing and other occupational adjustments (such as updating and upgrading of skills). This institution would be even more flexible than the first one in that exiting from this one would be virtually free of such limitations as calendar considerations. Because adults with work experiences hold perceptions of the world of work and their role within it that are different from those held by adolescents, their education and training in some cases would be different from that offered to neophyte workers.

An appropriate label for this kind of institution would be the universal college for adults, and it would replace most of the adult and continuing education efforts in vocational education currently offered by the several institutions analyzed in Chapters 5–14.

An integral part of each of the two varieties of universal college would be a sizable department of research and also a special department for the offering of experimental and exemplary programs. Each would be accorded the financial support needed so as to ensure continuous and viable efforts in research related to sundry aspects of vocational education. The building in of these departments in such a manner would ease the translation of findings and results into the curricula and other institutional activities. In addition, these efforts would be supplemented by support activities conducted cooperatively by the research department of the universal college and the state university serving that region. In this way the research efforts in vocational education would be parlayed into more effective thrusts, resulting in significant improvements in vocational education. The exemplary programs, designed around carefully based research, would be established such that the activities within them and their outcomes could be observed and measured with considerable accuracy. Being an internal matter for the institution, changes in the exemplary programs could be easily inaugurated to remedy shortcomings as they are identified. Associated with the conduct of exemplary programs would be the careful establishment and monitoring of appropriate control groups which would provide accurate comparisons with traditional modes.

These two ideal universal college configurations would together provide all the vocational education offerings needed by society. (That is, many of the present institutional types would not be needed.) The senior colleges and universities would continue to play an important role through their training programs for vocational teachers and administrators and also through their research efforts in vocational education. The establishment of two generic types of universal college which would provide all vocational education services would reduce the complexities of coordinating efforts.

In conclusion, only two basic universal college institutions would be needed to serve all of the vocational education needs in this utopian model: a universal college for adolescents and other neophyte workers and one for adults. The designated role of selected senior colleges and state universities would be to provide support for these two basic organizations by preparing teachers and administrators and conducting research.

Funding

The utopian situation, being ideal in every respect, would have no financial problems. One should not misconstrue this to mean all funds requested would be quickly provided. An excellent assessment mechanism would permeate the vocational education system, and it would be the major determinant of the allocations of funds.

The control of funds would still reside with the political sphere, since our utopian system could function only within the rubric of a democratic society. Political leaders with authority for making ultimate funding decisions would have at their disposal appropriate information in digestible forms so their decisions would invariably be the most correct in terms of optimum benefit to vocational education's clientele. Political decisions would be part and parcel of funding the utopian system, and the decisions made would be of a superior quality because of accessibility of superior information for use in making such decisions.

In the ideal system funding for vocational education would be predicated upon the ranking of its importance to society at that point in time. This means that vocational education services would be subjected to cyclic fluctuations, which would be predicted sufficiently far ahead to permit the system to accommodate easily to the changes. Sources of funding would be completely public. There would be no student tuition or any other personal cost directly concerned with the provision of vocational education. In addition, and even more important, the student would be qualified to receive an income while attending school. The amount of income would be determined by a formula which would consider the funds the individual required for legitimate living expenses (including support for a family at a level that family had been living on prior to this point in time). Such funding would pay students for school attendance in the same way people now are paid for employment performance. This approach would equalize vocational education opportunities for everyone, regardless of financial and other personal circumstances.

All funds would come from one source, such as the regional governance center described earlier. Criteria for receiving funds would be established in an equitable manner based upon services rendered by each institution. In addition, a fraction of the total funds (such as 5 percent) would be earmarked each year for research efforts and conduct of exemplary programs. Institutions that have failed to fulfill their obligations with regard to services to their clientele would lose financial support; and the activities previously assigned to them would be given to another institution, or a new institution would be established. Accountability, mixed with benign understanding of the difficulties that can be encountered, would be the major bases for institutional funding.

The Overall Delivery System

The delivery components of the vocational education system, which would include the institutions described in a preceding section, would be strategically located throughout each state. The entire state would be viewed as the service area. Regional universal colleges would be situated so that they would be accessible to all people in a given region. With the exception of those in the more rural areas, each of these institutions would have medium to large enrollments (i.e., at least 1,000 equivalent full-time students). In the more rural areas special outreach programs for small groups of individuals would be provided, although incentives would be offered to these persons to enroll in the universal college as resident students. These incentives would include special funding to meet additional costs incurred as residential students, including room and board and back-home expenses which would continue while he or she was attending school away from home.

The overall vocational delivery system would be drawn up as a state master plan for vocational education, and would be subjected to minor revisions annually and completely reviewed every fifth year. Provisions for discontinuing old programs, when deemed necessary, and inaugurating new ones would be built into the system so that such decisions could be made and implemented regularly with little fanfare or emotional trauma. If time permitted, programs and courses considered to be new and different would be tried within the framework of an exemplary program first, with all the mechanisms for observation and evaluation built into the effort. After careful assessment and adjustment of the experimental offerings, the new programs would be inaugurated as regular school offerings.

The research effort contained within each universal college would fit within the overall research effort on a statewide basis. This is not to say that all vocational researchers would be coerced into inaugurating activities that some authority at the state level deemed necessary. Coordination at the state level and between the states would provide information as to whether some researchers were conducting duplicative studies. Some research does need to be conducted more than once, especially under different environmental conditions, to test the universality of certain findings. But there are many instances where going over old ground in the same way is a waste of time, effort, and finances.

There would be a special organizational scheme through which new findings would be brought into the universal college's operation. This scheme would include a feedback network from the researchers to the teachers-administrators, with the identified opinion leaders and change agents of that institution serving as the chief coupling mechanisms. Such communication would also be set up between institutions so that new practices and ideas could be diffused throughout the delivery system in a most expeditious manner. Suspicion and resistance to such activities would be at a minimum, since they would be a routine part of the overall operation of the system and its constituent institutions.

The ideal system would be responsive to the needs of all persons regarding vocational education and related services. There would be a viable liaison between the universal colleges and the business-industrial community based on commonality of objectives—the maximizing of individual occupational fulfillment. Industry would recognize that workers who view their employment tasks as meaningful and interesting are most productive, and would therefore be as concerned as the schools about placing people in jobs that are most congruent with their abilities, interest, and personal achievement needs. The achievement of this ideal situation would convert the blue-collar work force into a happier work force than that found in our society. The utopian universal college arrangement would be a coupling agent for joining people with jobs most appropriate for them and consequently society as a whole.

The ideal vocational education delivery system would be a dynamic and highly flexible instrument in the promotion of occupational stability, and would be viewed as such by everyone. Vocational education would be highly regarded in general, and would be supported by society accordingly. This would be manifested in the quality of the universal college campuses, which would be points of interests and sources of pride in every region.

The utopian ideas presented here are just that, but such an excursion into fantasy helps to point to directions in which excellence in vocational education can be found. Dreams generated during waking hours can form the bases for goal making in reality.

17

Models for the Future:
A Prediction

Every social system contains a device akin (but not completely identical) to the biological negative feedback mechanism called homeostasis (Dubos, 1972). When a disturbance occurs within a biological system, that system seeks to restore biological equilibrium through automatic adaptive responses (which can be considered analogous to negative feedback). Such adjustive responses are, of course, good, but they also have certain disadvantages. One of the major dangers is that the long-term effect of adjustments addressed to an immediate impingement upon the system may be less than beneficial. For example, scar tissue which appears because of the body's emergency response to an organ injury may later impede that organ's normal functioning. In other words, while an early and rapid adjustment to a bodily emergency is critically necessary at the time, the adjustment may result in an alteration of the affected body component.

A phenomenon similar to biological homeostasis (in some respects) occurs in vocational education. It is displayed in the manner in which the present delivery systems in vocational education function, where the traditional mode is to provide occupational preparation *first* and job placement second. While this approach was highly appropriate in the past, it is becoming increasingly dysfunctional in modern society. As it becomes increasingly evident that jobs change in nature frequently and people change jobs more often than they did just a few years ago, vocational educators will become more aware of the inappropriateness of the present delivery system. Half or more of all vocational graduates don't go into the occupational areas for which they were prepared. The adaptive response to this dilemma is what this chapter seeks to examine. Will the response be of the "put out the bleeding" variety (i.e., get untrained persons trained), with resulting "scar tissue" (i.e., "trained" persons who end up not using their training) which will impede, not help, the vocational delivery system (i.e., since these persons will need still other training after they become employed)? Or will the response be a new delivery mode, more rational and less impetuous? A logical adjustment would be the new delivery system alluded to in several places in this book and in a previous work (see Gillie, 1973). In this system

1. Each person would receive careful guidance and counseling, which would include testing, interviews, and consistent individual evaluation, and through this counseling he or she would be advised to join the occupational cluster most appropriate for his constellation of talents and interests.

2. The student would then spend as much time learning about that occupational cluster as deemed profitable by himself, his teachers, and other appropriate professional support persons such as counselors.

3. Then, with the direct assistance of professionally trained job coordinators, he would be placed in a job that matches his interests and abilities.

4. The job coordinator, the student, and the new employer would determine the specific skills and tasks that the new worker would need on that job.

5. The job coordinator and the employer would determine the best place for the student to acquire those skills.

6. Some students would return to a skill center within the school or to some other appropriate setting, where they would acquire the necessary skills. Others would acquire the necessary skills by way of on-the-job training.

7. There would be provision for any worker to repeat any part or all of the cycle whenever necessary.

This strategy for preparing people for vocations is more than an emergency response in that it deals with immediate dysfunctions while simultaneously establishing an environment conducive to long-term career development of each individual. It appears to be among the most constructive, adaptive responses vocational education can make to the ever changing parameters associated with job requirements and styles and with people's interests.

The big question is: Will it happen this way by 1980? The prediction here is No, not on a universal scale, but Yes, on a more limited exemplary program basis. The rationale for this prediction is presented in the following paragraphs. This chapter also provides predictions of what future vocational education will look like, along with the reasons for making such predictions.

Along with a host of other difficulties, vocational educators run the danger of failing to provide the services needed by people in general while simultaneously failing to affect the decisions made by the three generic power groups in the United States (i.e., the military, the politicians, and the industrial conglomerates). Vocational education may well find the world of education and vocational training passing it by while its leaders engage in a flurry of directionless skirmishes with others for funds and the wherewithal to provide vocational services. Such internal battles serve to inhibit creative approaches to modern vocational education problems, since only the old and conservative methods tend to be retained when dissension continues. Are the traditional public vocational schools (secondary and post-secondary) destined to become educational dinosaurs? If vocational education fails on both counts (i.e., in providing vocational services and in affecting the nation's decision makers), the present form of vocational education may indeed be heading toward its denouement and may find a place in the museum of educational relics as a mere array of memorabilia of the way vocational education "used to be in the old days."

Why must vocational education always be subjected to annual and biennial fads? Witness the onslaught upon the procession brought on by vocational educators' infatuation first with career education and then with competency-based vocational education. Does a profession turn to fads, rather than well-designed, tested, and evaluated research endeavors, for its future direction because of a dearth of its own original ideas? Why is vocational education more susceptible than some of the other professions, such as medicine and law, which are traditionally much more cautious about incursions into their performances as professionals? One may suspect it has something to do with the overzealous attempts of some vocational educators, in their desire to gain additional funds, to capture the attention of society in general and the educational world in particular. The glibness with which such fads are taken on and later shedded bodes ill for the profession of vocational education. A new idea is not a good one until proven so. It ought to be subjected to rigorous examination, analysis, field testing, and reanalysis to determine whether it does in fact offer a significant and positive contribution to the profession and its clientele. The prediction made here is that certain centers of innovation will develop in vocational education by 1980. These will be associated with research-based experiments of the most excellent design, and will most likely be contractual consortia between large state universities and several vocational institutions (such as community junior colleges and area vocational schools). These centers will demand that certain faddish ideas be put through rigorous testing so their usefulness to vocational students in particular and vocational education in general can be accurately assessed.

Associated with these centers will be the problem of diffusing principles, practices, and ideas, when they are found to be acceptable, to the other, nonexperimenting institutions. This problem will call for the organization of a special research-oriented field service. In this service researchers would venture out to the vocational schools and work with the administrators and faculties on a long-term basis in order to bring the innovations to their curricula. This would require substantial funding, which could be provided only when those governing such funding resources believe the effort to be a viable approach to improving vocational education. Will it happen? Exemplary programs and other forms of experimentation in vocational education will be conducted on a limited basis. Sorely needed is vocational education legislation not unlike the Hatch Act for agriculture passed in the late nineteenth century. Such legislation, if properly drafted and implemented, would provide for at least one vocational experimental center in every state. Although there is some risk of redundancy in such efforts, such a move would provide a mechanism for experimenting with a diversity of approaches to certain generic ideas in vocational education. The prediction here is that several states, those fortunate enough to have a group of influential and farsighted vocational leaders, will succeed in pooling certain federal and state monies for the conduct of these important endeavors.

A problem viewed as serious by many is the dilution of vocational funds by the incursion of peripheral activities—a trend that is likely to continue. Most notable will be inroads made by educators from the areas of guidance, industrial arts, career development, and vocationally related general education. It appears that each of these groups will succeed in acquiring greater amounts of allocations from the overall vocational education fund, while the overall amount of monies appropriated will remain essentially the same. The obvious result, of course, will be a reduction of funds allocated to the traditional vocational programs themselves. Is this a good or a bad trend? Certainly, it is good for those peripheral activities that succeed in tapping this source of funding, but it will probably exert at least a restraining effect on the development of traditional vocational programs per se. On the other hand, some peripheral activities may serve in the future as catalysts, or even vehicles, for the spread of the new type of vocational education alluded to here.

Vocational education has several sets of major problems. One relates to federal funding and the direction it may take in the future (categorical funding, revenue sharing, or some blend of these two types). A second relates to state funding. In most states funding is accompanied by increasing demands for cooperative-consortium vocational efforts in the interest of maximizing vocational opportunities for the state's citizens and minimizing duplicative and redundant efforts. A third set relates to the local scene and is intricately tied in with real estate taxation, which is being viewed increasingly as a nonviable mechanism for obtaining funds for educational purposes. A trend is afoot to stabilize or even reduce local contributions, while the states increase their expenditures to make up for the reduced local source. Added to the need for increased state funding is the likelihood that the federal share of the total appropriations for vocational education will gradually decrease. State support for vocational education, bolstered by some noncategorical funding from federal sources, will become the major type of support for vocational education in the future.

Will this be an improvement over existing funding? In many states (i.e., those with strong and respected leadership in vocational education), the overall condition of vocational education will be improved. In other states (i.e., those already suffering from mediocre leadership in vocational education), vocational education may not compete successfully for its share of the state's dollars, and a reduction in the quantity and quality of vocational education may result. If we look at the nation as a whole, it appears that vocational education will not capture the imagination of the citizens any more than it has in the past. There will be some shuffling around—some states gaining while others are losing—with a net effect of little or no change. If there is to be a wider acceptance of vocational education, its mode of preparing people for occupations must change to one similar to that described earlier. It is difficult, however, to see such a drastic revision of the profession taking place without the introduction of a strong legislative mandate, which of itself would tend to usurp the entire vocational education movement and would be considered undesirable by most traditional vocational educators. Much of what happens in vocational education, unfortunately, will likely include emergency responses to external forces impinging upon the delivery system, and these responses may, with time, result in a scar-ridden system with increasingly less flexibility. Each response will alter the system just enough to obtain a new balance. As this happens again and again over a period of years, vocational education will become a hodgepodge Band-Aid type of system, unless basic changes are made soon. Such hodgepodge changes will continue until the system becomes (like the dinosaur) unable to sustain itself, and continued changing conditions will cause it to gradually die out. Unfortunately, the best changes are most likely to occur when there is no previous host of traditions to counter. The probable replacement for our increasingly antiquated system will be a new administrative form of vocational education with elements similar to those contained in the Comprehensive Employment and Training Act of 1973, which is described in Chapter 13. The most viable and innovative forms of vocational education, although limited in number and influence, will emerge out of the proposed state university types of experimental center-vocational institution consortia discussed earlier.

With this somber note to set the stage, we will now examine the kinds of models predicted for the future and the sundry elements and constituencies that will probably be included in the overall vocational education system in the 1980s.

Funding

A change of style in funding, already started, is likely to continue in the decade beginning in the mid-1970s. At the federal level of funding, certain vestiges of revenue sharing will persist. As vocational education adjusts to external influences, the reaction will produce an equivalent of scar tissue in the vocational education delivery system in the form of funding which contains aspects of both revenue sharing and categorical aid. The resultant new funding approach will be more flexible in that many of the constraints in traditional vocational education will have been shunted, but new inflexibilities inherent to the new funding mode will appear. When the "new approach" becomes established, rigidities unique to it, the forms of which cannot yet be predicted, will emerge.

Special groups in need of attention other than traditional vocational education will receive continued categorical aid for the next several decades. Included in this category will be special ethnic groups (e.g., Indians, blacks, Spanish-speaking), other types of minorities (such as women and the handicapped), possibly mid-career changers in need of income, offenders, and various other people identifiable as disadvantaged (socially, economically, or socioeconomically) in our society. Such categorical funding will gradually become increasingly loaded with an array of requirements that must be met before a group can qualify for receipt of monies. In addition, careful specification of how the funds are to be disbursed will be made. The extent to which such specificity of regulations is increased will depend on whether or not it is found that present categorical funds are being used wisely for their intended purposes. Indications are that they are falling short of intentions (see *Report to the Congress,* 1974). If this is felt to be true, Congress and state legislators, believing that these funds must be spent only for vocational

efforts directed toward the special groups mentioned above, will become concerned and this concern will be translated into reduced funding or additional bureaucracy to enforce the intent of the funding.
Indeed, if such specificity is carried too far, the outcome may be the
opposite of Congress' and the state legislatures' intentions, and this
component of federal support may become dysfunctional (as did certain
aspects of the Manpower Development and Training Act in its later
years).

Other federal funds, according to this prediction, will flow back to the
states in the revenue-sharing mode. Criteria by which political units,
called prime sponsors (see Chapter 13), can singularly or together qualify for such funds will be refined. The unique element within this approach, which is extremely threatening to many vocational education
leaders throughout the nation, is that control of these funds will be
vested with the political governing officials in the designated primary
sponsor units (as opposed to state departments of vocational education).
Furthermore, these leaders, in conjunction with their governing and
advisory boards, will have the authority to establish new structures by
which the funds will be allocated and disbursed. It is conceivable and
likely that in some places the governing officials may decide to bypass
the existing public vocational school system and contract for services
with one or more new educational configurations. While this alternative
appears to be a most radical one to some, it is quite likely to take the
place of the entrenched ultra-traditional vocational systems presently
found in some places. Furthermore, if it is found to work well in these
places, it will hasten the demise of the traditional delivery system
elsewhere.

A wholesale movement in this direction would result in a revolutionary change in vocational education and could have severely perni-
cious effects on the traditional public vocational education delivery system. One can't help but wonder what forces propel movements of this
type, since such thrusts are at least partially iconoclastic (i.e., anti-
public vocational education). Is it the entrepreneurial tendencies of
some legislators, who assume such changes will result in more economical vocational education (and thereby lower total required appropriation)? Or is it an attempt to replace the old system with a new one
because of genuine dissatisfaction with it? The latter may be the main
motive behind the funding changeover. The trend to rely less on the
public sector of vocational education in its present form will continue,
and the efforts of public vocational schools may be seriously eroded by
such inroads. In actuality, the public vocational schools have been more
than willing to pass on the more difficult and less attractive varieties of

vocational education to other groups and organizations. For example, the Department of Labor, first through the Manpower Development and Training Act of 1962, and through subsequent legislation such as the Comprehensive Employment and Training Act of 1973, has already taken on the task of training certain disadvantaged and minority groups. The funds for this task are appropriated directly to primary sponsors through the Department of Labor (bypassing state bureaus of vocational education), whereas the public vocational schools receive federal funds through the Department of Health, Education, and Welfare and state-appropriated monies through the state departments of education. The introduction of federal funds through the prime sponsor kind of revenue sharing will increase the ease with which newly formed vocational institutions can strongly bid for funds to conduct certain aspects of the vocational education effort. It is likely that private learning corporations (still suspect in some quarters), although focusing on hard-to-teach and hard-to-train individuals in present contractual arrangements, will seek contracts in the future involving some of the less difficult and more attractive elements in the overall vocational education effort. Public educators, as one would expect, greatly fear the possibility of such incursions into what has been their undisputed educational territory. It is likely that in some states public vocational education systems will be unwisely weakened through attempts to economize by contracting substantial elements of vocational education out to the public learning corporations. This will provide fuel for debate on the desirability of maintaining the traditional public vocational school system, as opposed to heavy utilization of primary sponsor-based vocational education and training. The public school system advocates will likely lose out and also be scathed in the process. The primary sponsor-supported programs probably will provide the more exotic vocational education efforts for the hard-to-teach and hard-to-train groups.

It appears that Congress is disenchanted with the ability of the Department of Health, Education, and Welfare to allocate funds wisely for education in general. This jaundiced view of HEW's capabilities may continue, thereby providing additional impetus to the expansion of the revenue-sharing approach. Although in recent years several of vocational education's national leaders have made a strong case for making vocational education a special exception to this approach, it is predicted that allocations for vocational education will also be largely in the form of revenue sharing. Categorical funding for vocational education, except for those very special groups cited earlier, will be viewed as an outmoded approach to financing vocational education. As the Department of Health, Education, and Welfare becomes more unfavorably viewed as a conduit for vocational funds in the years ahead, the Department of Labor will become increasingly successful in procuring such funds, which will strengthen the already existing dual system of vocational education. In the future, then, federal funding for vocational education and training will include revenue-sharing legislation via the Department of Labor and funds from the Department of Health, Education, and Welfare source. The latter, however, will be reduced and may eventually be eliminated. The prediction bodes well for those who desire a new approach to vocational education but is a harbinger of difficult times ahead for the traditionalists.

State allocations for vocational education will increase in most places, and local allocations will undergo corresponding decreases. Vocational education may receive larger portions of total state appropriations in some states, but this is not expected to be true in most states. With stabilization of the birth rate several years ago and the consequential downturn in the number of secondary school and college age students, education at all levels and of all varieties (including vocational education) will be viewed as a lower priority concern by the public and state legislatures. Congressional appropriations will emphasize such matters as environmental protection, services to retirees, accommodation to changing energy resources, and other contemporary issues capturing the imagination of the public and state legislatures in the next decade. Vocational education, as far as state and local funds are concerned, can be expected to remain at its present level (proportionately) for the next ten years. The prospect of the nation indulging in a love affair with vocational education with a fruition of increased funding is indeed a wild notion with no basis in reality. There are no discernible reasons to believe that vocational education is going to be considered more important than it was in the early 1970s.

The Dual System

The bifurcation of the vocational services system, which began in 1963 with passage of the Manpower Development and Training Act, has had a significant impact. There has been some debate over the ultimate effect of this movement on vocational education as a whole and on those served by the profession. The predictions vary from those of the "doomsday" variety to highly optimistic conjectures about monumental improvements in vocational education. It does appear certain that the phenomenon will indeed alter the delivery system of vocational education and allied services.

The resulting distortion in the vocational delivery system can produce an overall improvement in the long run. Specifically, persons over the usual school attendance age (over thirty) may receive special attention and benefits as a result of this new trend. The approach of supplying some financial subvention to adult students, a practice now in effect (although in a very inadequate form) via several of the programs included in the Comprehensive Employment and Training Act of 1973, may well be considered more seriously for mid-career-changing adults. The approach incorporated in the programs alluded to previously, which dealt primarily with disadvantaged and poverty groups, could serve as a guide for establishing special provisions for the many middle-aged workers in need of preparation for another job. Such changes must be accompanied by substantial financial support so the person will not be forced into traumatic changes in life-style during this important transition. The prediction here is that several federal programs with such income provisions will be inaugurated well before 1980. The rationale behind this variety of income subsidization will relate to the principle of sabbaticals presently extant in some professions. While these programs may be costly, even as high as 5 percent of the gross national product, the accrued results in terms of personal happiness and continued economic productivity of the enrolled individuals should provide sufficient reason for the government to support a large-scale investment.

The further expansion of vocational delivery efforts through Department of Labor funds can effectively limit the public vocational institutions to those activities in which they are now involved, with new endeavors emanating from the new funding sources. While reviews of past Department of Labor vocational education and training efforts vary from highly positive to highly negative, the fact remains they sought to serve the hard-to-teach and difficult-to-employ individuals, who had been cast aside by the traditional public vocational schools. Furthermore, as stated in Chapter 13, their success in placing these difficult groups has been as high as 50 percent, which must in all fairness be termed impressive. The big question is: Having found relative success in serving the most difficult elements in our society, how many of the other aspects of vocational education will the Department of Labor seek to take from the public vocational school systems? It is predicted that most vocational education and training for adults will eventually fall within the rubric of the Department of Labor thrust. Rapid changes in this direction will likely take place by 1980, as Congress, vocational education leaders, and the American people at large come to accept more fully the idea of subsidized mid-career changing on a continuing and permanent basis for a substantial segment of our working population. Only the Department of Labor and some of its manpower-training and -development programs have had any significant experience with such forms of mid-career vocational preparation in this country. However, some initial lessons may be drawn from similar efforts presently made in several European countries.

The public vocational schools, by virtue of these forecasted trends, will be forced to confine their efforts to the provision of vocational education and training to the younger elements of our society—those who are to be prepared for their initial entry into the occupational world. If this happens, the enrollments and finances of the public vocational schools will quickly become stabilized. This could provide an excellent opportunity for the traditional vocational institutions to indulge in some of the experimental practices associated with the universal college model described previously, although it is unlikely that such practices will become extant immediately. It seems more likely that if the public vocational schools are limited to vocational preparation of the young, they will feel threatened and thus maintain the status quo relative to existing practices and curricula. This will continue a cycle in which they will create even less impact upon the three major governing groups in our society (the politicians, the military, and the industrial-business conglomerates), which in turn will encourage these groups to seek out the Department of Labor for additional vocational services. A perilous time is seen ahead for the forms of vocational education that have traditionally received some federal support through the Department of Health, Education, and Welfare.

The revenue-sharing element of vocational education, which is predicted to continue, will have an additional negative effect upon traditional vocational institutions. These institutions are accustomed to receiving funds within a noncompetitive monopolistic setting. Each year they have received their local-state-federal funding more on the basis of the total allocations made by these governmental legislative bodies than on a basis of institutional and/or vocational program merit. This will not be the basis for support with revenue-sharing funds. The trend toward revenue sharing may continue to the extent where existing bureaus of vocational education in state departments of education will have much less to say about the administration and governance of vocational education and training.

Vocational Education Institutions

Several of the types of schools examined in Part II will likely maintain their present level and kind of involvement with vocational education during the next ten years. This is most true of senior colleges and universities, whose involvement with the vocational education delivery system has been largely limited with regard to the preparation of people for nonprofessional jobs. But these same institutions have performed another important function as trainers of teachers and administrators. While they will probably continue to be the major vehicle for the professional preparation of teachers and administrators, the manner in which the task is performed may undergo changes, some of which could further improve the professional qualities of teachers and administrators in vocational education. Another important function of senior colleges, particularly state universities, will be to conduct an increased amount of basic and applied research relating to vocational education. Although there has been considerable significant research up to now, the findings have not been translated into workable applications and mechanisms for the practitioner-teacher. This difficulty is examined more closely in the research section of this chapter. Considerable ferment may be anticipated during the next decade in the areas of vocational teacher-administrator preparation and research related to vocational education. It is hoped that a number of the changes will move the profession away from the present self-defeating cycle of making certain work experiences prerequisites for vocational teachers and thus systematically segregating certain individuals out of the vocational education profession. This could become one of the controversial issues in the profession during the next decade.

Since the 1950s the state-owned colleges in most places have been undergoing a transition from the teachers' college type of institution to liberal arts-oriented schools. The transition, while a profound one in some colleges, has resulted in barely more than a change of name and rhetoric in others. In many states these colleges are controlled to an excessive degree by their state departments of education, and some of their faculties are becoming restive. Struggles for additional institutional autonomy appear to be on the increase in certain areas. One of the arguments offered for greater autonomy is that autocratic central control breeds and perpetuates mediocrity. In view of the above, it appears likely that (1) in states where control of the colleges is excessive, the legislatures will legislate special boards of control for the state-owned colleges, which will, in turn, be granted virtually full authority for conduct of college affairs, thereby eclipsing control by state departments of education, and (2) with the advent of increased autonomy, many of the state-owned colleges will establish a number of new undergraduate vocational programs. As the state universities increase their emphasis on graduate studies and research aspects of vocational education, the state-owned colleges will be encouraged to become more involved with undergraduate vocational teacher education.

Changes of major magnitude are anticipated in the public community junior colleges and area vocational schools. Although a widespread incorporation of the universal college concept is not expected for another decade or so, decisive movements in that direction, as well as the sharing of faculty, facilities, courses, and programs, are in the offing. A harbinger of this is the establishment of various coordinating boards for educational services in several states. It isn't too much to anticipate that such efforts will become increasingly refined and will select specific target areas, such as vocational education and training. Although there are differences in the institutional philosophies of the community junior colleges and the area vocational-technical schools, these differences are more often complementary than contradictory, so these two types of institutions could be formed into organizational amalgams that provide a rich constellation of vocational programs and associated services for adolescents and young adults. Hybridized institutional amalgams will become commonplace, but although they will be formed in many places, most of them will contain offerings and services unique to those schools and the regions they serve. The major commonality among the many amalgamations will be their desire to join together to provide vocational services for adolescents and adults in what they perceive to be an optimum manner. Once such hybrid institutions are commonplace, and it is expected that they will by 1980, the adoption of the universal college idea will become relatively natural.

The comprehensive high schools in many places are not, at present, meeting the vocational needs of a majority of their students. One suspects that many local school authorities and decision makers agree with this statement, as manifested by rapid growth of the area vocational schools, whose avowed purpose is to provide vocational education. In view of this development, the comprehensive high schools will become increasingly concerned with the academic, nonvocational subjects, and the public will come to rely increasingly on area vocational schools for the provision of vocational programs and services. In other words, the trend to separate vocational education from the general purpose secondary schools and place it in its own institutions will likely continue. The philosophic debate relative to separatism in education will reach a new crescendo, although the overall tune will be the same. During this time some well-designed research into the desirability of separating vocational education and academic education will be conducted. It is hoped that the findings will contribute to knowledge as to optimum institutional environments for vocational students. There is some basis now to suspect that vocational students enjoy greater satisfaction and happiness when they are separated from the total educational system and placed in a special sub-system purposely oriented toward serving vocational students. Such findings, no matter how well tested, will be contested by the general and academic educators with the same old reprobate expressions relative to the importance of "educating the whole person" and the like. But, in spite of these protestations, separatism will continue to expand to a considerable extent, with a resultant reduction in the importance of the comprehensive high school.

The most profound institutional changes in the next decade will probably occur in the private school sector. The number of both secondary and post-secondary private schools will be reduced to the point where their impact upon vocational education will become negligible. In spite of the rhetoric about the possibilities for vocational education and training in private and proprietary schools, most of these institutions are not and will not become financially viable. Even those operated by the large learning corporations, with large sources of money behind them, will abandon most if not all of their efforts in the field of vocational education as the possibility of making these endeavors profitable dwindles. Continued and consistent injection of public funds into vocational education will prohibit the proprietary schools from ever effectively competing with the public sector, resulting in most of them disappearing from the educational scene in the next decade.

People To Be Served

Theoretically, the majority of Americans should have direct contact with vocational education and related services several times during their lives. If public vocational education were universal, which is visualized by some as an idealized form of vocational education, then virtually everyone would encounter some facet of vocational education as early as their secondary school years. The proponents of this position see vocational education as a panacea for several of the present ailments of secondary schools. Most pronounced among these is the frequent complaint that American high schools fail to bring adolescents to terms with the social and occupational realities of the world. Those who advocate universalization of vocational education, and some other educators as well, urge that a study of the nature of occupations be an integral part of the school curriculum in the same way that social studies, American and state histories, and English are. Should this suggestion find acceptance in the American high school, then vocational studies would become an important part of the nation's educational system. While the concept of career development will probably gain increased acceptance in both elementary and high schools, the chances of moving it from the guidance-counseling stage into actual courses and programs dealing with skill development and training on a universal basis appears small.

Why is this so? There is a multitude of factors contributing to the reluctance to universalize vocational education in the secondary schools. But one element that appears to be pervasive throughout our society is a passive but firm unwillingness to embrace the belief that vocational studies are for everyone. Many parents are still hesitant, in spite of the enlightened philosophy of present-day vocational education, to earmark even a small portion of their children's school work for vocational education unless or until it is abundantly clear to them that their offspring is not likely to succeed in entering one of the professions. Stating this phenomenon in a more direct manner: Most parents (and therefore their youngsters) continue to perceive vocational studies as the "other alternative" when they have "given up" on breaking into the ranks of a profession.

In view of this fact, it is likely that in the future secondary school age persons entering vocational studies will be those with demographic and intellective characteristics quite similar to today's secondary school vocational students (i.e., those who are clearly not destined to enter one of the professions). And since a general leveling in the number of high school age persons is expected (because of the downturn in the national birth rate), very little change in the number of youngsters receiving vocational education is projected.

There is a perceptible increase in the number of post-secondary school youngsters enrolling in vocational offerings. The most important public institutions engendering this trend are the community junior colleges and area vocational schools. This fact and some of the important aspects of the movement are noted in several earlier chapters. But the sum total of all the factors involved will result in stabilized enrollment in these two institutions.

Another element to be considered is the increasingly greater role played by the Department of Labor-funded programs in the arena of vocational preparation and job placement. A major change in vocational enrollments will be those having to do with mid-career training and occupational adjustments, and it appears that a substantial amount of this effort will be conducted under the auspices of Department of Labor funding (such as the Comprehensive Employment and Training Act of 1973). If the history of previous vocational training by the Department of Labor is an indication of the future, there will be little involvement of the public vocational schools in these endeavors. But history is not always destined to repeat itself. Should other sources of vocational funding fail to expand or even maintain their present levels, a number of the more entrepreneurial schools will seek Department of Labor funding. It will be interesting to observe what longitudinal effects such external funding will have upon these schools.

Preparation of Teachers and Administrators

A significant change in the preparation of vocational teachers and administrators may be in the offing. Up to this point in time, among the traditional initial requirements for admission into a vocational teacher preparation program has been prior work experience in one's occupational specialty. The rationale, of course, is that such experience is necessary for any teacher to have an understanding of the associated occupation. Occupational competency examinations have emerged as a partial replacement, and in some states as a supplement to on-the-job experience. But in spite of the claims made in some quarters, such demands do not guarantee that the potential teacher has a broad and intelligent knowledge of his occupational area. All too often an individual's work experience, even when it includes many years, is restricted to a specialized sector of an occupation. Such experience is really an encounter with a unique and sometimes provincial and distorting aspect of the occupation. A case may even be made for the claim that a person can acquire a broad view of an entire occupational area without working in it, by being provided with a comprehensive and systematic treatment of that occupation.

Furthermore, imposing the requirement that potential vocational teachers have occupational experience also introduces de facto segregation into the process of vocational teacher selection. Such a practice virtually precludes the migration of originally professionally oriented persons into that teaching area. Many traditional vocational educators apparently feel that any individual who wants to teach in a vocational specialty should spend a predetermined number of years performing that type of work at the subprofessional level. It seems very unreasonable to demand that a person practice a cluster of skills as a craftsman when all the while he intends to become a professional teacher. As long as this criterion is used for vocational teacher selection, the cadre of vocational teachers in certain specialties will consist largely of those having long on-the-job experience. This in effect will restrict teacher entry to only those who come from the ranks of craftsmen, semiprofessionals, and skilled laborers. If we keep in mind the American tradition with regard to occupational and educational egalitarianism, maintaining open access to the profession of vocational teaching is unquestionably attractive, and closing or severely limiting the possibilities of entry for those who haven't passed through the direct experience route is blatantly chauvinistic. This narrowness in the teacher selection process has led to a lack of diversity in the types of people found in many vocational specialty areas. The absence of a sizable fringe element in any profession tends to foster perpetuation of traditional ideas and practices, which in turn tends to establish opposition to new and provocative notions. The demand for many years of work experience also promotes an almost systematic exclusion of younger persons in the profession. This is indeed regrettable because many areas of vocational education are viewed as conservative-traditional and not in tune with the interests of our youngsters.

Another element in the de facto segregation relates to the categorization of vocational specialties along sex lines: Male faculty dominate the trade and industrial, agriculture, technical, and distributive education specialties, while health-related, business, and home economics are female-dominated. An early defense for the existence of these separations by sex was that occupations in actuality are separated in the same manner. But the notion that occupations ought to be segregated along the lines of sex is now soundly rejected. This brings us to a basic difficulty: If new kinds of vocational faculty are to be sought, qualifications for entry into the profession must be changed so they can be admitted. For example, if five years of welding experience is required for certification as a welding teacher and there are very few female welders, it is highly likely that female welding teachers will continue to be virtually nonexistent. Similar examples abound in most of the vocational specialties, as well as in the areas of industrial arts and vocational guidance.

In order to break this relationship between work experience and qualification for vocational teaching, which is a serious dysfunctional element in vocational education, new configurations for teacher preparation must be tried. A number of such attempts will be made. Some of them will be rushed into without careful and intelligent planning, and will be deemed failures. But several new configurations will emerge that will provide viable alternatives to the existing method of teacher selection and preparation. The most successful teacher preparation programs will likely be based upon sound theoretical constructs dealing with symbiotic relationships between what should be transmitted to a vocational student and what is required of a good teacher in the transmitting of knowledge.

While the emergence of new vocational teacher preparation programs will be based on sound teaching-learning theory, these programs will be strongly colored by realities surrounding the vocational student, the teacher, and the world of occupations. The new programs will be initiated by one or several of the larger state universities which endorse the precept that the preparation of vocational teachers ought to be based upon a strong foundation of research findings and not upon the preconceived empirically derived notions of traditional vocational educators.

New approaches will be devised whereby aspiring vocational teachers can develop the occupational skills required for their specialties in laboratory-shop-clinic situations. This will reduce the required experience time to a few months (or a year at the most), in place of the many years now demanded. Furthermore, the contrived arrangements will be vastly superior to internships and actual work experience, because of the manner in which they will be designed and conducted. The occupational area (based on carefully designed, conducted, and evaluated research) will be set up so that the future vocational teacher will have meaning-laden experiences that will introduce him to a synoptic treatment of the significant elements within his occupational area. The development of such a program promises to be one of the most exciting events in the future of vocational teacher education.

Another important happening in vocational education will be the development of a new way of preparing vocational school administrators. In most places the present mode of preparing administrators consists of a series of courses (often mundane), supplemented by internships of questionable worth (in some instances) to the internee and intern-granting institution alike. In one or several places, likely a large state university, new approaches to the preparation of vocational administrators will appear. The idea of focusing the preparation of administrators around course work will persist, but there will be major changes in course content. The new approaches will furnish potential administrators with a sound basis for more adequately understanding and dealing with union–management relationships and financing and funding at all levels (local-regional, state, and federal). In addition, course work will include philosophy of vocational education, theories of leadership and their application, theories of administration and their application, and a thorough study of educational organizations and their place in American society. Such programs will include well-designed and -operated sequences of practical exposures to the major aspects of administration and leadership in vocational education. These practical contacts can replace present internships, which are time-consuming and in some cases provide the internee with a distorted rather than a true, overall view of the administrator's role in a vocational education institution or agency.

The introduction and eventual adoption of a new mode for preparing vocational teachers and administrators promises to be an exciting event in the late 1970s and 1980s. Included in the new configuration will be ways in which new kinds of persons can enter the profession. Furthermore, there will be provision for persons with nonteaching backgrounds to enter into vocational administrator training. Contrary to popular belief, good teachers don't necessarily become good administrators. Many educators, in fact, believe good teachers should be offered special incentives to remain in teaching. The characteristics of a good administrator, for the most part, are sufficiently different from those of a good teacher to consider persons with no experience in teaching, although persons with teaching experience should not be excluded. Certification arrangements in many states are such that one must first become a certified teacher before he or she can even apply for licensure as an administrator. The new kind of program can be the beginning of the knocking down of artificial admission barriers to persons who should qualify for entry into the profession.

Teacher-administrator preparation, always thought to have the potentiality of serving as the vestibule for the modernization and improvement of vocational education, can indeed serve that function.

Competency-Based Teacher Education (CBTE)

Vocational education seems to be destined to suffer through the vicissitudes of trends. A recent fad was career education. Although a number of worthwhile transient educational changes can be attributed to the career education thrust, its permanent positive impact on vocational education is probably minimal. Why? Because in an era of anti-Establishment feelings, career education programs were launched in a hurried (sometimes frantic) manner without sound theoretical and research-based underpinnings. The politically ascribed leadership of the Office of Education, in trying to point the way rather than allowing the profession to chart its own course, helped to rush many vocational educators into ill-conceived schemes under the umbrella of career education. After many millions of dollars (much of it diverted from badly needed vocational funds) and almost uncountable effort-hours spent by numerous vocational educators, the resultant improvement to vocational education may be surprisingly closer to zero than those involved with career education would care to admit. The mediocre results obtained from the career education fiascos have projected an unjust and unfavorable public image of vocational education.

The new fad in the mid-1970s was competency-based teacher education*—and vocational education is fully enmeshed in it. A considerable amount of vocational education monies has been diverted toward massaging this new panacea. A harbinger of the future extent of this movement is that 71 percent of 783 teacher education institutions were involved, in one way or another, with competency-based teacher education in 1973 (Massanari, 1973). In addition, most state bureaus of vocational education indicated some activity related to competency-based certification for vocational teachers.

Like many movements in education, this one has two rationales—one announced and one hidden. The proclaimed rationale emerges out of the vocational teacher educator's long-standing goal of preparing vocational teachers in the best possible way for the task of preparing students to meet the challenges of the world of work. Until the emergence of the CBTE fad, this goal (for secondary vocational teachers in all states and post-secondary vocational teachers in a few states) was pursued through the traditional certification route, which most commonly includes a blend of work experience requirements and the completion of certain teacher education courses. The proponents of the competency-based vocational teacher movement, on the other hand, want to define vocational teacher competencies, examine teachers in terms of these,

---

* Unfortunately, the terms "performance-based teacher education" and "competency-based teacher education" are used interchangeably. The word "performance" is a neutral term which means an act, whereas "competency" can include knowledge and values as well as performance. It is suggested that "competency-based teacher education" be used only to describe the movement, and this term is used here.

and provide licenses on that basis. At first glance, this seems to be an exciting approach, and it has considerable appeal to professionals and laymen alike.

But what is really behind this movement? Some vocational educators believe it is an attempt by its advocates to upset the status quo. Basically, it would provide a chance for persons critical of present vocational teacher education to assert their values and put in their bid for some or all of the control over vocational teacher education. Specifically, it is an attempt to weaken (or destroy) the hegemony of university–state college vocational teacher education departments and state bureaus of vocational education. Reasons for desiring more control over vocational teacher education are at least partially political. The opponents of the status quo would like to realign the existing control system of shared powers between the state colleges-universities and state bureaus so as to include teacher and lay groups. Since the movement has an egalitarian quality to it, which increases its attractiveness, a reformation of the controlling groups in vocational teacher education may result. A clear danger exists in the possibility that control of preservice and in-service vocational teacher education could move completely to other groups to the exclusion of the senior colleges and universities. There are elements in the educational community that desire this outcome. Should this happen, those who feel vocational teachers do not need degrees and course work could replace all such studies with equivalency tests. Then, in the opinion of many vocational educators, vocational education would have been set back several generations. Such a move is analogous to certain groups "overthrowing" the medical schools and establishing their own training mechanisms external to the universities. The resultant dangers to the public as well as the profession are also analogous in that in both cases the result would be inadequately prepared professionals.

Some vocational educators have jumped on the "accountability bandwagon," even though many researchers believe that validating teacher competencies is beyond the state of the art (Barro, 1972). Even those who ascribe some value to the competency-based vocational teacher education concept have reservations about its use as the sole criterion for vocational teacher education (Terry, Thompson, and Evans, 1972). In spite of these caveats, the movement has sufficient attractiveness to appeal to increasingly greater numbers of vocational education leaders.

If this becomes the chief mode of vocational teacher education, the profession may find itself locked into an array of new gimmicky certification mechanisms. Since there is no way to establish validated competencies in vocational education, the competency-based teacher education movement can degenerate into mere negotiating slogans between forces contending for control over vocational education. If this occurs, preservice and in-service vocational teacher education will become politicized and deprofessionalized. It seems too high a price to pay for emancipation from the vocational-teacher-training programs of the universities and state colleges, if indeed such freedom is even deemed desirable.

What alternative is available? Criticisms aimed at the present hegemony of state colleges-universities and state bureaus of vocational education over vocational teacher education must be satisfactorily answered. Also, those critics who support the establishment of competencies in a nondiscriminate manner must be responded to in a forthright manner so that the fallacies of CBTE are brought to light.

First, the immediate brush fire (i.e., "let's all get on the CBTE bandwagon") needs to be extinguished so rational solutions can be sought without undue harassment. The replacement of traditional in-service and preservice vocational teacher education practices with a series of competency-based gimmicks should be blocked. The present system, although known to possess deficiencies and discrepancies, is understood in the profession and does work to some extent. It should be kept intact while the search goes on for something better. Another caution is in order. Attempts to assemble groups of vocational educators to "think out" lists of competencies that can be used as "given competencies" must be seen for what they are. Such tactics have characteristics resembling a "kangaroo court" and can degenerate into exercises in utilizing superficially derived consensual opinions to falsely identify competencies. Such nonresearch-based activity can be sheer quackery and is unworthy of serious consideration.

Second, statewide vocational teacher education committees should be formed with professional representation from teachers' groups, state departments, and the senior colleges-universities. Symbolic representation should also be provided for students, parents, and the business-industrial sectors. The formation of such committees can reduce the hegemony of the senior colleges-universities and state departments. Furthermore, such committees can be the focal point for the demand that changes in vocational teacher education and certification be permitted only when supported by well-designed and -conducted research. This seems to be the least that we must do as professionals (Gillie, 1974).

The statewide committee could be used as a direction setter, and then specific areas of study could be commissioned. For example, vocational teacher education as a totality should be examined through protracted research to see if certain measurable components can be separated out of its value-laden elements. Arbitrary identification of competency areas, followed by attempts to verify them, must be studiously avoided. Such an atomistic approach would fragment vocational education into countless and meaningless bits and pieces forgetting, if one can, that obsolescence of many competencies occurs long before they are validated. Furthermore, students do not learn via progression from one competency to another, as evidenced by refutation of faculty psychology many years ago.

In conclusion, the headlong rush into competency-based vocational teacher education should be stopped. Vocational educators should consider this movement in a professional and research-based manner. Otherwise the traditional vocational teacher education mode may be replaced with a system that will be politicized and deprofessionalized, and CBTE will become yet another bygone fad whose adverse effects remain to haunt the profession for some time.

Women and Minorities in Vocational Education

The inequities imposed upon women and minorities in the professions in general also extend to vocational education. Minorities are underrepresented in all ranks of faculty in every vocational education specialty. The difficulty appears to be further aggravated by a tendency for minorities not to seek to become vocational faculty members and administrators. This may have some relationship to the comparatively low prestige accorded vocational education within the overall field of education, as well as the role vocational education has played in keeping minorities out of the professions in the United States (see Chapter 3). With the possible exception of health-related occupations, the minorities have not, in general, been found in the several vocational areas. Until civil rights legislation was rigorously enforced, it was difficult for certain minorities to find a vocation which they could enter on the same basis as white persons. Therefore, with on-the-job experience being required before one can teach in vocational education, there continues to be a limited source of potential teachers from the minorities. Such a dilemma can be solved in a most expeditious manner by waiving present certification requirements in favor of others which would remove the barrier against minorities while still maintaining some semblance of competency demands. As indicated earlier, this can be accomplished by utilization of carefully planned, conducted, observed, and evaluated laboratory-shop-clinic experiences that would preclude the need for work experience. Even this approach, if implemented intelligently, would require several years of careful examination before being introduced into a formal teacher preparation curriculum.

Inequities are also imposed upon women faculty in vocational education. The tendency to exclude women in many cases and to provide them with lower salaries, less interesting teaching assignments, and chorelike responsibilities continues in many places. Such practices ultimately work against the welfare of all concerned, both men and women. Individual fulfillment comes about only when there is a surplus of pleasure over pain. This doctrine, if it is to work in vocational education, means that male and female faculty members must live amicably together. If this is to happen, large quantities of respect, consideration, and understanding must be introduced into the system. It will not occur by happenstance, but only through planned policies in which true equality of male and female status and roles is demanded, inaugurated, enforced, and perpetuated.

Even our political forefathers, considered heroes in many respects, were not enlightened as to the equality of women. It was a rare individual in those times who managed to perceive the inherent injustice imposed upon women. One such individual was Mary Wollstonecraft:

> . . . two years before the French revolution Mary Wollstonecraft published *Thoughts on the Education of Daughters,* in which she argued that a woman should be entitled to the same education as that of a man—far beyond anything Rousseau claimed in *Emile.* [Jones, 1974, p. 48]

Not until the late 1960s was there a true movement toward equalization of rights and opportunities for women. Because of stronger enforcement of "affirmative action," women's groups, and various civil suits introduced by a number of aggrieved individuals, private groups, and the federal government, greater equalization is literally "being forced down the throats" of many educational institutions. Many neared the panic stage, began to experience some pangs of guilt, and then began to aggressively recruit women as students and for faculty and administration positions. Many educators believe that true equality can begin only when the number of women in these places is in proportion to their number in society at large—which means about 50 percent in all occupational areas. Measures need to be taken to encourage more males to move into the health, business, and home economics programs, and similar actions should be taken to encourage entry of a massive number of women in the vocational fields of agriculture, trade and industrial, technical, and distributive education until numerical balances are achieved. After such an achievement, equality of salaries, working conditions, assignments, actual jobs, etc., will be easier to obtain.

Many educators believe that true equality of sexes in vocational education will not be achieved for many years, although substantial advances will be made. We have yet to learn how to deal with males feeling extremely threatened by fellow female professionals, a feeling that probably has much to do with the emphasis on male chauvinism during the childhood years of males over thirty. The situation will gradually improve as males with true feelings of equality for women come into vocational education—which may not happen until well after 1980. Those who must live with enforced equality, against their beliefs, may tolerate the situation on a superficial level while privately wishing for the return of the time when male-dominated vocational education was unquestioned. In the meantime many younger persons with fewer male chauvinist feelings to overcome will enter vocational education and bring with them a true acceptance of the equal status of women in vocational education. Women still have a difficult time ahead of them in vocational education, and it is their daughters who will most likely begin to reap the benefits of present thrusts in this direction.

Governance Patterns

Several countervailing forces appear to be at work relative to location of governance centers for vocational schools and colleges. First, there is a move in some places to change the locus of governance from the local community to a regional station from which the vocational educational services for several towns or school districts can be administered. This trend toward centralization of governance is accompanied by another significant change. The state departments (or bureaus) of vocational education (or their equivalent structures) are, in many states, delegating much of their administrative activities to these newly emerging regional stations. A useful descriptive term for these new groupings is "intermediate units," since they are, in fact, between the local and state administrative levels in vocational education. This administrative mode has been adopted in many states, and others are seriously considering the feasibility of doing the same. When such a mechanism is inaugurated, its initial role is often limited to the more routine, relatively nondecision-making tasks associated with the administration of vocational education. Its role is then gradually expanded until the transition is complete. The advantages of the intermediate unit are (1) a better chance of minimizing the adverse effects of provincialism, which is most likely to emerge from small local units and (2) a reduction in the disadvantages associated with long-distance control of vocational schools by the state bureau, since the previously held state level responsibilities are delegated to the intermediate units.

The inauguration of this type of governance center, which could become identical to the prime sponsor jurisdictions, could result in a corresponding reduction in administrative staffing at both the local and state levels. One can suspect that such economies are likely to be slow to come by, however, since reducing staff in vocational education, like most other public services, is difficult to implement (except by not replacing persons who leave) because of resistance in the organizations. Eventually, over a period of five years or so after the intermediate unit has been established, there will likely be reductions in the number of persons associated with the administration of vocational education at both local and state levels.

A major impellent for establishing intermediate administrative units is the emerging change in revenue acquisition. Local real estate taxation will become increasingly less important as a source of funds for all educational services. Statewide income taxes, or some combination of income, sales, and real estate taxation imposed at the state level, will likely become the major source of funds for all public services on a statewide basis. As this occurs on a widespread basis, formulas will be devised for determining the amount of appropriations to be allocated back to each governance unit. The present formula used for public school state funding may serve as a guide. The allotments will probably contain major commitments in certain categories plus some discretionary monies. The latter would provide governance flexibility for the intermediate units.

Along with state funds there will be federal monies that can be used for vocational education, from both the Department of Labor and the Department of Health, Education, and Welfare sources. The Department of Labor funds, for the most part, probably will bypass state level government structures and filter into the intermediate units via prime sponsors. This can ultimately reduce the influence of state bureaus of vocational education upon the regional units, especially if the intermediate units and prime sponsors should merge and strive to provide vocational services in that manner. Any regional district which elects to furnish the kinds of vocational services deemed fundable by the Department of Labor appropriations (such as the Comprehensive Employment and Training Act of 1973) can solicit such funds and not be accountable to the state bureau of vocational education for the regional district's operation. This could weaken state bureaus of vocational education and local boards of vocational education, as authority moves from them to the prime sponsor and federal levels. In view of the vicissitudes of federal funding since 1970 or so, heavy dependence upon this source of revenue for vocational education could introduce additional elements of instability into vocational education, unless special assurance of continued funding at some minimum level is provided.

Predicted here is that HEW funds, with the requirement that matching funds be provided by the states, will continue with no major changes. This aspect of funding will remain as the chief mechanism for maintenance of state control, although even much of this control will gradually be delegated to the regional levels. Coordination between sources of funding may result in the funds being used to supplement the Comprehensive Employment and Training Act funds, with eventual merging of all finances. While the state and federal funds take shape in this manner, a movement toward substantial reductions in the direct use of local taxation for vocational education is anticipated. Local taxation, for the most part, will be replaced with statewide levies of the varieties described earlier. As one can suspect, the changes in funding sources will result in alterations in governance patterns. Those who control the funds do indeed control the overall operation.

Regional units will probably exist in all states at the secondary level of vocational education before 1980. But vocational education at the post-secondary level is more complex, and several patterns may emerge. Some states may elect to separate post-secondary vocational education from other higher education institutions. In some other states the post-secondary and secondary vocational elements will be blended together and be governed by regional units. Certain states may elect to keep post-secondary vocational education structurally distinct from secondary vocational education, thereby establishing a dichotomy by level within the state's vocational education system. Some geographic areas may keep vocational education within the framework of education in general. In places where this happens, the secondary vocational efforts will be found in comprehensive high schools, and the post-secondary thrust will remain within the area vocational schools, community colleges, or senior colleges. The last pattern is likely to be the form adopted by most states.

What are the implications of this last approach, in light of the forms of funding expected? In short, it means that vocational education financing will become even more of a hodgepodge affair than it was in the early 1970s. The secondary schools, and in some cases the area vocational schools, will obtain their financing from and be governed by the intermediate units. In some places the area vocational schools are or will become actively involved with post-secondary as well as secondary vocational education. When this occurs, there is a strong likelihood that the area vocational schools will establish a governance structure of their own with some measure of state level control, even though their services will be on a regional basis. Some educators believe the community colleges will become more like the area vocational schools and increasingly less like the senior colleges and universities in terms of curricula, clientele, and professional staff. The funding for community junior colleges will probably continue to be partially based on student tuition assessment, with the remainder being obtained from a regional board of trustees which is provided with funds from several sources, including the state legislature. Also, the community junior colleges (and some area vocational schools) will receive additional special federal funds for projects from both the Department of Labor and HEW sources. These "soft money" activities will in some cases be special attempts at trying new things (such as new instructional modes and innovative curriculum combinations). It is entirely possible, and highly probable in some states, that funding strategies will force increased coordination and cooperation upon area vocational schools and community junior colleges. If this happens, the universal college alluded to in this book will become closer to fruition.

Vocational education funding for senior colleges and universities will likely not change substantially from what is now found in most states. There will be increased emphasis on bachelor degree programs, and fewer enrollees will be sought for associate degree vocational curricula, since they will become the acknowledged hallmark of community colleges and area vocational schools. One can expect some continuing tension between the area vocational schools and community junior colleges, as they increasingly seek funds to perform similar or identical services. The halcyon period in the relationships between these two institutions will not be upon us until well into the 1980s. The senior colleges and community junior colleges, on the other hand, have for the most part achieved peaceful relationships in the mid 1970s, now that the educational turf of each has been mapped out and is being respected by the other.

Research in Vocational Education

Serious efforts to support research in vocational education originated with a separate title (C) under the Vocational Education Act of 1963 (PL 88-210). The subvention for such efforts has been continued in a somewhat fluctuating and waivering manner since then. The initial investment in vocational education research produced mixed results, and the perceptions of the overall value of research completed to date are also mixed. Several of the difficulties associated with funding research in vocational education are similar to the problems found in educational research in general.

The major difficulty has to do with impatience. Many of the authorities who exercise some control over research funds are not research-oriented, and they possess an inadequate understanding of the nature and purpose of vocational education research. Although it is undesirable to stereotype such individuals, it is common knowledge that one of the uppermost thoughts such persons have in mind is an early and even dramatic "payoff" for all research funding. For example, there was considerable naïve thinking along the lines that a one- or two-year research project dealing with the identification and matching of student characteristics with vocational curricula would once and for all establish the magic combination(s) that would lead students to successfully completing their programs. When such studies showed that many of the characteristics, such as student motivation, were largely unquantifiable and the studies' conclusions seemed to hedge on providing concrete step-by-step procedures, some disappointment and concern was expressed. In response to this concern, some of the nonresearch-oriented authorities considered the entire effort a waste of public funds and time. The notion that research is of limited usefulness has been common in vocational education, perhaps because vocational educators, who in general tend to be practically oriented, have been seeking quick and practical solutions to sundry kinds of problems through research. Once in a while a research effort does discover something that can be virtually plugged into the vocational effort with obvious and immediate effects. But such experiences are indeed rare, as they are in most educational research. Unfortunately, a considerable portion of the research effort has been, and will likely continue to be, devoted to investigating and testing things that turn out to be of marginal or no significance to vocational education. But many of these investigations need to be conducted so that assessments can be made upon the basis of actual documentation rather than suspicions and hunches. In spite of such a need, however, it is often difficult to convince legislators and nonresearch-oriented persons in governance positions that learning about the nonworkability of a concept is important. One remedy for this difficulty is to convey the basic purpose of vocational education research (i.e., to investigate various matters in vocational education to ascertain their relationships and utility to the profession and its clients) to those persons concerned with the effort—especially legislators, state level vocational leaders, and vocational teachers in general. Admittedly, this is a difficult task—too formidable to be completely achieved in the next decade. Therefore, a practical approach needs to be substituted for the ideal remedy.

If vocational education research is to be supported at all, it should probably concentrate on the applied kinds of efforts aimed at alleviating problems of deep concern to the profession. What kinds of research efforts would these be? Special attention needs to be focused on curriculum development and modernization, demonstration programs, programs for incorporating research findings into the curricula and other school activities, leadership development, student placement, student follow-up, and preservice and in-service teacher education.

Research directed toward these areas will, in the opinion of some vocational educators, receive some support from both state and federal funds, particularly those monies that originate in the Department of Health, Education, and Welfare and are matched by state funds. It is hoped that increased attention will be paid to the qualifications of the persons seeking these funds. A considerable amount of past research in education in general and in vocational education has been poorly conceived, of inferior design, and conducted amateurishly. Research endeavors initiated under such adverse conditions are clearly destined to produce nothing more than reports filled with educational jargon devoid of anything meaningful or useful to anyone. Ironically, such reports are often brought to the attention of persons influential in determining research funding as examples of how such monies are wasted. This has apparently occurred frequently at the national level and may have contributed to the reduction in new research funds since the onset of the Vocational Education Act of 1963. One must realize that vocational education research funds have been exploited by some educational entrepreneurs, just as funds for research in other professions are exploited. But it can be safely predicted that charlatanism in funded vocational education research will become less common as more sophisticated and effective evaluation of research proposals becomes a standard practice.

The real values of vocational education research can be explained to legislative and educational leaders who make funding decisions in such a way that they understand the importance of inquiry into the profession and its clients. Furthermore, only high quality research efforts should be supported, and noncompetitive funding to special groups (such as national research centers) must be prohibited. The results of each vocational research project should be evaluated upon completion, and an overall review of the impact of research upon vocational education should be made at least once every two years. It is believed that such measures will be taken, and that vocational educators who accept the value of research will even offer to establish mechanisms for evaluating research efforts in such a manner.

Applied research will receive financial support. The most important applied research will be conducted by the colleges and universities, especially the large state universities. Land-grant colleges and universities will increasingly perceive applied research in vocational education as a normal extension of the land-grant tradition inaugurated with the Morrill Act of 1862, and such research may well become a priority activity for many of them. In such institutions the focal point for the research efforts will be those departments in colleges of education where vocational teacher education and vocational administration training are provided.

Research will become increasingly the cutting edge of vocational education and will remain in that favorable position well into the future. Research will be the source for new concepts, ideas, techniques, and systems, for an improved delivery of vocational education services at all levels and for all segments of American society. Vocational education research will become an increasingly viable element in the profession, and will be a catalyst for the achievement of increased excellence in vocational education.

Competency-Based Vocational Education

Competency-based teaching, like its counterpart in teacher training, is making inroads into vocational education and may do more harm than good to the profession in general. The concept embraces the idea of identifying desired competencies, designing a program to pursue their achievement, and making measurements to assess the extent to which they are achieved. There are several serious deficiencies inherent in the concept, particularly the following:

1. The desired competencies in various vocational specialties cannot, for the most part, be validated as competencies needed in a particular occupational area, and it is foolhardy and unfair to students and faculty to make assessments on the basis of unvalidated competencies. Vocational education has no prophet to decree those competencies required in any area of vocational education (Gillie, 1974).

2. Misidentified competencies may be used as a mechanism to break away from the present institutional type of vocational education. In other words, competency-based vocational education provides a basis by which individuals can learn to "beat the test" and in the process lose out in becoming vocationally educated.

3. Competency-based vocational education deprives teaching of its art form, and forces faculty to teach for specific competencies and likewise coerces students to learn in the same way. Such teaching is mechanical and robotlike, and results in uninterested teachers and bored students. Good teaching leads to individual learning, which is a form of genial anarchy. This must be so, in the opinion of some educators, if individuals are indeed different from one another. Competency-based teaching runs counter to this most fundamental human requirement.

4. Teachers are afraid of competency-based instruction. They fear it will be used as an evaluation mechanism against them without regard for the myriad factors that influence the extent to which a student learns.

The acquiescence of vocational teachers and administrators in competency-based vocational education is not a harbinger of its future success but symptomatic of the outward passivity of the professionals. The fundamental flaws within the constructs of competency-based teaching will eventually bring about its abandonment, and it will go the way of previous fads that have cycled their way through the profession. However, some long-lasting debilitating scars will be inflicted upon the profession. The extent of these damages can be assessed only after the fad's incursion has been experienced, blunted, and eventually deflected.

Vocational Education for Retirees

The traditional view of vocational education is that it prepares persons for entry into the world of work. But a newer concept of vocational education is on the scene. It is perceived by some as a mechanism for providing people with assorted skills, ranging from purely manipulative to cognitive, which they seek in the interest of personal and/or occupational fulfillment. This modern view is sufficiently broad to include the development of skills for the needs and interests of two important groups of persons ignored by traditional vocational education: retirees and hobbyists. This section proposes that vocational education can be made to serve these groups along with its traditional constituents.

Several trends relative to worker retirement point to the possibility of changes in some aspects of the vocational education delivery system. The first factor that can trigger these changes is the trend in most occupations toward early retirement (Barfield, 1972). Another major factor deals with changing perceptions of what people want to do after retirement (Sheppard, 1971). Many retirees consider retirement an opportunity to pursue another occupation, which is contrary to the traditional view of retirement as the time one enters a life of idleness. In many cases the retiree contemplates a job he had some interest in over a period of time but hesitated to switch to at an earlier point in his working career because of the inconveniences and difficulties such a switch would have entailed.

At an earlier period in our history, sixty-five was considered the usual age for entering retirement (and still is in many businesses and industries). (See Mathiasen, 1953b, for details on compulsory retirement.) This was encouraged by parameters established by the national Social Security system as well as by many other retirement schemes. In recent years various alterations in retirement plans have been offered, many of which were initiated in several of the more liberal state, city, and federal retirement systems. Even the national Social Security system, albeit at its own slow pace, is moving in the direction of an earlier retirement age. Many present retirement systems already provide their recipients the option of retirement (with initiation of retirement income) at age sixty or fifty-five. Public sentiment is pushing for changes in the direction of still earlier retirement. This continuing trend is presaged by the military, where one can leave the service with retirement income after twenty years of service, regardless of one's age at the time of separation. Another encouraging sign is the consideration of legislation which will force all retirement systems to provide workers with immediate or early vesting in the retirement system.

Although opportunities for early retirement are increasing, life expectancy of the average worker has remained essentially the same over the past decades. Thus earlier retirement creates longer periods of retirement. The idea of being "put out to pasture," so to speak, is unappealing and even threatening to many Americans. Furthermore, gerontologists are finding that the changeover to a life of leisure and often enforced idleness, after many years of working, produces serious emotional trauma and early death for many older citizens. It is well known that retirement is not of equal benefit to all who indulge in it. The form and mode of a person's retirement should be more closely tailored to his desires, health, and environmental circumstances. Specialists concerned with gerontology are continuing to conduct research into the effects of enforced idleness (and other traditional retirement effects) upon the mental health and life expectancy of retirees (see Mathiasen, 1953a). The findings are expected to verify further that one of the essential ingredients for a happy and therefore lengthy after-retirement life is a continuation of activities meaningful to the retiree. On the basis of this assumption, it is predicted that vocational education will play an important role in the endeavors of future retirees.

If decisions to retire continue to be made on the basis of the person's chronological age and/or length of employment (and poor health in some cases), then delivery systems for retirees can be provided by vocational education. An increasing number of retirees, because they are leaving their career at earlier ages and because improved medical services will enable them to remain physically and mentally active for a greater number of years, will prepare for new post-retirement occupations. Their actions could be described as late career changes or first post-retirement changes. Because retirement benefits meet some of their financial needs, many will enroll in occupational-training programs for personal interest reasons alone, although some of the jobs they will prepare for offer low remuneration (Fine, 1970). Certain more adventuresome individuals will seize upon this transition in their lives as an intriguing opportunity to pursue an occupation and life-style completely different from their earlier one (Fine, 1970). A retired teacher, for example, may, after the appropriate training, enter into a new career as manager of a franchise restaurant. In many instances, particularly with professionals and high level paraprofessionals, their new post-retirement career may be considerably lower in status than their pre-retirement employment. After devoting several decades to an earlier career, many retirees will welcome the opportunity to enter another occupation in which they have had a long-term interest, in spite of its comparatively lower prestige. This can be of great societal value, since such retirees may prove to be an excellent source of manpower for many of the low status difficult-to-fill jobs. Such a trend, therefore, can be a double bonanza in that benefits are accrued by the individual retiree and by society at large (Adams, 1969).

If the public's views of retirement continue to become increasingly enlightened, such a movement will indeed become a sizable one. Some inducements may be needed to encourage certain businesses and industries to participate in this liberalizing trend during the next few years, but it should become widely accepted by 1980. Skilled, service, and clerical-sales occupations will most likely experience the major influx of these post-treatment retrained individuals in the years ahead if past trends continue (Sheppard, 1971).

The role of vocational education in all of this will be to provide special programs designed to prepare retirees for occupations they deem desirable and for jobs which are on hand. In many places a considerable amount of "selling" to business and industry needs to be done to overcome the myths that persons over sixty are of little occupational utility to society. State and federal interventions in the form of legislation, tax concessions, etc., may be needed to assist in the initiation of the movement, but the chances of such intervention occurring appear good. The vocational schools throughout the nation may become involved in the training and education of thousands of retirees each year, as will Department of Labor-supported efforts via the Comprehensive Employment and Training Act of 1973 and subsequent similar legislation. Together these efforts will add another important dimension to the role of vocational education in our society. Such a movement may account for as much as 20 percent of the vocational schools' efforts in 1980 and thereafter.

Another retirement-related factor that will have an effect upon vocational schools has to do with avocations, hobbies, and possible self-improvement interests. Retirees will be assisted in pursuing these interests through short-term special courses, many of which will be organized spontaneously when a group of persons expresses an interest in a particular endeavor. Such assistance will become increasingly commonplace, and is considered in detail in the following section.

Programs devoted to retirees will also affect vocational schools' efforts in the future in that greater numbers of persons will have to be prepared to provide services to retirees, both in the institutions where some of them will live and in the other sundry activities engaged in by retirees.

The role of vocational education in serving retirees is perceived as one of the growth areas in the profession. As the number of young persons entering school levels off and then tapers off, retirees as a group will continue to grow; they will become an expanding element in vocational education until well into the next century. The idea of continuing to work beyond one's first retirement is an attractive one from medical, social, financial, and personal points of view—four excellent reasons for believing that it should become a common phenomenon in the future.

Vocational Education for Leisure—Hobbies

Another variety of training and education not usually considered a part of vocational education is the development of skills for hobbies and leisure-related activities. The term "leisure" is used to refer to the portion of an individual's life in which he is free from an occupation-for-payment. The term "hobby" is used to indicate activities that an individual pursues for self-fulfillment and pleasure, although the activities may be an occupation-for-payment for others. These definitions point to the difficulty in classifying the education and training of persons for hobbies or other leisure-time purposes as components in vocational education. While this may appear to be merely a matter of semantics, it is important because ultimately the interpretation of this matter becomes the major basis for deciding whether or not to include such training within the overall framework of vocational education.

The similarities between occupations and hobbies (and many other leisure-time activities) are seen in the skills required for them. For example, the basic skills required in ceramics are the same, whether it be for hobby or wage-earning purposes. The same is true of virtually every hobby or leisure-time activity. One person's vocation is another person's hobby. Skill development for hobbyist endeavors, therefore, can be quite similar to preparing persons to enter occupations where the same skills are practiced.

But there are important differences as well. The hobbyist is usually an adult already committed to an occupation, and his or her interest in the matter lies in the realm of self-enrichment and fulfillment. His mental attitude, therefore, toward acquisition of the necessary skills can be significantly different from that of an individual who is preparing for job entry. This implies that hobbyists will seek to derive greater personal enjoyment from the processes associated with the developing of the skills than the potential worker will, although this is not always true. When a person engages in an activity for its intrinsic value, his attitude regarding that activity is generally different from that of the potential worker (who perceives the skill as a necessary ingredient in his repertoire of vocational skills). This ties in with the overall concept of "work" held by many individuals (especially those in the paraprofessions and skilled occupations). That is, the job is perceived chiefly as a vehicle to provide financial sustenance, and personal fulfillment is sought in activities that are not related to the job (see Kreps, 1972).

While many seek out leisure-time activities in search of satisfaction they do not find in their occupation, others take up hobbies for other reasons. Many individuals who apparently enjoy their work and derive feelings of accomplishment and self-satisfaction from it still find a strong need for diversity in their lives, and they seek to obtain this diversity through a hobby. It is commonly accepted that all persons need to engage in a variety of activities in order to enjoy a full and interesting life. The most fortunate individual is the one who derives enjoyment both on the job and in leisure-time activities, and the least fortunate misses out on both.

In addition to providing a vehicle for self-fulfillment, many hobbies and leisure-time activities are perceived by some individuals as very important mechanisms for bringing families, couples, clusters of families, and other people together in purposeful activities. It is well known that activities that bring couples and families into closer relationships can have profound effects upon the participants. Acceptance of this belief in our society is evident from the consistent expenditure of funds on promoting and conducting such activities. Governmental funding at local, state, and federal levels for development and maintenance of sundry recreational facilities is a clear manifestation of our belief in the importance of hobbies and other leisure-time activities.

Because of the tendency to neatly categorize (or stereotype) various endeavors, the development of skills associated with hobbies and other leisure-related activities has not been tied in with the vocational education delivery system in most places, and remains in a classification of its own. This has resulted in a weakening of such offerings in many cases. The teaching of skills for hobby–leisure-time activities is unquestionably related to vocational preparation, but with an important difference in the conduct of the classroom, laboratory, and shop activities. While the personal intrinsic values and the societal importance of a cluster of skills needs to be emphasized to a group of neophyte workers (particularly adolescents and young adults), the emphasis should be different for potential hobbyists. A pursuer of leisure-time enjoyment of certain skills needs to develop those skills within the context of his intended use of them, not within the larger framework of the world of work. The most important implication derivable from this difference is the need for a special breed of vocational teachers for hobbyists. Recognition of this difference may well have had something to do with the separation of such special offerings from the vocational education delivery system in many communities.

Vocational education is in a position to serve this very significant societal need. In order to do so most effectively, vocational faculty will need to be trained in approaching skill development from the viewpoint of a hobbyist. Such a task is not a particularly monumental one. The fundamental philosophy of the industrial arts component of the profession embraces many of the ideas suggested here, and members of the industrial arts faculty could be prepared with relatively small adjustments in modern industrial arts teacher-training programs.

Interest in the development of skills for the pursuit of hobbies and other leisure-time activities will likely increase, particularly as the length of the average workweek decreases and the value of out-of-work activities increases. With some intelligent planning, vocational education can absorb this important function to the benefit of all concerned. It may become one of the most significant growth areas in vocational education in the next decade.

Coordination of Vocational Education and Other Elements in Education

The idea of coordinating various components of education into a coherent, minimally competitive, nonduplicative system of education for a region and in some cases an entire state has gained favorable attention since the 1960s. The fundamental idea behind coordination of educational services is to place the elements within the system so as to maximize the opportunities for persons to use these services, and to promote economies in the overall education delivery system. In order for this to happen, coordination must be exercised between each level and every segment of the system. Effective coordination could enhance the quality of vocational education and expand the services it makes available. Duplicative programs in the same region, for example, could easily be avoided at the very onset by a viable coordination council. Such a council would play a considerable part in decisions to inaugurate new and drop old programs, and would thus exercise important long-range control over regional or statewide vocational education.

Vocational education coordination councils are becoming commonplace in the more populated areas, where there are many institutions offering diverse vocational services. Although coordination councils will not eliminate all the bickering for the establishment of vocational education turfs, they do inhibit such acrimonious action and encourage all concerned to accept the necessity of their giving up some of their own intentions in the interest of maximizing vocational services for the public. Also, successful coordinative experiences can encourage institutions to enter into truly partnerlike efforts to provide a more complete array of vocational services.

In some places coordination of all educational efforts has been mandated by regional and state legislation. Several advantages and dangers are inherent in this movement. The advantages include economy and increased diversity of programs. A major disadvantage, always present in any coordinative endeavor, is the surrendering of some degree of institutional autonomy in the interest of an improved overall system of education. A very real danger exists for vocational education in this regard. While the reduction of institutional autonomy is indeed necessary for such efforts to be successful, it is essential that vocational components within the overall system retain their integrity and not be diluted with sundry general education offerings. A tendency for this to occur has been observed in some places, especially in community junior colleges, where serious attempts to provide both pre-professional and vocational programs are made. Frequently general education courses (in the areas of social sciences, English, communications, and humanities) are forced into the requirements for vocational as well as pre-professional students. The essence of the argument favoring this approach is that a minimum level of comprehension and achievement in these general education areas should be required of all students. As a result of attempts to enforce this approach in the secondary schools and community junior colleges, vocational students have been required to take general education courses that are frequently meaningless to them, causing some of them to drop out of school. The surest way to minimize interference of this nature from educators who have little understanding of the nature of vocational education is to guarantee that each institution included in the coordination effort have complete internal program integrity. This can be guaranteed by granting vocational administrators and faculty full authority to establish complete curriculum content with minimal outside interference. The prerogative of the coordination council would lie in making decisions relative to initiating and discontinuing programs. The specifics within each vocational program would be an internal matter established by qualified vocational educators. In this manner an important element of self-governance is retained in the overall coordination effort.

Relations between Vocational Education and the Power Groups

As was pointed out earlier, the success of vocational educators in obtaining recognition and funding for their intended endeavors has much to do with the quality of the relationships between the profession and the power groups. The three generic power groups are the business-industrial conglomerates, the military-national defense establishment, and the political establishment. The possible relationships between each and their impact upon vocational education are considered in the following paragraphs.

Since the industrial revolution began in the United States in the 1800s, the business-industrial conglomerates have had considerable influence upon the national and state level decision makers, who in turn affect the extent to which vocational education receives public funds. These relationships exist at all levels and throughout the nation.

On the local level the president or director of a vocational school often solicits assistance from community business and industrial leaders in obtaining funds, equipment, job placement of graduates, and in bringing pressure to bear on community-regional government bodies for increased financial support for vocational education and for that institution. Such tactics, when conducted within the context of advisory councils, task forces, etc., are viewed as legitimate strategies for obtaining support for vocational programs, since education at the local level does contain a political component. In many instances local business-industrial leaders serve as members of such special groups with the tacit (and even openly expressed) intention of rendering this kind of support for the institution when the need arises.

Similar strategies are utilized at the state level, with such groups providing advisory services to vocational education bureaus or departments at the state government level. The state advisory council for vocational education, which received funding for its operation under the aegis of the Vocational Education Amendments of 1968, is among the most notable of such groups. Other state level councils have been formed from time to time in many places with the intention of bringing pressure to bear upon state legislatures. Such groups are ostensibly formed by and consist of laymen interested in maintaining and improving the posture of vocational education in that state. Closer examination of the interworkings within such groups, however, often discloses that their establishment and maintenance are closely related to the efforts of one or more influential professional vocational educators. Such activities are not completely clandestine in nature, but the association between professional vocational educators and the business-industrial leaders in such groups is not purposely publicized. These two sectors often have tacit agreements relative to the nature of the demands and pressures to be applied on the state legislature. When such groups appear before the legislature as constituents of the state's business-industrial elements, they can sometimes exert considerable influence upon lawmakers (an example of one power group interacting with a second one, resulting in increased funding for vocational education).

At the federal level the business-industrial associations that represent the various national conglomerates (such as the National Association of Manufacturers) can have an impact on federal legislation dealing with vocational education. While this has occurred to some extent in the past, the tactic has been largely undeveloped up to now. Perhaps efforts at the national level have been relatively low key because vocational education is administered at the state-regional-local levels. There are no bureaus or departments of vocational education at the federal level, other than those housed within the bureaucracies of the Department of Health, Education, and Welfare and the Department of Labor. While these federally established bureaus do have some limited impact on what goes on in vocational education, their actual responsibility has to do with the management and administration of funds appropriated by Congress. The leadership here needs to be exercised when such appropriation bills are being drafted and again when they are introduced to the Congress. When pressure from the business-industrial community has been brought to bear in behalf of those who support a Department of Labor effort, such as the Comprehensive Employment Training Act of 1973 (PL 93-203), that effort has been successful. Some vocational educators feel that the prospects of obtaining such support for future financing of HEW vocational endeavors (such as updating the Vocational Education Amendments of 1968) are not promising.

The Military Establishment can also assist in the support of vocational education. Since World War II support of the national defense establishment has accounted for a substantial percentage of the gross national product. A considerable portion of the military's efforts has to do with training persons for sundry skills, trades, and occupations utilized in the military. The military organizations originally conducted many of these training efforts as a matter of expediency—public institutions at that time were not able or willing to provide the courses and programs necessary to prepare persons for various military-related activities. Modern military complexes require as many as twenty or more support personnel for every individual specifically trained for combat. Much of the training required for support persons could be provided by the public sector of vocational education. The military schools have trained millions of individuals for hundreds of jobs. Authorities on military job preparation indicate that these efforts have been very effective (i.e., in terms of training an individual for a specific military task). But one can question whether society ought to be satisfied with the achievements of only these objectives. Would it be better for everyone concerned if the individual received vocational preparation of a broader scope? While there are those who will strongly disagree, it seems that long-range objectives ought to be given substantial consideration in preparing people for vocations, even in the military (except in unusual periods of national emergency of course). But the military establishment is sufficiently strong, in terms of national leadership as well as influence upon the federal lawmakers, to pretty much control its own future in these matters. The training mechanisms within the military are very elaborate, and the tradition of training most of its own subprofessional personnel is so strong that attempts to move substantial portions of that training to nonmilitary public institutions would likely be strongly opposed. Support from the military establishment for increased public funding of vocational education, especially for relieving the military of its own vocational training efforts, seems improbable at this time.

The political establishment is also in a position to aid vocational education. A curious dilemma exists in that educators have traditionally been expected to "stay out of politics," while simultaneously being under the influence of politicians in terms of funding. This stance has been modified in recent years, and there are several approaches that vocational educators can use to deal with politicians. One of these is the indirect one, via the business-industrial groups, just described. Although relatively ineffective, another approach is a formal treatment of vocational education concerns via legislative hearings and similar activities. It is a rare event, at either the state or local level, when a professional vocational educator is in a position to assist in the making of funding decisions. The paradox of not permitting public professionals to make direct overtures to legislative bodies when they are indeed the ones who should be guiding those bodies toward legislation which would provide optimal vocational services, apparently cannot be reconciled. A partial response to this difficulty, in addition to bringing vocational education needs to the attention of the lawmakers via business-industrial pressure groups, is the use of professional associations, which is discussed in the following section.

Professional Vocational Education Associations

There are four types of vocational education professional associations. First are associations that are differentiated by type of institution. The American Association of Community and Junior Colleges and the Technical Institute Division of the American Society for Engineering Education are examples. Second are those that are differentiated according to vocational specialty, such as the American Technical Education Association and the American Association of Home Economics Teachers. There are kindred associations for the agricultural, distributive education, health, business, guidance, and industrial areas. Third are the associations that relate to the professional vocational educator's overall job functions, such as those that are oriented toward administration, curricula, or research. These associations draw upon certain specialized elements within the field of vocational education. These three types of associations lack sufficient commonality to attract vocational educators from every sector of the profession.

The fourth type includes the one professional organization that tends to have some commonality with most vocational educators—the American Vocational Association (AVA). This is a national group with a governance structure that includes representation from the major specialties of the profession and geographic regions of the nation. AVA embraces those activities and services aimed at improvement of the profession of vocational education. One of its major impacts over the years has been upon federal legislation, most particularly the Vocational Education Act of 1963 and its subsequent law, the Vocational Education Amendments of 1968. The reader may recall that these public laws have been the chief sources of federal funds for the public school component of vocational education.

Because vocational education is administered at regional and state levels, there is no federal administrative structure for vocational education, and this is likely to remain the situation well into the future, unless there is an unexpected revolutionary change in the administration of public education. Professional vocational educators are therefore limited in the ways they can influence federal lawmakers. The traditional letter-writing campaigns are difficult to get into motion and not very effective as a whole. A strong (i.e., unified) professional association is one of the few vehicles through which the profession can present its perceptions of vocational education legislation to Congress. The American Vocational Association is the most viable of such groups (associations like the National Education Association, American Federation of Teachers, and the American Association of University Professors are considered under the category of unions, and are examined in the following section), although AVA membership in 1975 was made up of less than 25 percent of the nation's vocational educators.

In recent years, with the surge of secondary school faculty unionization, many vocational teachers have elected to restrict their association membership to the one which also serves as their bargaining agency. As a result, membership in the AVA has not increased greatly for a number of years, and a majority of the members come from states and regions in which the unions have not gained strong footholds. While it is indeed wise, from a bargaining-negotiations point of view, for vocational faculty members to join in with other secondary school teachers, if they do this without joining other professional associations, vocational educators will tend to be deprived of the professional forums and other relationships unique to vocational education. This is viewed as a serious drawback to vocational education because the vocational faculty is most often a minority component in a school system, and those concerns peculiar to the profession of vocational education tend to go unnoticed.

Such is the dilemma the profession found itself in during the mid-1970s, and it appears that the professional association proponents (especially those who advocate strengthening and promotion of the AVA) will need to make some hard decisions relative to new directions for their endeavors if such associations are to grow in membership and viability (Gilgannon, 1975). What are the alternatives? One possibility, of course, is to modify the objectives of the American Vocational Association so that it can compete directly with the unionlike groups. (That is, AVA could offer to become involved in collective bargaining, negotiations, etc.) It appears unlikely that the American Vocational Association will move in such a direction, however, since the number of vocational educators is too small for them to form effective bargaining groups outside the rubric of all public education. A second alternative is to more aggressively establish and pursue professional goals, and attempt to demonstrate to vocational educators that certain professional concerns fall outside the realm of the union type of associations and demand the attention of vocational educators. This approach could be made most effective by incorporating some of the membership recruitment strategies used by the unionlike organizations. Should the AVA, for example, succeed in establishing viable and aggressive state level vocational associations as affiliates of the national group, the confederation of state groups could (with wide coordination and planning) wield considerable influence over vocational education legislation at both state and federal levels. Should this indeed occur between now and 1980, the Department of Health, Education, and Welfare component of federal funding could have a renewed chance of keeping pace with the financial needs of the traditional vocational schools.

The difficulties besetting professional associations are substantial, with unionlike groups successfully competing for potential AVA membership (thereby depriving the association of its maximum impact on federal lawmakers) and a splintering of the vocational education thrust into HEW and Department of Labor segments. The professional associations, particularly the American Vocational Association, could initiate a movement toward coordinating all vocational services. There are federal funds earmarked for vocational education and training in every major government department. Currently these departments more or less go their separate ways in this matter. Should the AVA broaden its scope sufficiently to embrace all of these efforts, it could become a powerful mechanism for the furthering of the profession. An early start would include serious attempts to coordinate efforts funded by the Comprehensive Employment and Training Act of 1973 and the Vocational Education Amendments of 1968. Such an overture would likely be unpalatable to some of the traditionalists in both quarters, but moves in this direction must be made in the interest of optimizing the vocational education delivery system. An association such as the AVA is in the proper strategic position to initiate this very necessary action. It is likely to move in this direction by the late 1970s.

Unionism and Vocational Education

Excluded from this discussion so far, although they are within the province of the problem-oriented groups just discussed, are those groups that are concerned with governance and faculty benefits. Such groups, for simplicity purposes, are referred to as unions here. The increased concern over governance and faculty benefits is not unique to vocational educators, but has literally swept the public school sector of the nation. Furthermore, unionism has made significant inroads at the college level as well, most particularly in community junior colleges and technical institutes. One recent survey found that about one-fourth of all public community junior colleges are unionized (Tice, 1973). These community junior colleges represent nearly three-fourths of all colleges and universities that are formally involved with faculty bargaining. Of special interest is that the union in most of these schools is the National Education Association, which was, until recently, a non-union type of professional association.

Although it is beyond the intent of this book to delve into the reasons for recent trends in faculty unionism, we will examine certain aspects of the movement. First, vocational educators have not, as a group, been the leaders in the unionization movement. Except in the special purpose area vocational schools (of which there were nearly 2,500 in 1975), vocational teachers are a minority in the faculty of most schools. It is likely that teachers who have felt most threatened by employment conditions (i.e., liberal arts-humanities teachers because of the great surplus of teachers in those specialties for several years) have provided the major thrust in this movement. Thus most vocational teachers in the comprehensive secondary schools and two-year colleges have probably played a passive part in the unionization movement.

Much of the effort in unionism is leading toward salary parity, faculty control of appointments and tenure, alterations in governance structures, and increased tension between students and faculty, as well as between faculty and administrators. In some places an attempt to reduce the control of despotic administrators and boards of education may have been the original catalyst in the unionization process, particularly by faculty members who felt threatened or that they were not being dealt with in a just manner. In many cases the relationship between faculty and administration quickly became a confrontation. Instead of a true sharing of authority by the administration and faculty, a general state of conflict became established in many schools. Although the conflict lines were ostensibly between the faculty and the administration, elementary logic leads one to suspect that the students are recipients of many of the resultant changes.

Unionism has affected the vocational education delivery system in ways similar to the way it has affected the entire education system. Since most public vocational education goes on in comprehensive secondary schools, and the educational unionism movement has made its greatest impact at the elementary and secondary school levels, many vocational faculty are directly influenced by unions.

Literature on faculty unionism has been of mixed quality up to now, and much of it is addressed to the development of skills in negotiating. It is evident from the impasses that have developed in some places that faculty and board members are not properly trained to confront each other in the spirit of union-style negotiations. While this claim is subjective in nature, it likely contains some element of truth. The fact is faculty unions are a reality. Thirty-four states already have permissive legislation regarding bargaining rights of school employees (Edwards, 1973), and it is realistic to expect that this will be the case in all states by 1980.

Some faculty unions have been very militant in the pursuit of their objectives, while others have adopted comparatively mild approaches. A casual review of the items frequently negotiated by faculties and boards of governance shows that most of them have to do with faculty benefits, particularly salary schedules and work load definitions. Many negotiations seem to operate in a spirit of confrontation, and many educators view this as counter to the basic tenets of the profession. Perhaps the role of the professions in American society will undergo changes in the decade ahead, with a shift toward more concern for the professionals themselves rather than for the clients' welfare. This trend appears to be going on in education. While some superficial thought is given to the educational client (i.e., the student), the client hardly appears to be a serious concern, except in such matters as how he affects the faculty. Some educators fear that a continuation of this trend can further deprofessionalize public school teachers. The trend could initiate a self-perpetuating cycle in which teachers become less concerned about the welfare of students and more involved in protecting their self-interests, which is a clear indication of deprofessionalism.

In light of this trend (where faculty concern for an optimum learning environment may be on the wane), a number of studies need to be conducted on the effects of unionized faculty upon students, the effects upon the students' rate of intellectual development, and related matters. Research of this variety must be carried out in an atmosphere of free inquiry, with complete absence of the pressure (and even direct harrassment) that could be brought to bear upon the investigators and their sources of funding. A priority should be to determine whether present union activities, which are often mere replicas of industrial unionism, have produced changes in the intellective environment of the schools. Other studies should delve into the effects of unionism upon faculty members themselves. It will take considerable courage to fund such studies, since it is politically unpopular to question unionism in any way, and even greater courage on the part of selected researchers to plunge into the thicket of faculty unionism and emerge with validated answers to some key questions.

The following queries, among others, need to be researched in detail:
1. What are the differences in attitudes of vocational students in union and non-union schools toward the following matters?
   a. Vocational studies.
   b. Vocational teachers.
   c. Educators in general.
   d. Quality of and satisfaction with instruction received.
   e. Job satisfaction.
   f. Concern of faculty for students.
   g. Concern of administrators for students.
   h. Quality of interpersonal relationships between students.

  i. Relevancy of training received to present job.
  j. Quality of intellectual and learning environment in school.
  k. Desire to pursue additional education or training.
2. What are the differences between vocational school faculty in union
   and non-union schools regarding the following matters?
   a. Job satisfaction.
   b. Concern for student learning and welfare.
   c. Desire to pursue additional education or professional training.
   d. Attitudes toward the teaching profession in general.
   e. Attitudes toward fellow vocational teachers.
3. What is the place of the AVA in these overall concerns as viewed
   by union and non-union vocational educators?

This writer suggests that some significant differences will be uncov-
ered. Vocational education is right in the middle of the concern over
unionism and professionalism, and it may very well be a good place to
initiate such timely research. It's time that we got on with this vital
investigation.

The New Institutional Configuration for Adolescents and Young Adults

    Changes going on in American education relate to society's
changing perceptions of the educational system's role within society. A
generation or two ago, with much impetus provided by the Conant report of the 1950s, the comprehensive secondary school was perceived as
the public school vehicle for the provision of equal educational opportunities for all adolescents. But, as indicated in the Conant report, many
so-called comprehensive high schools were not truly comprehensive
and were failing to provide sufficient educational opportunities for their
clientele (Conant, 1959). The same rationale (i.e., equal opportunities
for all) was used in the establishment of many community junior colleges, and they also were not able to offer sufficient curricula diversity
for true comprehensiveness. The rhetoric used by the secondary schools
and community junior colleges did much to mask the fact that they
were seriously deficient in the provision of quality vocational education.
Fortunately, this was recognized by some educational and political
leaders, who perceived that special federal funding subvention was
needed for remediation of this difficulty. The Vocational Education Act
of 1963 provided a powerful mechanism for the strengthening of the

nation's vocational education thrust. One important requisite in the legislation was that the states had to match every federal vocational dollar they accepted. Many states that were previously investing very meager allocations in vocational education responded favorably to this incentive, and since that time have routinely maintained higher levels of funding for vocational education. Thus federal legislation has succeeded in encouraging the various states to bolster their financial commitment to vocational education, although not to the complete satisfaction of everyone (*Report to the Congress*, 1974).

This federal subvention provided a mechanism for those who questioned the workability of the comprehensive high school to develop separate vocational schools. Since vocational programs were reputedly more costly to establish, operate, and keep up to date, some vocational leaders felt they ought to be administered under separate budget categories within their regions with additional special state-federal subvention. The federal legislation was written in a sufficiently broad fashion to encourage establishment of separate vocational departments in comprehensive high schools, an idea deemed consistent with the rationale of this type of institution. Also, the Vocational Education Act of 1963 provided funds for construction of separate vocational schools, which have come to be known as area vocational schools, to serve larger geographic areas. Area vocational schools have caught on, as evidenced by the presence of nearly 2,500 of them in 1975, but one can suspect the tendency to place vocational education in special departments in comprehensive schools will continue. The claims that educational separatism is contrary to democratic education are now counteracted by more recent findings (alluded to earlier) that the placement of vocational and pre-professionally oriented youngsters in one institution is harmful to vocational students' self-concepts. Separate vocational institutions may indeed provide a greater chance for students to find equal opportunities than exists in comprehensive secondary schools and all-purpose community junior colleges.

But the community junior colleges are caught up in a special bind of their own. If they are to provide pre-professional course offerings, the offerings must be similar to those found in the freshman-sophomore years of senior colleges and universities, since such courses are intended to be transferable to those places. Therefore the two-year colleges have little freedom to experiment with innovative approaches to teaching such courses, and they hesitate to introduce more exotic courses in fear of jeopardizing the chances of students taking those courses being accepted for advanced credit by senior institutions. At the same time, the community junior colleges are increasingly being sought out by low achievement students, who would in most instances derive maximum profit from carefully prepared and conducted vocational programs of high quality. Since such programs would introduce an increased nonacademic flavor to the community junior colleges, faculty support for such endeavors may be difficult to obtain. A solution to the dilemma will likely be forced upon the schools by public governing bodies via funds earmarked for the programs they perceive as being important to the community (i.e., vocational studies).

The community junior colleges will become increasingly more oriented toward vocational education. At the secondary level a trend toward separatism of vocational and pre-professional studies will continue as the area vocational high school movement expands. An important change, and one that is sorely needed, is a modification of the general education and support courses in vocational curricula so they blend better with the specialty courses. Placing vocational and other students in the same English, humanities, and social sciences courses in the interest of promoting interaction is more harmful than beneficial. A new configuration for vocational education delivery for adolescents and young adults calls for the preparation of a new breed of teachers of nonvocational courses for vocational students. Such courses should be oriented toward the world as it is and the vocational student's place in it. Preparing the student for more advanced courses (i.e., beyond the associate degree) in a subject area should not be the main concern in vocational programs. It is already evident that students who desire to continue vocational studies beyond the associate degree can find a college that will accord them appropriate credit.

The New Institutional Configuration for Adult Career Changes

The public vocational schools have not been a realistic vehicle for adult career changes, largely because they have been unable to provide income for such persons during their education-training period. Since the public schools were originally established for education of the young, it comes as no surprise that provision for student income has usually been considered an out-of-school problem, and educational authorities have not dealt with it in a serious manner. Such an approach is satisfactory for most adolescents and young adults, who are not faced with heavy financial commitments. Having established this tradition, public school vocational education will continue to be aimed primarily at adolescents and young adults.

Adult career changers will likely find the going difficult during the transition from one occupation to another. Some improved form of financial assistance will be devised, in the form of direct federal subvention in some cases and special industrial-business-based endeavors (which may also be subvented by federal funds in one way or another). Direct federal subvention will likely become more common under the rubric of the Comprehensive Employment and Training Act of 1973 and other subsequent legislation that will be designed to improve the provision of vocational services. The configuration of such programs will be varied, since they will initially begin within prime sponsor districts (see Chapter 13).

Although coordination and cooperative efforts are expressly required in the legislation, the revenue-sharing aspects of the law permit primary sponsors to ascertain their own priorities, and will probably result in a considerable amount of hodgepodge, duplicative efforts and some nonproductive activities for a few years. Since this is a relatively new method of providing federal vocational funds to the regions, some errors in management and other administrative difficulties can be expected. This may be the most serious disadvantage of the Comprehensive Employment and Training Act of 1973, and could result in the establishment of vocational-training modes that are not in the best long-range interests of career changers and society as a whole. But the other side of this risk is the opportunity to invoke fundamental changes in the vocational education delivery system. The legislation does provide incentives, through permissive funding, for establishment and evaluation of innovative model programs in vocational training and clear-cut opportunities to bypass the traditional vocational institutions. Therein lies one of the greatest opportunities, since the passage of the Vocational Education Act of 1963, to embark on some radically new and exciting designs in vocational education.

It appears likely that programs for adult career changers, with much more liberal income provisions than found in the previous Manpower Development and Training Act legislation, can emerge upon the educational scene. Unfortunately, many of the traditional vocational educators don't know how to incorporate such innovative ideas and practices into the existing school-based vocational delivery system. The result will probably be the establishment of special institutions for adult career changers, and integrated within these institutions will be the vital provision of income for the learners, based upon a sizable percentage of their last salary. While such an idea may be seen as revolutionary when considered within the context of traditional educational institutions, it does bear some resemblance to training programs now supported by several of the larger businesses and industries for carefully selected employees. Another example of the possibility of providing salaries to workers while they are being retrained is France's Continuing Vocational Education Act of 1971, which entitles the worker to 90 percent of his prior salary for as long as one year. Therefore, establishing such a configuration within an environment more congruent with that of business and industry could enhance its chances for success. The biggest obstacle to overcome is to persuade (by providing projective estimates of income differentials that could result from such efforts) the public at large, and the political leaders who make decisions at the prime sponsor level, that such an approach is necessary and desirable. The point needs to be made with all concerned that such efforts will indeed improve the lives of many people and enrich society as a whole. With the expectation that career changing will be required of most persons in the future, including those in the professions, the concept will likely gain increased acceptance, and the formation of these special institutions to accommodate this need will probably be in evidence by 1980. It is hoped that the universal college mode of vocational preparation will be one of the chief characteristics of the new configuration.

The New Institutional Configuration for Part-Time and Continuing Education

Secondary schools have traditionally offered part-time and continuing education during the late afternoon and evening hours. The community junior colleges and, later, the area vocational schools more or less copied the approaches used by the high schools for many years. There are two important drawbacks to the ways part-time and continuing education have been offered. First, most offerings of this variety are conducted at other than the usual workday hours. While this may be advantageous for some, it is an impediment for many persons. For example, a housewife seeking to prepare to reenter an occupation may find it more convenient to take courses when her children are in school or at a day care center. Some individuals are able to obtain released time from their places of employment if they are near a school where suitable courses are offered. In recognition of this limitation, a new mode of part-time and continuing education is emerging, particularly in some of the larger urban and suburban regions.

Second, part-time and continuing education offerings tend to be fragmented into various courses, with little concern for the development of the total program to be completed on a part-time basis. In those places where one can complete an entire program through part-time attendance, courses and programs are usually the same as those provided for full-time day students. In many schools, faculty have demanded that offerings, regardless of whether the program is a full-time or part-time one, be the same for all students. The reason offered for such demands is faculty concern for maintaining "quality" programs, etc., and where such practices are most rigidly adhered to, part-time enrollments are small or nonexistent.

One can question the relevance of having an evening program, whose enrollees are most often adults fully engaged in other activities during the regular workday, that is identical to the daytime program (which enrolls younger students with little or no work experience). One way to minimize any adverse influence the daytime faculty and administrators may have upon the continuing education offerings is to maintain sufficient autonomy for the part-time courses and programs to prohibit such interference. A good approach, and one that will likely increase in popularity in the future, is to establish autonomous continuing and adult education centers within existing institutions or in some cases to establish separate schools or colleges of continuing education for an entire region.

The separate college (or center) of continuing and adult education is the most desirable configuration of those mentioned, because of the relative freedom from constraints imposed by the more traditional elements in vocational education. The training and educational needs of adults who bring a store of work experiences with them to the classroom are indeed different from those of adolescents preparing for work entry for the first time. The above configuration offers the greatest hope for adults to meet their unique vocational education needs.

The Universal College: It Can Happen If We Try!

The vocational education delivery mechanism whereby the skill development needed for a specific job is withheld until the student is employed, which is an integral component in the universal college concept, can become a reality in several places at any time in the near future. As indicated in several other sections, the traditional public vocational schools presently located throughout the country may not be the most fertile ground for planting the seeds of this concept. Because of its almost completely reversed approach to traditional vocational education (i.e., obtaining a job first, followed by specific skill development), the universal colleges that are most likely to be tried with successful results will be in new vocational organizations with no traditions to overcome. In addition to housing the effort in an unconventional administrative structure, it might be best to hire nontraditional vocational faculty. This is very difficult to do at the secondary level in all states because of rather stringent certification requirements relative to such matters as previous work experience. In most states the certification dilemma is not present at the post-secondary levels, but the traditions of conventional vocational education exist there also.

Where would be the most plausible place to inaugurate the universal college concept? A brand new effort with a new source of funds within the rubric of a demonstration project may offer the best hope. While demonstration monies may be obtained through the Department of Health, Education, and Welfare funds (such as the Vocational Education Amendments of 1968), a Department of Labor source (such as the Comprehensive Employment and Training Act of 1973) would include fewer initial restraints. The application for such funds should clearly spell out the freedom the director of the universal college model would require in selecting his faculty and staff, in establishing curricula to achieve the universal college's objectives, and in delegating freedom to his faculty in the design and conduct of the overall effort. Being free of the state level requirements relative to teacher-administrator certification, vocational program limitations imposed by the state plan of vocational education (which was devised for spending of Vocational Education Amendments of 1968 monies), and constraints imposed by other elements in the traditional vocational structure, a demonstration model under the auspices of CETA would have a good probability of succeeding.

In conclusion, the universal college concept has the best chance of receiving favorable consideration for funding through a new agency such as a local prime sponsor provided within the CETA of 1973 legislation. The granting of autonomy to local prime sponsors does provide an opportunity to experiment with matters that would likely not be seriously considered by the traditional vocational education governance structure in many places. A very important and interesting experiment would be to conduct several carefully designed models in each of the governance arrangements (i.e., several with HEW funds and several others with Department of Labor funds). A careful monitoring of the operation of each and evaluation of the results would advance the state of the art so as to provide greater insight into the optimum approaches for implementing the universal college. The universal college can be tried if a few innovative educators with sufficient courage are willing to move into this relatively new and unproved mode of vocational education delivery. It can happen if we try!

References

Adams, Leonard P. "Employment Prospects for Older Workers." Section in *Employment of the Middle-Age Worker*. New York: The National Council on the Aging, 1969.
Barfield, Richard E. "Some Observations on Early Retirement." Paper in *Employment of the Middle-Aged*. Edited by Gloria M. Shatto. Springfield, Ill.: Thomas, 1972.
Barro, S.M. "Review of the Power of Competency-Based Teacher Education." Paper prepared for a committee on National Program Priorities in Teacher Education, City University of New York, May 1972.
Conant, James B. *The American High School Today*. New York: McGraw-Hill, 1959.
Dubos, Rene. *A God Within*. New York: Scribner's 1972.
Edwards, Harry T. "Legal Aspects of the Duty to Bargain." *Faculty Bargaining in the Seventies*. Edited by Terrene N. Tice. Ann Arbor, Mich.: The Institute for Continuing Legal Education, 1973.
Fine, Sidney A. "Older Workers in Pursuit of New Careers." Chapter in *Toward an Industrial Gerontology*. Edited by Harold L. Sheppard. Cambridge, Mass.: Schenkman Publishing, 1970.
Gilgannon, Nancy. "Perceptions of Vocational Education of Professional Vocational Associations." Unpublished doctoral dissertation. University Park: The Department of Vocational Education, The Pennsylvania State University, 1975.
Gilli, A.C., Sr. "Competency-Based Teacher Education: A Plea for Caution." *American Vocational Journal* 49 (1974).
Gillie, A.C. *Principles of Post-Secondary Vocational Education*. Columbus, O.: Charles E. Merrill, 1973.
Jones, Howard Mumford. *Revolution and Romanticism*. Cambridge, Mass.: Belknap Press of Harvard University Press, 1974.
Kreps, Juanita M. "Lifetime Trade Offs Between Work and Play." Chapter in *Employment of the Middle-Aged*. Edited by Gloria M. Shatto. Springfield, Ill.: Thomas, 1972.
Lerner, William. *Statistical Abstract of the United States: 1973*. Washington, D.C.: Bureau of the Census, 1973.
Massanari, K. "Performance-Based Teacher Education." *Journal of Teacher Education* 24 (Fall 1973). Washington, D.C.: American Association of Colleges for Teacher Education, 1973.
Mathiasen, Geneva, ed. Monograph I, Section 7, "The Retirement Environment and Its Relation to Health and Disease." Chapter in *Criteria for Retirement*. New York: Putnam's, 1953.
———, Monograph II, "Responsibilities of Employer, Workers, Unions, and Government." Chapter in *Criteria for Retirement*. New York: Putnam's, 1953b.
Report to the Congress: What Is the Role of Federal Assistance for Vocational Education? Washington, D.C.: Controller General of the United States, 1974.
Sheppard, Harold L. *New Perspectives on Older Workers*. Kalamazoo, Mich.: The WE Upjohn Institute for Employment Research, 1971.
Terry, D.R., Thompson, R.L., and Evans, R.N. *Competencies for Teachers*. Urbana-Champaign: University of Illinois Press, 1972.
Tice, Terrene N. "The Situation in the States." *Faculty Bargaining in the Seventies*. Ann Arbor, Mich: The Institute for Continuing Legal Education, 1973.

Index

Accountability bandwagon, 266
Adjunct faculty of community colleges, 127
Adult education: in vocational education, 93; in vocational schools, 31
American Vocational Association, 55
Anti-university tone of community colleges, 116
Appalachia, vocational schools in, 79
Autonomy: of community colleges, 148; of university vocational programs, 203
Authoritarian syndrome, 135
Authority in vocational schools, 9

Behavior of leaders, 27
Bifurcation of vocational education, 32, 254
Blacks and vocational education, 44

Cable television in community colleges, 154
Career aspirations of community college students, 139
Career education in community colleges, 146
Categorical funding versus revenue sharing, 253
Certification: of vocational teachers, 39, 69, 90; rationale for, 69
Communications in vocational organizations, 15
Community leaders and vocational education, 285
Commuting students, 148
Competition between community colleges and universities, 197
Comprehensiveness: of community colleges, 115; of technical schools, 175
Conant study, 102, 104
Conflict: in organizations, 5; in vocational organizations, 17
Constellation of traits theory, 26
Cooperation: between CETA and vocational education institutions, 212; between proprietary schools and community colleges, 185
Cooperative vocational education, 34
Coordination of community colleges, 150
Core of vocational subjects, 77
Correspondence schools, 188
Counseling in vocational education, 47
Counseling services in community colleges, 113

Decision making: in vocational schools, 10; levels of, 14; relationship to hierarchical position, 13
De facto segregation in selection of vocational teacher, 262
Dictionary of Occupational Titles, 30
Diversity in higher education, 162

Economic value of college, 141
Educational administration, studies of, 54
Effectiveness: of a vocational school, 16; of vocational programs, 82
Efficiency of a vocational school, 16
Egalitarianism versus meritocracy, 137
Equal opportunity in community colleges, 136
Equalitarian goals of community colleges, 112
Equalitarianism in vocational education, 223
Exemplary programs, 241
Expectations for leaders, 27

Faculty categories in community colleges, 132
Fads in vocational education, 248
Feasibility studies, 30
Fields, vocational, 65

Generalized versus specialized vocational education, 101
Goals: displacement of, 6; hierarchy of, 4
Governance, student involvement in, 146
Grades of vocational students, 40

Headship versus leadership, 19
Homeostasis, analogy to vocational education, 246

Identity problem of community colleges, 114, 126
Idiosyncratic behavior of leaders, 27
Individualized instruction in community colleges, 153
Innovation, resistance to, 11
Institutional control and relationships with school selectivity, 9
Interaction theory, 26
Intermediate units, 270
Internships in vocational education, 35, 59

Job satisfaction, 47

Labor force, 99
Land-grant concept, 197
Leaders, selection of, 25
Leadership, 18, 23
Learning resource centers, 150
Legitimacy of proprietary schools, 186
Low achievement students in community colleges, 136, 139

Melting pot, theory in education, 107
Mergers of community colleges and technical institutes, 171
Meritocratic criteria of schools, 41
Mid-career changes, 83, 95
Militancy in vocational education, 291
Military establishment and vocational education, 286
Minorities and higher education, 142
Modular instruction, 152
Morrill Act's effect on higher education, 197
Multi-campus community colleges, 149
Multi-campus districts of community colleges, 123

Nonvocational education, economic benefits of, 101

Occupational aspirations and vocational education, 45
Occupational choice, stability of, 40
Occupational competency of teachers, 38
Organizational set, description of, 12
Organizations: classification of, 4; nonprofessional, 4; professional, 3; service, 3; table of, 7; vocational school functions, 13

Peer group: description of, 14; leaders of, 53
Political establishment and vocational education, 287
Practical arts and vocational education, 34
Prestige, effect upon organizational adaptability, 12
Primary groups, description of, 14
Professional associations for proprietary schools, 187
Program of activity in vocational schools, 14
Programs in area vocational schools, 76
Public school patterns, 104

Race and higher education, 141
Recycling of workers, 31, 36
Regional boards in vocational education, 85
Regional schools, 77
Regional units, 272
Regional vocational centers, 78
Regionalization in vocational education, 110

Revolving door of community colleges, 112
Role conflict of community college faculty, 135
Role of community college presidents, 119
Roles: of community college faculty, 147; of leaders, 21; of private junior colleges, 160; organizational, 14
Rural regions, vocational education in, 82

School board members' attitudes toward vocational education, 87
Secondary schools and vocational preparation, 47
Segmental groups in vocational schools, 19, 49
Self-aggrandizement, 12
Separatism in vocational education, 79, 101
Slogans in vocational education, 225
Social processes in American schools, 106
Socialization of students and faculty, 9
Sociocentrality and leadership, 19
Specialty schools 183
Status: exchange value of, 13; of vocational institutions, 12
Strategy: of organizations, 6; of vocational schools, 13

Teacher evaluation in community colleges, 128
Teacher training: for community colleges, 131; future trends in, 261; varieties of, 108
Television instruction consortiums in community colleges, 154
Training: levels of, 30; on-the-job, 36
Transfer programs, 147; in community colleges, 113
Trichotomy of vocational educational organizations, 232
Trustees of community colleges, 118

Unionization of college faculties, 129
Unions and vocational education, 57
Unitary trait theory, 26
U.S. Office of Education, vocational education personnel in, 56
Urban colleges, 147, 149

Vocational administration, levels of, 56
Vocational doctoral programs, courses in, 59
Vocational fields, 29
Vocational programs, special categories of, 66

Women in community colleges, 145
Work experiences of vocational teachers, 39
Work practicum in vocational education, 35
Working life of students, 93